Still Single

Still Single

You Don't Have to Be!

Casey Maxwell Clair

FOREWARD BY JEFFREY W. WHITING PH.D.

ST. MARTIN'S GRIFFIN
NEW YORK

www.stmartins.com

Design by Heidi Eriksen

Library of Congress Cataloging-in-Publication Data

Clair, Casey Maxwell.
    Still single : you don't have to be! / Casey Maxwell Clair ; foreword by Jeffrey W. Whiting.
        p. cm.
    Originally published 2002, with the subtitle: Are you making yourself unavailable when you don't want to be?
    ISBN 0-312-28236-2 (hc)
    ISBN 0-312-30373-4 (pbk)
    1. Single people—Psychology. 2. Man-woman relationships. 3. Dating (Social customs). 4. Mate selection. I. Title.

HQ800 .C53 2003
646.7'7—dc21
                                         2002031894

First St. Martin's Griffin Edition: February 2003

10 9 8 7 6 5 4 3 2 1

To Christopher, the love of my life.
You were worth the wait.

Contents

Chapter 3
Behaviors and Beliefs That Can Keep You Unavailable

PART II
Becoming Available
NEW RULES — A NEW WAY

Chapter 4
Facing Your Fears

Chapter 5

Twelve Steps to Becoming Available

Chapter 6

The Questions to Ask — The Answers to Listen For

PART III
Success Stories

Acknowledgments

I wish to thank all those who took a chance on me when I set out to write a book on relationships even though I wasn't in one.

I wish to acknowledge all those who gave me love, support, and encouragement. To those unnamed who shared their experiences with me, I am forever grateful. I'm sorry I couldn't use them all, but each one of your stories helped to make this book a reality.

I thank my wonderful family for their love and constant faith in me: my children, Melanie and Tiffany, my grandchildren, Kelly, Nick, Nina, and Cameron, my sons-in-law, Al and Jamie. My new family: Elizabeth, Tim, Taryn, and Ian; Catherine, Tom, and Charlotte; and Rubin and Marilynn.

I'd like to thank my dear friends for always being there for me, in life as well as in support of this book: Gail and Alan Nassaney, Susan and Stan Roskens, Mary Trainor, Brian Byers, Kathie Culleton, Dan Ruben, Bob Griffard, Fred Rubin and Marley Sims, Darlene Maxfield, Elayne Boosler, Julia Newton and Michael Fibish, Ronnie Hallin, Sally Robinson, and Candace and Stan Frileck. And to Melanie Wilson for her encouragement early on.

In addition to their love and encouragement, I thank the following friends for providing a beautiful change of scenery in which to write: Barbara Bowman, Joyce and Bob Freeman, Marianne Miller, Jacqueline and Daniel Osborn, Gregg Selleck, and Stephen Weinheimer.

To Jeffrey W. Whiting, Ph.D., for the excellent foreword; thank you for your time, wisdom, and kind words. To relationship counselor Mary Padlak, and to Michael Topp, marriage and family therapist, thank you for your participation and insight. To all those I've quoted, thank you for your humor and your knowledge.

For believing in this book, I'd like to thank my agent, Michael Broussard, my editor, Jennifer Weis, a big thanks to Jennifer Reeve in publicity, and to my publicist and friend, Lyla Foggia.

Foreword

After more than two decades of working with individuals and couples who want to improve the quality of their relationships, I am quite convinced that being involved with an intimate other offers us the truest, most reliable context to promote our growth and development as human beings. And . . . it's not easy to pull this off—this relationship stuff. The constant balancing of and sensitivity to personal needs and desires with those of our partner provide for a seemingly contradictory experience that holds both mystery and hope. The concept of the "we"—that third entity, that dynamic system of the twosome—creates a rich and fertile place that makes us stretch and go beyond the limitations of the isolated self.

But the questions that many of my clients have asked through the years describe a more preliminary proposition—"How do I meet that special someone?" "Why do I waste so much time in relationships that are going nowhere?" "Where are all the good men (women)?" "Why do I keep making such bad choices?" "When will I meet my Prince Charming or my Cinderella?"

And . . . at the same time . . . the difficult answers to these questions always start with the one who poses these questions. It really is about *me*.

But this flies in the face of most of the romantic ideas that literature, songs, and movies have popularized and indoctrinated us with over the eons. Isn't love supposed to happen to us? Isn't love supposed to be magical? Aren't we supposed to just bump into, quite by accident, or meet by mere coincidence, the love of our lives? It does not come naturally and it is, indeed, quite hard for us to grapple with taking personal responsibility for how we choose, how we behave, and how we think about love and coupling.

It is fairly unpopular and feels counterintuitive at times to think that we are the playwrights of the relationships we create, sustain and, sometimes, suffer within.

When Casey Clair asked me to review this manuscript I was instantly intrigued by the subject matter and the author. It has been my assessment that although these concerns of coupling are shared by millions, little has been written that presents the reader with quality information delivered with a refreshing, uplifting style that actually helps people. And now I am introduced to Casey, a successful writer immersed in the entertainment culture who is attempting to write a book that addresses the nuts and bolts, the behavioral dos and don'ts, and the underlying philosophies that have everything to do with successfully going from a onesome to a "we."

Frankly, in perhaps the not-so-professional vernacular, I was blown away by the quality of this book. Casey Clair's willingness to address her own vulnerability, her energetic quest to research this topic, her ability to synthesize and communicate both information and ideas, her generous sense of humor, and her down-to-earth spirit, make for a very readable and artful work of personal assistance. It's destined to guide and offer helpful structure to this meandering journey of finding someone, by first of all finding yourself. It will make easier the essential task of identifying what you can and must do to improve the quality of your search for someone to share your life with, by knowing better your self.

The crucial battles we wage are always most profoundly the ones we fight within. Changing ourselves is the precursor to being ready and truly available for someone else.

I encourage you to make notes as you go through this book. Make it a project. Underline as you go. Treat this book as a road map for the most interesting, rewarding trip you can take. The one that provides the hope and promise for a happier, more fulfilling chapter of your life. Going from where you are—to where you want to be.

This journey will not be an easy one. No endeavor of this nature that is worth undertaking is ever easy. Personal change is difficult, but not impossible. Casey Clair reminds us often of that fact. But refer back to your notes when the going gets rough. Turn back to key sections of this book that seem particularly relevant for you. The things that speak to you. I trust that you will feel repeatedly energized and supported, and reassured that you are on a new and better path.

I am confident that your reading of this book will be a wise investment in your self, and in your future relationships. Best wishes for your learning along the way.

Jeffrey W. Whiting, Ph.D.
Santa Monica, California

Autobiography in Five Short Chapters
PORTIA NELSON

I

I walk down the street.
  There is a deep hole in the sidewalk.
  I fall in
  I am lost . . . I am helpless
                It isn't my fault.
It takes forever to find a way out.

II

I walk down the same street.
  There is a deep hole in the sidewalk.
  I pretend I don't see it.
  I fall in again.
I can't believe I am in the same place.
                but it isn't my fault.
It still takes a long time to get out.

III

I walk down the same street.
  There is a deep hole in the sidewalk.
  I see it there.
  I still fall in . . . it's a habit.
            my eyes are open.
              I know where I am.
  It is my fault.
  I get out immediately.

IV

I walk down the same street.
  There is a deep hole in the sidewalk.
  I walk around it.

V

I walk down another street.

Introduction

With so many "self-help" books on the market, written by so many "experts," you should know a little about the person who wrote the book you are about to read.

Let me begin by telling you what I am not. I'm not a therapist. I'm not a psychiatrist. I'm not even a marriage counselor. I'm a writer, a television comedy writer, actually. I am also a woman who spent nineteen years single and unavailable. I knew that I was single; that part was easy. But I had no idea that I was the one who was unavailable. Even after reading dozens of the aforementioned "self-help" books, watching hours of Oprah, all the therapy; even after all that, I still believed that it was just a whole lot of bad luck and a series of unfortunate choices that kept me out of a satisfying relationship. I truly believed that.

It took the emptiness of a five-year relationship with a *totally* unavailable man (i.e., married) for me to look at what was really going on in my life. Only after years of heartache did I realize that I was consistently choosing unavailable men because I was unavailable for a relationship.

No book, no "expert," not even the world's greatest therapist can spare you from all the pitfalls, missteps and, yes, pain, that come with making yourself available for love. But I'm hoping that this book can spare you *some* of that pain, *some* of that time, and bring you that much closer to finding the relationship you deserve.

The words that follow are those of experience. My own as well as those of the dozens of others with whom I spoke during the research for, and writing of, this book. In addition to my own story, I will share the observations and experiences of many others who feel as if they wasted years of their lives before realizing the part they played in their own "singleness." I will also talk about people who found ways to change their old patterns and were able to make themselves "available" for the first time in their lives.

•   •   •

I was married for seventeen years to an unavailable man. I married young to get out of a home situation that made *The Addams Family* look like an episode of *The Brady Bunch*. I had two lovely children whom I adored, but a husband who cheated on me repeatedly; this in spite of the fact that our sex life was the only part of the marriage that seemed to function well. The term "sex addict" hadn't been coined yet, but that's exactly what my husband was. I stayed anyway. I just figured that was the price I had to pay to keep the life I had (see also: Chapter 5, Boost your self-esteem).

As my professional life began to evolve (I worked as an executive at a television network at the time), I came into contact with people who treated me with respect. I began to believe that maybe I deserved a better life. It was a bizarre concept to me at the time, but it sure sounded good. Slowly I began to realize what a soulless relationship I had with my husband. But the thought of divorce was still nowhere in my mind. I believed that if I left my marriage, my life would go back to the way it had been before, and that was too awful to contemplate. Then he did me a huge favor one night. During a party celebrating my promotion to a better job, he made a play for one of my former coworkers in front of all my friends and colleagues. Despite my pleas for an ounce of discretion, they left together. As embarrassing as it is to tell this story, it's important to know when the Universe gives you a gift, even when it doesn't look much like a gift.

That was it. I left that night, determined to start my life over. I was single for the next nineteen years. And during that entire time I believed that I was ready, willing, and just waiting to meet the right man. No matter how many princes turned out to be toads in training, I always assumed that it was my bad luck and poor radar that kept me from finding happiness in a relationship. I used to say, "Put me in a room full of men and I'll attract the married ones, the ones who live out of town, or the ones who have a girl-friend—or even a boyfriend—at home." If someone had told me back then that I was part of the problem, that I was *purposely*, albeit subconsciously, choosing unavailable men, that I was the unavailable one, I would have said they were "nuts and go crazy," as my father used to say. After all, I was dating many different types of men. Bright men, creative men, interesting men. It wasn't until after my relationship with the married man, the most painful and shameful experience of my life, that I finally saw the pattern. All of them, no matter how bright, or wonderful, or interesting; all of them were unavailable in one way or another.

For the record, when I met David, he told me he was having problems in his marriage and was *this close* to a separation. Naïvely, I rewrote that to mean "almost available." I got in deeper and deeper and convinced myself that I was in love with this man. How else could I justify my actions, especially after my own experiences with a cheating husband? It's difficult, even now, for me to write the words "affair with a married man" without feeling shame. By the time I got a clue, five years of my life and much of my self-esteem were gone. When it was over, I began to do a lot of soul searching.

How the hell did this *happen?* I asked myself. One relationship after another, after another, after another. I reviewed my entire dating and relationship history since my divorce. There was nothing to point to a pattern, no common denominator. As I said, I didn't have a certain "type" of man. If I had picked the same wrong man over and over, like *all married men* or *all musicians*, I might have figured it out sooner.

Then, one dark and stormy night, I came to a realization that changed my life forever. I saw clearly for the first time that the one thing they all had in common was . . . me. If I were truly open to love, would I be picking emotionally and physically unavailable partners? The answer is no. Just being single and dating doesn't mean you're available to love. You can be single—*and* unavailable. I was. And maybe you are as well.

This was a huge revelation, and an empowering one. It wasn't about *them*. It was about me. That was the bad news, but it was also the good news. If I was the problem, then I could work on that. I couldn't change someone else, but I could change myself. By taking responsibility for a situation that I had always blamed on intangibles like "bad luck" or "timing," I could gain some control and actually change things in my life. I gave up the feeling that I was waiting for love to happen to me. I decided that I was going to *happen* first.

I was so enthusiastic about my breakthrough; I couldn't help but share it with friends and colleagues. As I explained my theory about being single and unavailable, I saw how many people were able to relate. I could see the spark of recognition as we talked about relationships and the roles we play in mapping them out. One woman I ran into at a party told me that she had left an alcoholic and now realized that the man she was seeing was a workaholic. A man I had worked with told me that he dated only women who lived out of state. He had all kinds of reasons for why he thought this plan worked for him, but the truth was, he finally admitted, he couldn't handle a real relationship with a geographically "available" woman. Another man actually told me that he only picked women he didn't like. At first he was flippant about it, but as we continued to discuss why he would make such a choice, he got very angry and then surprised both of us by bursting into tears. Even though each situation was different, they all shared one important element; each had been unaware of their own unavailability. I knew my discovery had changed my life; I didn't know it might help so many others.

Friends told friends and soon I was getting calls from complete strangers wanting to discuss their relationships. I learned a lot, as you will, about the diversions and roadblocks that keep us out of meaningful, satisfying, loving relationships. It's amazing how many creative and resourceful ways there are to be unavailable and not even know it.

Obviously, identifying the problem was only step one. The real work began with the question, What do I do about it? If I'm the one who's unavailable, then how do I become available? Part I of this book deals with identifying the problem. Part II takes a look at various methods of working on that problem. And let me issue this warning right up front; this will not be a book about how *easy* it is to change your life. What I referred to earlier as my period of "soul searching" was, for me, a difficult, painful, brutally honest time of my life. And, in all likelihood, it may be a difficult process for you as well. But the rewards are tremendous. At worst, you will know yourself in a deeper and more meaningful way. At best, you will be open and available for a loving relationship. Add a little luck to both and you just might find what you're looking for in a partner.

In Part III I go in search of success stories; people who were previously unavailable talk about the changes they made in their lives to become open to love. These are the models of healthy behavior that help us to understand what's possible when we do the work. Mary Padlak, renowned relationship therapist, has written, "We repeat until we repair." This book is intended to be a road map to repair.

I can tell you with certainty that it worked for me. I'm happy to say I'm one of the success stories. Not long after my revelation I met the love of my life. I firmly believe I couldn't have drawn this man to me if I hadn't been able to identify and overcome my own unavailability.

NOTE TO READER: I have structured this book so that you can return to a given chapter in order to reference a specific situation. This means that some points, pertinent to several different scenarios, may be repeated.

Also, while most of the material in this book applies to both sexes equally, I have elected to choose one gender, my own, so as to spare you a multitude of he/she references. Unless otherwise specified, all examples will be written from the point of view of a woman.

Names, and some events, have been changed in order to protect the privacy of those offering their personal stories.

PART I

Who's Unavailable?

IDENTIFYING THE PROBLEM

They always say that time changes things, but you actually have to change them yourself.

—ANDY WARHOL

When you're convinced there's nothing you want more in this world than to be in a wonderful, loving relationship, it's almost impossible to believe that you could be the one who's stopping you. But, all too often, it's true.

As I mentioned in my introduction, the episode that forced me to look at my life and reassess the way I approached relationships, was a shameful affair with a married man. The whole time I was having the affair, I told myself that we were star-crossed lovers, just unlucky to have met at the wrong time. (Not very original, but neither, in the end, is infidelity. It's called cheating for a reason; we cheat ourselves as well as the other person.) Now I know that I chose David because there was no chance of ever being in a relationship with him. Not only was he married, he was also incredibly wrong for me. I wonder what on earth I would have done if he had actually left his wife and we had gotten together. Our values were different. Our interests were different. So, what was the attraction? I came to realize that, by picking David, I was fulfilling a subconscious desire *not* to be in a loving relationship. That was our unspoken agreement. He wouldn't leave his wife and I wouldn't leave him, because then I would be available for a real relationship. Just as he chose me because he was unable to have a real, complete relationship with his wife, I chose him in order to avoid a real relationship with an available man. As I said, we cheat ourselves as much as we cheat on another person.

In the case of David and me, our pathologies fit perfectly for a very long time. We were both unavailable and unaware that we wanted to be. To this day I don't know what David's true agenda was and, I suspect, neither does he. If we had ever had those types of conversations, then we would have had the beginnings of a real relationship, wouldn't we? And we certainly couldn't have that. I only found the strength to dig deep and discover my own motivation after my heartache and shame sent me in search of the self-destructive patterns in my life. David certainly wasn't my first "unavailable" relationship, only the most obvious and painful one. After my seventeen-year marriage to a man who repeatedly cheated on me, I couldn't believe that I had managed to become involved in a similar type of triangle.

It took a long time to even see my patterns. I had dated such *different* types of men, or so I thought. The more diverse your dating history is, the harder it is to identify a pattern. The truth is, you don't need to be aware of the dynamics for the agreement to work—but it *demands* your awareness to make a change.

Step One in determining whether you are unavailable or not is to take an inventory of your own history. (There will be much talk of "lists" and "inventories" in this book. They can be tough at times, but they can also be incredibly useful in that they force you to think, write, and focus on the true nature of your patterns.) Think about this; if your relationships include a year with a workaholic who never had time for you, another year with someone who lived clear across the country, and an additional year with a person who was waiting for his children to grow up, you would've spent three years *not* getting what you want—unless what you want is to stay single!

Remember, I'm not talking about dating for fun. If that's what you're doing, then, by all means, date all kinds of different people and enjoy the ride. But you may not find intimacy. What I'm talking about in this book is the search for a healthy and meaningful relationship. Not that that shouldn't be fun, but along with the fun comes the responsibility of awareness.

In the following pages I will try to profile some "types" you should watch out for. Keep in mind, like most rules or guidelines, there are always exceptions. These are intended to be signposts that inspire new insights into your behavior.

Awareness is the key. You are picking the people that pick you!

Chapter 1

The Ones to Run From

Unless you had the incredible luck of finding the love of your life in high school, chances are you'll kiss a few frogs in your life. My goal is to help you to keep the number and nature of those frogs within a safe limit. Love is a risky business, there's just no way around it. Always has been; always will be. Most things in life that are worthwhile involve some risk. Let's use the stock market as an analogy. It's certainly risky, but the rewards can be great, so people spend hours and months and years trying to learn the ins and outs in order to avoid making mistakes and to get the most out of their investment. They do all that for money. But when it comes to their hearts, it seems that people feel it's okay to "fall" into it, or "jump headlong." The same people who "fall" into love wouldn't dream of just "falling" into an investment. Mind you, I'm not talking about following some rigid set of rules that operate from the outside in, some kind of MBA of Love. I've tried those rules, and maybe you have as well. In my opinion, they don't work. And they don't work *because* they exist outside your heart. The heart is always a key player in love and that's the way it should be. But the heart that beats inside you is the same heart you had as a child and it may carry scars that make it difficult to know exactly what's going on. Which heart is responding to the man flirting with me across the room? Is it my eight-year-old heart that only knew love when it came with a huge price tag attached? Is it my sixteen-year-old heart that only knew comfort when it competed and won? Twelve-step programs have a wonderful saying they use to describe this difficulty in perception; they say, "feelings are not facts." And while I wholeheartedly endorse this meaning, I also believe that feelings need to be listened to, felt deeply, and fully considered. Feelings may not be facts, but they're important. They're real.

Some of the personalities I am about to describe may have the power to make you *feel* good. Maybe they even make you *feel* absolutely wonderful. And how could that be bad? Well, it can be very bad if there's a hidden price tag that doesn't reveal itself until it's too late.

You wouldn't intentionally risk your physical safety by running onto a crowded freeway, jumping into shark-infested water, or swallowing poison, would you? Of course not. And yet, every day, there are people who put themselves in situations that are every bit as dangerous and damaging to their emotional existence.

If you are in a relationship, or if you are considering one, with one of the following six "types," you are putting your heart and soul on the line for an experience that could bring you suffering and pain. Not to mention wasting months or years of your precious life. If you really want a relationship, understand that you won't find it here.

1. Someone Married

> *I don't sleep with happily married men.*
> —Britt Ekland

Chances are, somewhere in your own circle of friends, you probably know of at least one married person who is having, or has had, an affair. Ask yourself these questions: Did it end well? Did the one in the marriage leave that marriage? Did the two "unavailable" people end up getting together, marrying, and living happily ever after? Probably not. The statistics are unbelievably low: Fewer than five percent of couples who meet during an affair end up together. Pretty bad odds. Not that it doesn't happen. It does, but not often. Still, there are countless people falling every day for the old "I'm in a terrible marriage and I swear I'm getting a divorce just as soon as—" (fill in your own excuse). I certainly fell for it.

The trouble, as I mentioned, is that these things do work out from time to time. In the real world, in the adult world, people sometimes encounter each other at unfortunate times and under difficult circumstances. Sometimes people meet who absolutely belong together in the most healthy, loving way. They just happen to be married to other people. It's not the purpose of this book to examine the moral or religious aspects of this dilemma. You must look into your own heart and your own belief system to answer those questions. But I implore you, if you are considering a relationship with a married man, to examine the reality of your situation in terms of what you want in your life and whether or not you are subconsciously catering to your own need to be "unavailable." If a man is married, he's unavailable. If you choose a married man, or he chooses you, then you are entering into an "unavailable" relationship. (As I noted in my introduction, all examples apply to either gender.) If you truly think the situation is going to change (i.e., he'll become available) then I suggest you keep a close watch on your calendar. Better yet, why not simply wait until the divorce has happened before getting involved in an intimate way? Easier said than done, I know. But, as difficult as it is to rein in those physical longings that accompany every attraction, why not keep the relationship nonsexual until he is truly out of his marriage and available for a relationship with you?

My affair with a married man was a choice I made. It wasn't something that *happened* to me. I chose to believe David when he said his marriage was in trouble. I chose to ignore my feelings of pain and suffering. And now I know that I made those choices because I was *choosing* an unavailable relationship. By reading these words maybe you can learn a lesson that took me almost five years to learn. No matter how attracted you feel, no matter how good you *think* the sex is, it's not real. Sex is frequently a determining factor in an extramarital relationship, but if you take away the secret rendezvous, the excitement of "stolen moments of passion," and add the reality of a daily routine—mortgage payments, car pools, dinner with the in-laws—I wonder how great that exact same sex would be. No matter how much you tell yourself that it's worth it even if it's only for X number of hours, X days a week, what you are doing, what you are *really* doing, is keeping yourself unavailable by participating in an unavailable relationship. And really, if you think about it, someone who is cheating *with* you will cheat *on* you. If you've never heard the expression "date a cheater, marry a cheater," you have now.

How will you trust this person even if you do end up together? Trust is the foundation of any solid relationship and you'd be starting out without it, like building a house on air. If your goal is to be important in someone's life, don't choose a person who doesn't know how to make his own wife important.

Here's what happened to my friend, Maxine, who is a smart, attractive, successful woman. Shortly after she was hired to be the chief financial officer of a large corporation, she met the big boss. Let's call him Phil. He was a powerful, sexy, dynamic man. He was also married.

That didn't stop Phil from pursuing Maxine. And it didn't stop Maxine from responding. Sparks flew and pretty soon they were having the hottest love affair you can imagine. They made love in their offices, in the stairwell, and the elevator. It was very hot and full of intense passion for almost two years. And then it was over. Maxine, for all her business savvy, and all her social sophistication, had actually believed Phil when he told her that he was going to get a divorce. And, guess what? He *did* get a divorce. And he promptly married someone else. So, Maxine was left just exactly where she started. Alone. Only now it was two years later. And just to make it really interesting, she received an extra helping of unpleasantness because everyone at her company knew about the illicit relationship. In fact, when people talked about Maxine, the affair was one of the first things anyone mentioned. Her coworkers forgot that she had landed her big job on her own and was hired before she had ever met Phil.

Do yourself a favor and try on the title "mistress" before you buy it. Say it out loud: "I'm his mistress." It doesn't feel very good, does it? Wouldn't you rather be able to say, "I'm in love with him, and he's in love with me, and we're there for each other?" You don't get to say that with an affair.

After Phil, Maxine made some conscious changes in her life. With the help of a good therapist, she came to understand her part in choosing these men. She took her loss and turned it into a gain by using the opportunity to learn her own story. There are reasons behind the choices we make. The painful part is looking at those reasons, experiencing the pain attached, and finding ways to deal with those feelings. Maxine learned that she had been afraid to be as smart and successful as she was and needed to diminish herself by having a more powerful man in her life. The whole time she told herself that she didn't *want* an available man (there had been other unavailable men before Phil), she was feeling that she didn't *deserve* an available man. After a lot of hard work, she has an even better job now and is happily married to a wonderful man.

Like me, it took years of frustration and a painful betrayal before Maxine began to look at the pattern of her relationships and the part she played in it. Phil had taken two years of her life (with her willing participation), but there were a dozen years before Phil that were "lost," spent kissing frogs that bore only the slightest resemblance to a prince.

A word about great sex. (There will be many more words about great sex throughout this book.) We often mistake great sex for love, but try to remember that great sex is just that, great sex. It has no bearing on whether your partner is emotionally available. It could just mean that you've both mastered some great sexual techniques. It could mean that both of you are going through an emotional struggle that *seems* to be lessened by the distraction and the release of a physical experience. Granted, it can *feel* like an emotional connection; but feelings, as we've said before, are not facts.

As easy as it is to get lost in the fog between feelings and facts, it is a good idea to give some consideration to an extremely important word. A word that can make the difference between success and failure in this, or any other, difficult assignment. That word is "help." If you're struggling to see what's really going on in a relationship you're having, or considering, then turn to a friend who is truly a friend, someone who is on your team and wants what's best for you, and ask them for an opinion; not a judgment, an opinion. And then do something *really* unique; listen to what they say. Obviously the final decision in these matters will, and should be, yours. But so many "self-help" books seem to take the position that we are all operating in a vacuum. It's only us (and whatever book is dispensing the "expert" advice) that can work the problem and find a way out. But, in my humble opinion, that's a false premise, and a lonely one. We are a part of a community that can serve us well. Friends, family, therapists, and psychologists are all part of a network of voices that can give us different points of view as well as strength and support when we make difficult decisions to better our lives and our relationships.

By the way, I am not naïve about words like friends and family. There are healthy, decent, supportive friends, and then there are jealous, petty, competitive friends. We've all had some of each, I'm sure. And family is a word loaded with danger. But sometimes we're lucky enough to have one or more family members with whom we are deeply bonded. These are the people I'm talking about.

Also, when it comes to therapists and doctors, there are good ones who can be of tremendous help, and there are bad ones who should be stripped of their licenses and run out of town for all the harm they do. If that sounds a bit extreme, so is the damage that can be done by a bad one. I think we need to keep in mind that a psychologist or therapist is a person who has completed a series of tests and holds a degree. Whatever personality quirks, issues, and damage they grew up with can be carried into their practice.

Being a professional doesn't automatically make you a kind, sane, or ethical therapist if you are not a kind, sane, ethical person to begin with. I was seeing a psychologist when I began my affair with David. I talked to her for hour upon $120.00 hour about my attraction to him. Her advice was to "go for it." She said as long

as I felt adored, it might be good for me. Now don't misunderstand, I take complete responsibility for my actions in regard to
the affair; but let's face it, that was bad advice. A dear friend of
mine, Jack, got the same bad advice. His therapist encouraged him
to "explore the relationship with Denise," a married woman he was
seeing. Jack also knew better, but it sure gets confusing when a
trained therapist is telling you that it's okay to date an unavailable
person. Obviously these people were telling us what we wanted
to hear. Relationship counselor Mary Padlak says that, often,
when we set our minds to do something, we'll find the people in
our lives who will support that view—and that includes friends,
family—even therapists.

But if you think I'm not a fan of therapy, you'd be wrong. For
the most part, I think it is an undervalued, underutilized service
that has a profound effect on our society when we give it the chance
to do so. I have since spoken to other, more responsible, therapists,
who have helped me as I struggled with the difficult questions
regarding my relationship choices, questions about self-esteem,
and even deeper questions about why a married man would interest
me in the first place.

As I said, when I met David, he told me his marriage was in
trouble. He led me to believe he was on the verge of a separation.
It's amazing how fast we went from being strangers to lovers. The
speed and intensity of the intimacy between us was very seductive.
The frantic pace is one of the most exciting things about an affair—
it's also the clearest indication that it's not real. David said a lot
was missing from his marriage—passion, laughter, and sex. Over
the next few years I provided those things. I filled in the blanks
of what was missing in his life and, ironically, I helped his marriage, such as it was, to survive. So, let's do some math here; I tell
myself that I want this man in my life but, unconsciously or not,
I provide him with the necessary "vacation time" so that he is able
to tolerate, and remain in, his marriage. And I do this for five
years! I would be embarrassed to even write these words if it wasn't
a story that we've all heard dozens of times. Maybe for you it's not

a married man; maybe it's a workaholic, or an emotionally disconnected husband, or some other variety of "unavailable," but the story is a familiar one.

As I've stated, this is not a book dealing with morality, per se. But sometimes social mores can help you see things that you didn't want to see. I was able to convince myself that what I was doing wasn't so bad because I didn't know his wife. Well, of course it was bad. I was taking part in a betrayal of another person and of myself. When you're having an affair with a married person you are in a relationship with the other spouse. He or she is your invisible partner in an unkind and unhealthy competition. You want to be prettier, sexier, better. You want to win, believing that if you do it will prove your worth. In fact, it only *devalues* your worth. In the eyes of others and, more importantly, in your own eyes.

There are as many excuses for infidelity as there are plastic surgeons in the 90210 zip code. And even though some of the following excuses are weak, any one of them may be the "reason" given. The all-time champion, of course, is and always has been, "My wife doesn't understand me." Then there's a lack of sex within the marriage, an illness, busy schedules, kids, etc. I once heard a woman say that she had an affair with a man who lived in Malibu Beach because she thought the clean beach air was good for her asthma. Ultimately the appeal of an affair is that it "feels" like an easy fix for a multitude of possible problems, including, I suppose, asthma. It feels like a great escape that you "deserve." And, of course, it *is* a great escape. But when you return to the marriage, if you do, then you'll be returning to the same bad sex, the same kids, schedule, smoggy air, whatever. But now you get to add guilt to the equation. And if you're the one having the affair with the married person, then you get to return to . . . your life. With the added ingredient of guilt over the affair and over the sense of loss when you take a look at the calendar and see how much time has gone by.

Near the end of my affair I had a dream in which a dear girlfriend of mine, Ann, came to speak to me. Ann had passed away a few years earlier from breast cancer. Her husband had been in a long, painful affair and I had seen her suffer through it. In the dream she urged me to remember her pain and to stop seeing David. There is a theory about dreams that says that every character in your dream is actually you. I don't know if that's true, but I do know that somewhere in my heart I knew that I was causing harm to myself and to others by continuing this relationship. This affair was just the last incarnation of a long series of relationships with unavailable men. And I know now that the ability to change my life came from looking honestly at what I thought I wanted in my life and how it differed from what I was bringing into it. I'm not sure if that dream was a message from my friend, or a message from my heart. Either way, it helped me to finally wake up before it was too late. I would not be in the incredibly satisfying, healthy relationship I'm in now if I didn't listen to all the voices that told me that I had work to do, and miles to go before I kissed a real prince.

In my research for this book I interviewed a lot of people who had been unfaithful to their spouses, and I heard a lot of stories. Like Tom, who says he cheats because he feels inferior to his wife. He feels she's too good for him, too smart and too successful, and one day she'll realize it and leave him. He says he just wants to be prepared. Tom remains "unavailable" for a real relationship with his wife by having affairs. But what if his wife doesn't feel that way about him? Maybe she would love him no matter what job he had. Maybe she loves him for qualities that have nothing to do with being smart or successful. Tom will probably never find out.

Then there's Catherine. She has affairs because she craves the excitement of not getting caught. She says she loves her husband, doesn't want to lose him, but needs the thrill of an affair to feel truly alive. She even thinks that this makes her a better wife. Like most gamblers, Catherine may *look* like she's playing to win, but she's really doing what most of the people in Las Vegas do when they hit the casinos: flirting with disaster. Like all those nice folks who finance all those 5000-room hotels, she'll just keep playing until she loses. She would be shocked to learn it, but Catherine is "unavailable" for success. Like the real hard-core gamblers she just may keep playing until she loses everything, and then wonder what happened.

Larry said having an affair makes him feel attractive and desired, which he hasn't felt for a long time. He says that he's happy in an affair until the moment the woman puts any demands on him. In other words, he's happy in a relationship until it becomes a relationship. What Larry is doing is called dating. There's nothing wrong with dating, but it's usually better if you're not married at the same time. If Larry doesn't feel attractive, and the woman he married doesn't make him feel attractive, then Larry needs to do some work to find out what it will *really* take for him to feel good about himself. Maybe therapy is a good place to start. The chances of Larry feeling good about himself on his current path are slim at best. Larry has found a tried-and-true method of keeping himself "unavailable" for a real relationship. What would happen if Larry turned to his wife and told her, honestly, that he feels unattractive? Who knows? Larry certainly doesn't know, and never will as long as he loses himself in a series of affairs. To confide his fears and insecurities to his wife would mean that Larry would have to become vulnerable. And that, dear readers, is the common thread behind all our "unavailable" choices and behaviors, including my own. None of us want to be vulnerable. None of us believe it's truly safe. And so we choose unsafe people to justify our fears, and hide behind affairs that will never offer us the safety we need to become vulnerable. It's not a life; it's a facsimile of one. And that's why it doesn't feel good for very long.

Lynn was shy and overweight when she married twelve years ago. Now she's great-looking and successful and wants to catch up on all the sex and excitement she feels she missed. Once again, Lynn is someone who *assumes* that there is not enough sex and excitement in her own marriage. If that's the case, then she might want to remind herself of the things she found worthwhile in her marriage in the first place. I'm not saying that people don't change. They do. And not all marriages withstand those changes. The truth is that we are living longer and staying healthier and more mentally alert well into decades that were previously thought of as "twilight years." Not all marriages that end in divorce should be considered failures. Because we're living so long, the person you met and married at age twenty might not be the person at forty whom you want to be with another twenty years. That doesn't have to mean that the twenty years you spent together weren't worthwhile. But many people are sabotaging relationships and marriages before they even *try* to save them. This may be why the statistics are showing a growing number of people who are getting married *twice*—to *each other*! They leave the marriage, sometimes after an affair, sometimes for other reasons, but usually looking for something that exists only within a real relationship. Then, when they don't find it, they come back "home," discovering that what they were looking for was right next to them all along.

Ken claims to be happily married. He says that he considers his affairs to be like the dessert after his main meal, something he doesn't need but has room for; sort of like Jell-O. Wouldn't it be nice if the human heart and all our intimate relationships were as easy as planning a menu? Actually, no. But you'd be surprised how often I heard this analogy used when justifying an affair. "Just because I like steak doesn't mean I shouldn't enjoy a little chicken once in a while." But people have feelings. They have hopes and dreams for their lives and they agonize over how to make those dreams come true. And when they give their heart to someone, it means that they are making themselves vulnerable (there's that word again). There is such a casual attitude these days about commitment and relationships, in the music played and the television shows watched. I'm a child of the sixties and I'm the last one to say we should go back to the postwar mentality of pretending that sex doesn't exist and relationships need never be discussed. But we do need to acknowledge that there are consequences to our actions when it comes to the choices we make. It seems as if every other song on the radio and every third joke on television makes light of affairs. It's as if they're the "thing to do." No wonder David, the man I had an affair with, was fond of saying that, because all his friends had had many affairs, he believed he "deserved" to have one too. I'm not advocating censorship. I'm just saying that there is precious little awareness of how much damage is done when we "have a little affair." There are no "little" affairs.

If you find yourself considering an affair with a married man, and none of my warnings about making yourself unavailable for a real relationship are getting through, remember my friend Maxine. After she recovered from her affair with Phil, she realized that she had been kidding herself for all those years, thinking she was an important person in Phil's life and in his heart. In the end, she realized that she was little more than the emotional Styrofoam packing in someone else's life. Not exactly a scientific evaluation of the situation, but it's a hell of an image.

There's one more type of affair I want to talk about, and that's the "close friendship." That's one in which you're the best friend, confidante, and trusted advisor to someone who is unavailable. Even if he doesn't know about or share your feelings, even if you're not having sex with him, *you* are still involved with an unavailable person and you are still keeping yourself unavailable. In some ways this can be even more dangerous than a full, sexual affair in that the signs are more difficult to read. After all, you're not having sex with him. You're not meeting in out-of-the-way restaurants or motels. What's the harm? If you are participating in what noted therapist Robert Firestone calls a "Fantasy Bond," then you are retreating from the reality of your life and making it extremely difficult to remain available for a healthy, reality-based relationship. Many of the married couples I spoke with said they believe an emotional affair, even without the element of sex, can be just as threatening to a marriage as a sexual affair.

The damage to yourself is that while you're misspending your affection on someone whom you can't have, you remain unavailable.

When speaking of an affair, try to remember that even if you win, you lose.

2. SOMEONE WHO TELLS YOU THEY'RE UNAVAILABLE

Believe it on the whisper.
—MAYA ANGELOU

Sometimes people tell you, in a variety of ways, that they're not available for a real relationship. But instead of getting that message, you choose to ignore it.

Here are four reasons you would get involved with someone who tells you he's unavailable:

1. You weren't listening.
2. You didn't think it meant you.
3. You love a challenge.
4. You're single and unavailable and don't want a relationship either.

Let's look at reason number one. You weren't listening. Believe it or not, this happens all the time. Person A meets Person B and asks if he's available for a relationship. Person B says that no, as a matter of fact, he's not available for a relationship, due to such and such a reason. And then Person A does something rather strange. Person A doesn't hear what Person B has just said. Person A simply continues on as if nothing happened. Why does Person A do this? Well, the real reasons are probably buried deep within her psyche, but let's agree that she is not doing all she could to choose an available man for the relationship in her life. It's possible that she just wasn't listening to what he was saying. That's why I'm writing this book, to help you read the clues. You have to listen and you have to know *how* to listen. That's why I put it at the top of the list. Deborah Tannen, in her wonderful and authoritative books about the art of listening, uses the term "active listening." It's a conscious, "active," process in which you don't just receive information, you consider it. She has written volumes about the huge benefits of active listening, as well as all the unnecessary pain and heartache that come from not listening well. If you really listen, you'll get clues that will let you know whether the person you're dealing with is available or not, as well as how he defines that word. Then, and only then, can you step back and consider the pitfalls or the advantages of moving forward in that relationship.

A group of us went to a baseball game one afternoon. My friend Marshall brought Gina, the new woman in his life. Afterwards we all gathered for dinner. Gina spoke freely and told us all that she was just getting over her divorce and had no desire to jump right into a committed relationship. She needed to get out and go to a ballgame and have a meal out from time to time. She made it clear that she was available for afternoon trips to the ballpark, but unavailable for a relationship. It wasn't some secret that she told me in confidence. Gina talked about it openly at the table, in front of everyone, including Marshall. She wasn't being cruel; she was just being honest about where she was in her life. But when I spoke to Marshall the next day, he practically had the church booked and the honeymoon suite reserved. He hadn't heard a word she'd said. I gently reminded him that she had been quite open about where she was, and that perhaps he might not want to move so fast, but he only got snippy with me and told me that she had said nothing of the kind. He proceeded with his plan to woo her, doing his best to sweep her off her feet. When she didn't respond, and then broke it off, he was devastated. I've never said the words "I told you so," and I never will. But as it happened, the same group, minus Gina, went to another ball game later in the season. The topic came up and I remained silent as every other person who had been at the previous game related how they had heard Gina talk about how she really wasn't interested in a relationship. Marshall didn't hear Gina because he didn't *want* to hear her. It's a dangerous game to play with your heart.

Reason number two: You didn't think it meant you. We've all been guilty of this one. We all have egos, and that's a good thing. We're all special and we need to know that we're special, and that's a good thing as well. But, to quote a friend of mine, "If the dog on your block has bitten everyone in the neighborhood, what makes you think it's not going to bite you?"

Oliver started dating Barbara and was quite taken with her.

Early in their relationship, however, Barbara told him that she had a "confession" to make. She told him about how she had stalked and assaulted her former fiancé. She even told him about how she had been charged, found guilty, and had had a three-year restraining order issued against her, protecting the former fiancé and his young son. The confession was a tearful one and Oliver chose to take it as her attempt to be honest and forthright. Over the next few weeks he saw the way Barbara treated her friends and family and he didn't like what he saw. And even between the two of them it was one mixed message after another, until the relationship finally ended a few short but painful months later. If you ask him now, Oliver would admit that he thought that *he* would somehow be different. He would be clever enough, or nice enough, or whatever enough to change her into the person he thought she could be. In other words, "The dog has bitten everyone in the neighborhood but he won't bite me." Oliver was so upset with himself for not paying attention to who this woman really was that he went to a therapist for some help.

Reason number three: You love a challenge. If your self-esteem lies in winning, controlling, or getting the ungettable, the person who tells you they're unavailable could end up being your next big challenge. But what then? After you win, if you *do* win, then it's over, and you're right back where you started, looking for another challenge. That's not a relationship; that's a contest. At least call it what it is. And if all you're looking for is to win, and you can find someone who is also looking to be in a contest, and the two of you want to duel to the finish, go right ahead. Just know that you're both single and unavailable, and you should present yourselves as such. The problem is that very few people even realize that they're only in it for the "win." And so other people get involved with these game players and feelings are hurt, and time is wasted. The truth is you shouldn't feel the need to *win over* a person who is truly resistant to you. If you were an available person, looking for another available person, you would move on to someone who's at least moderately interested.

That's not to say that wooing will ever go out of fashion. It's been a part of the mating ritual since time began. I'm talking about getting turned on or encouraged by rejection. For those of you who subscribe to the Groucho Marx school of thought, "I wouldn't want to belong to any club that would have me as a member," the resistant person can hold a certain fascination. It's not unusual for someone who doesn't feel good about himself to try to win over a person he considers above him or out of his league. If he can "win" that person over (as if we can ever really win a person), he thinks he'll finally feel good about himself. But for people who are lacking self-esteem, they will eventually turn the win into a loss because the object of their affection will ultimately be deemed unworthy. If they're in my "club," how great could they be? These single and unavailable people can never really win because they must constantly seek out partners to reject them in order to confirm what they believe about themselves. If someone does return their interest, then he or she is obviously undesirable or they wouldn't want to be with them. Joseph Heller called it catch-22, and the only way to win that game is not to play. No matter how you play it, disappointment is guaranteed. It's a syndrome that has a lot to do with self-esteem and it should be dealt with in a serious fashion because, Groucho Marx aside, it's a painful way to live one's life. It will also keep you single and unavailable.

Lindsey always knew she would go to medical school. She had two burning passions, to be a doctor—or to marry one. Soon after she started medical school, she met Donald, a really good-looking fellow student. He met all her requirements for a potential mate. They started doing research together and soon they were performing Anatomy Labs on each other after hours. From the moment they met, Donald was clear with Lindsey about the fact that he absolutely, positively, definitely didn't want to be in a relationship—at least until he finished medical school. Lindsey agreed, thinking all the while he'd change his mind once he got to know her and she became indispensable in his life.

She was sure it was working when he asked if she wanted to move in with him to save money on expenses. Lindsey jumped at the chance. Donald was the smartest man she'd ever been with and the sex was, you guessed it, incredible.

Once Lindsay moved in, she began doing Donald's research work and typing his papers in addition to her own work. She cleaned the apartment, did the cooking, and still managed to be a ball of fire in the bedroom. They both learned to put Donald first.

Lindsey was exhausted and her studies suffered, but it was worth it to her to please Donald. At least one of them was going to be a doctor. After two years of togetherness, Lindsey felt confident of their bond and of Donald's growing dependence on her. One evening, she brought up the subject of where their relationship was going. Lindsey was more than shocked when Donald hadn't changed his mind and further added that while he liked her a lot, he wasn't in love with her. He was under the impression they were both enjoying the temporary arrangement.

Her self-esteem was shattered and they broke up. She had been the best Lindsey she could be and it hadn't worked. She felt if Donald didn't love her after she'd been perfect, who would ever love the real Lindsey with her real faults?

Lindsey wondered what more she could have done. What more did Donald want? The truth is he didn't want *more*—he didn't *want* a relationship at all and had told her so. As much as Lindsey claims she wants to be in a relationship, she picked a man who was adamant about not wanting the same thing.

This is not to say that Lindsey should bear all the responsibility for the way things turned out. Donald could see exactly what was happening and he chose to do nothing because he was reaping what he considered the "benefits" of having Lindsey there when he needed her. She should have listened, he should have seen.

Of the two of them, Lindsey was the one who made the most of her mistake. After some soul-searching, and some good therapy, Lindsey recognized her role in the Donald situation. She was able to look at other areas of her life and see a long pattern of expecting success while going after things that were guaranteed failures. She had developed a Fantasy Bond in several areas of her life, and she began to look at life in a realistic way for the first time. It wasn't an easy road, but it was a satisfying one. Lindsey has since made some much healthier choices in her life and is happier for them. Donald, when last I heard, was still single and unavailable.

Lindsey's years of heartache were not something she was doomed to—and neither are you. Awareness is the key. Learn to listen. Examine your history. Are you living out a pattern of behavior that has led to heartache before? Remember that while it's human nature to try to present your best self to someone you're interested in, you must learn the difference between being your best and being someone else. If your history points to a series of unavailable partners, then stop, take a look at the pattern, and think about what you're going to do about it. It's only then that you can bring about a change that will make you available.

Reason number four: You're the unavailable one. In the previous story about Lindsey and Donald I spoke about Donald's responsibility to see what effect his actions were having on Lindsey. Regardless of what he told her, he could still see that Lindsey was behaving as if they were both in a real relationship. We all have a moral obligation to make damn sure that, to the best of our ability, there is no misunderstanding in such matters. If you say one thing and your behavior says another, then you're sending a mixed message, which is an innocuous little term for a practice that can cause great harm. If you've clearly stated that you're not interested in a relationship, but are intimate with someone, or have dated them for a long period of time, then you're sending mixed signals and fostering hope in someone who wants a future with you. Saying you don't want a relationship and then *being* in one is misleading—even to you. Be honest with yourself about your intentions. Maybe you're just not available to the person you're currently with. If so, then move on, and thereby help them to move on to someone who *is* available. You won't find love while you're busy being in the wrong relationship.

Of course, nobody wants to be in a "wrong" relationship. Given the choice, most of us want the best relationship possible.

How good is good enough? Should you hold out for great? As Stephen Covey says in his book, *The 7 Habits of Highly Effective People*, "It's easy to choose between good and bad. It's a clear choice. What's difficult in life is to make the choice between good and great." It's not only important that you ask yourself whether or not you're truly available for a relationship; it's also important that you know just what kind of a relationship you're interested in. Define your terms. It will make your life, especially your dating life, a lot simpler.

3. ALCOHOLICS, WORKAHOLICS, ANY "HOLICS"

If you cannot change the people around you, change the people you're around.

—ANONYMOUS

Addictions to alcohol, drugs, sex, gambling, etc. are all now considered illnesses. This is a huge leap forward in our perception of these behaviors, but the dangers for those in relationships with addicted people is still extreme. If you find yourself more often than not in a relationship with one of these types of people, you might have your own addiction issues to deal with. There is a personality type known as a "Rescuer." Even though countless scholarly volumes have been written about the syndrome, for our purposes I think it's safe to say that a Rescuer is someone who responds to another person's need, real or imagined, regardless of the cost to their own lives. Rescuers frequently end up with addicted people. No matter how damaged you are, you can usually experience some sense of worth and control when you feel better off than your partner is. There is an intoxication to giving, for some an irresistible intoxication; and there is no end of giving when dealing with an addict. As long as they are drinking, or using, or gambling, or whatever it is, they are in the process of trying to fill a "hole in their soul" that will never be filled by the substance or the behavior. And the Rescuer will always have to be there to bail him out, sometimes literally. Ultimately, this is what I call a "hierarchical" relationship. One person is "higher" in the sense that they appear to be the stronger one, the "helper," the "giver," and the other person, the addict, is the "needy" one, the "receiver." It is, by its very nature, an unequal relationship and, as such, it is precarious. It's not unusual for an addict to get well and leave the relationship. Why? Because the "relationship" was built on an off-kilter hierarchical structure. Change that structure and things are bound to get shaky.

If you've attended any twelve-step programs such as Alcoholics Anonymous, Narcotics Anonymous, Gamblers Anonymous, etc., you know that one of the basic premises is that you can't fix anyone but yourself. If you're a good person, and you're attracted to someone who is battling an addiction, then there will be a natural pull to help that person. (And, of course, to make matters worse, addicts are frequently incredibly charming, creative, attractive people who make it easy to want to help them.) But just as the addict must be very tough with himself if he's going to get better, you must be brutally honest in your evaluation of whether or not you are using that person, and his illness, to keep yourself single and unavailable. If you're waiting for them to clean up *their* act so *your* life can start, you're asking for trouble.

Maybe you want to be alone. Being with an addict will guarantee you time alone—even when you're together. There are dozens of reasons that people end up with addicts. Perhaps one of your parents was an alcoholic. It's the scenario for which you may have developed an entire set of coping skills; so, naturally, there is a tendency to find a way to make use of what you know. It's quite common for the child of an alcoholic or addict to seek out the same situation when he or she is an adult. Some have a need to recreate their childhood, hoping to change it. They want to rewrite their childhood history, but all they do is recast it—same script, different players, more of the same pain they knew as a child. There is a certain comfort in the familiar even if it's painful. You're used to dealing with a person who puts themselves and their addiction first, but know that when you're with an addict or alcoholic, you're not having an equal relationship. You both agree, whether you know it or not, to focus on them and their addiction. It's a situation tailor-made for the person who wants to remain unavailable. The sad thing is that so many of the people involved with addicts are unaware of what they're doing to their own lives.

Like Jenny. Her first boyfriend, Eddie, was into drugs. Jenny's energy was spent trying to help Eddie deal with the effects of his addiction. He refused to get into a program and eventually he lost his job and his reputation, and ended up in jail. His sentence was long enough so Jenny had no choice but to move on. In time she felt she had learned a good lesson from that experience.

Her next boyfriend, Charles, seemed to be an immediate improvement. First of all, Charles didn't do drugs! He had a job, a nice apartment. What a change of pace it was to be with Charles. Everything was one big wonderful party. They celebrated everything with champagne and martinis. Jenny probably knew right away, but it took her a long time to acknowledge that Charles had a drinking problem. Again her first thought was to fix him rather than leave. Of course, Charles didn't think he had a drinking problem. He was just a "social drinker," he said. And Jenny chose to believe him. And the years went by. After a while, Charles's alcoholism was out of control. He lost his job and became abusive. One day Jenny came home to find him passed out drunk in bed with another woman. In the end it was his infidelity that Jenny chose to focus on. She ended the relationship because he cheated, not because of his drinking. She still wasn't ready to look at the Rescuer dynamic in her life. If you had told Jenny that she was a Rescuer, she would have denied it and said that she was just trying to be a nice person. She would have said that being supportive is important in any relationship, and that everybody had their problems; Eddie and Charles happened to use and drink, she would have said, but they were no different from anybody else with problems. She would be right about the first part of her statement. Everybody does have problems, of course. But problems are not the same as addictions. Problems can be confronted, dealt with, and solved. Addictions are, for the most part, serious illnesses that require treatment of some sort that takes place over a substantial period of time. If you are with an addict and you're not part of his recovery, then you're enabling him to continue to live in his addiction. You are in a relationship with an addiction, not a person.

Another phrase that is popular in twelve-step programs is about what happens when you give up your addiction: "The good news is, you get your feelings back; the bad news is, you get your feelings back." Every relationship, even a great one, has its share of problems. But, when one is involved with an addict, he or she must first deal with the addiction before the problems are even visible.

But Jenny wasn't done yet. Next up was Drew. She made sure Drew didn't drink or do drugs before she agreed to date him. He had his own business and was really committed to making a go of it. He seemed perfect. She was aware from the start that he worked seven days a week. Drew was a major workaholic—he even referred to himself that way, proudly. Soon Jenny found herself back in a familiar and lonely place in her life. When she tried to protest, he made her feel guilty. Drew told her repeatedly how good she had it and how lucky she was to have a boyfriend who didn't do drugs, drink, or cheat on her. She wanted to believe her life was improving because each man *seemed* less damaged than the previous one. From drug addict, to alcoholic philanderer, to workaholic seemed like progress to her. But she was just as miserable.

Jenny's father had been an alcoholic. She had always felt lonely in her relationship with her father and picking these men was a way of repeating that pattern in her adult life. When Drew worked late on the night of her birthday, completely forgetting to show up at the expensive restaurant where she was waiting, Jenny had finally had enough. Devastated, she followed a friend's advice and went to an Alanon meeting. For the first time in her life she felt as if she was in a group of people that understood what she felt each time she was attracted to these damaged men.

When she was ready to date again, she brought a brand-new sensitivity towards the danger signs to look out for. That's when she met Tim. He seemed like a real catch. He didn't do drugs, drink, or work weekends. Like Goldilocks and the Three Bears,

Jenny thought she found the one who was "just right." On their first night out, Jenny *really* listened. She knew the price of *not* listening. She had learned that people will reveal themselves; we're just too busy trying to make a good impression to hear it. This time she was paying attention to every detail and she *heard* Tim when he revealed that he worked out every night and ran every morning—without fail. Rain or shine. Even the day his mother died! When he used the term "addicted to working out," her radar went up. But Tim seemed so great that she was reluctant to break things off so soon. (And so should you be, by the way, if your radar goes up with an otherwise healthy date. When you see something that gives you pause, then, by all means, pause. But sometimes it takes a while to determine whether a behavior is a quirk—we all have them—or a personality type that should be considered dangerous to your emotional health. This book is about warning signs, not excuses for giving up on dating and relationships. My goal is to help you step away from the unavailable people as quickly as possible so that you can find an available soul mate and begin to enjoy the warmth and love that comes from a fulfilling relationship.) So Jenny gave Tim another try. He said he was glad she wanted to see him again, that he was very attracted to her. Then he told her that the first available opening he had for her was two weeks away. It wasn't because he was going out of town or working on a special project; he was just booked solid with his trainer, yoga, and spin classes. Jenny thanked him *very* much and never saw him again.

There are as many addicts as there are activities in this world. If someone is doing something, anything, *instead* of living his life, then you may be talking to an addict. If he's doing something *in addition to* living his life, then you may have just met an interesting man who is available for a relationship.

YOU'RE THE "HOLIC"

You don't have to be falling-down drunk or strung out on drugs for your excesses to interfere with your love life. I know many people who have a glass of wine because it helps them to relax. I have also known people who drink or smoke to excess because they're lonely. Rather than feel bad, they'd rather not feel at all. This is an effective way of postponing your life. It's like being in a holding pattern. You "numb out" in order to end the bad feelings. The problem is, you're deadened to the good feelings too. You're successfully keeping anything bad or good from getting in.

Hopefully you are aware of your problem and you're seeking help for it. Make sure you're not using your illness or your recovery to keep you from a healthy relationship. You could be married, living with someone, or still searching, but if you're in denial about your own illness, you're not available to anyone else. And maybe that's where you need to be. It's not always a good time to be looking for a relationship, even a healthy one. There are many seasons to this life of ours and one of them is the season of solitude. Anthony Storr, in his book, *Solitude*, writes eloquently about the great benefits of being alone. If you are struggling with major life changes and you feel that you need to focus on those changes in order to succeed, then it's probably a good idea to hold off on any type of relationship that could distract you from the work you need to do. Because even if no one has ever left you because of your addictions—even if no one else knows about them but you—it still can have a negative effect on your ability to be present in a relationship. It keeps a barrier between you and the other person. If the fear of intimacy is what drives you to numb yourself with drugs and alcohol, it's working. If you're trapped in an addiction, then you're already *in* a relationship. Getting help for your addiction is the number one thing you need to do to save your life—and to start your life.

4. SOMEONE WHO WANTS TO CHANGE YOU

Argue for your limitations and sure enough they're yours.
—RICHARD BACH

There's a wonderful novel by Anne Taylor called *The Accidental Tourist*. In it the lead character's wife keeps beginning conversations with her husband with the question, "Do you know what you need?" believing she has the answer. It's a niggling little phrase, but it speaks to a much bigger problem that exists in many relationships. People who want to change you. What they're really saying is, "You're not okay the way you are and I'm the one who knows how to make you better." Now, on the face of it, we can all see how absurd it is to give up control of our lives and our self-image to someone else; but in reality, these people who "know what you need" can be quite powerful and frequently very attractive. They seem to have answers where you might only have questions. And, rather than help you to figure out your own answers, which is what happens in a healthy, loving relationship, they're happier to supply you with *their* answer and leave it to you to make it work. Why would you want to accommodate them? Well, many people don't know what they want to do with their lives. Finding someone who will tell them what to do *feels* like relief. They're willing to let someone else take charge and tell them who and what they should be in exchange for being relieved of the burden of having to make those decisions themselves. It's a Faustian bargain and it's hell in the end. Often it's an extension of a childhood pattern. Maybe Mom or Dad did all his thinking, never let him venture out on his own, and now he's looking for a new "parent." But here's the problem; the person who's changing you—doesn't like you the way you are. Oh, he'll tell you he likes you, maybe he'll even say that he loves you. But the truth is that he's in love with some *idea* of you that he has in his head, and he's going to spend the next (Five years? Ten years? A lifetime?) molding you until you match up to that idea in *his* head. And here's the kicker;

he thinks he's doing *you* a favor! I mean, after all, look at all the time and effort he's putting in to make you the best "you" that you can be (for him, that is). It's confusing. Confusing because the real "you" is not available to this new person. And worse, after a while, the real you is not even available to *you.* (This person who wants to change you, by the way, probably doesn't like himself very much either. If he did, he wouldn't be spending so much time trying to "fix" you. He'd be doing what we all should be doing; working to make himself a better person.) If you turn yourself over to one of these "Svengalis," you end up being like a lump of clay. When you give the power to someone else to approve or disapprove of you, you're not honoring who you are. And if you don't know who you are, then start with that realization and work from there. Sit down with a piece of paper and a pencil (laptop, whatever) and write about how you don't know who you are and why that might be. It doesn't matter how old you are or how embarrassing it might be to write the words "I don't know who I am." I've known people in their sixties who have gone through this painful but fulfilling exercise and it has changed their lives. Then write about who you *want* to be. And if you don't have any answers to that question, then sit there, or read, or travel, or talk to a friend, or a priest, or a rabbi, or a therapist, or walk on the beach, or do whatever the hell you need to do in order to come up with some answers. They don't have to be right answers. There are no right answers, only right answers for you. And, if you change those answers drastically in a year, or ten years, or a week and a half, then that's okay, too. The important thing is to have *some* idea of who you are and who *you* want to be. It's your duty and your privilege as a human being, and don't let anyone take it away from you. If you are turning these questions over to someone else, then you are unavailable for a real relationship. In a real relationship, each person has control of their own life and shares control of the life they have together.

Don't confuse giving up control of your life with getting help with your life. We all look to others for ideas, for different viewpoints, even for constructive criticism, but be sure that the final judge of you is you. You don't want to end up being the emotional equivalent of tofu, someone who takes on the flavor of each new person you meet.

Let's look at Tanya's story. She married very young. She left home to escape a critical mother and ended up marrying a critical husband. After eleven unhappy years, Tanya finally left. At thirty-one she was alone for the first time in her life. She didn't have a clue as to who she was or what she liked. Tanya had relied on others to define her. Her mother called her lazy for the first twenty years of her life, and then her husband took over with a similar message. She was lucky to have him, he told her, and Tanya assumed that he knew what he was talking about. She didn't have enough confidence in her own instincts to contradict him. She always kept a neat home, but assumed he was right when he told her that it wasn't neat enough. Just about anything that came up, she deferred to his "superior" knowledge. It was only after she was divorced from him and living in her apartment for a while that she discovered she was neither lazy, nor sloppy, nor stupid. At first she actually waited in dread for her place to be heaped in garbage, but it never happened. She realized she enjoyed keeping her home nice and that she was damned good at it. Who knew? She had never questioned her mother's judgment, or her husband's. This new feeling of independence and competence thrilled her but scared her as well. Sometimes revelations seem to come at a price in this life. She was lonely in that apartment, and suffered from all the anxiety one might expect from someone who was thirty-one years old and on her own for the first time.

What else didn't she know about herself, Tanya wondered? She decided she would treat herself as if she was a new friend whom she was just getting to know. Whatever problems Tanya had in her romantic relationships with men, she had always managed to make good friends. She had always tried to be kind and considerate, as well as honest with her friends. And so she decided to try an experiment and treat herself the same way. It felt a little like a childish game, but it seemed to bypass her own feelings of insecurity if she thought of herself this way; as her own best friend. By using this little device, she was able to uncover long-denied preferences and tastes she had buried years before. She enjoyed staying up late and reading in bed, eating cold pizza for breakfast, and watching old movies. In the end, she was thrilled over her newfound freedom and sense of well-being. Luckily for her the exhilaration won out over the fear.

Soon she was attracting a whole new set of people into her life, people who treated her kindly and with respect. Why? Because that's how she was *learning* to treat herself. Once she set a standard for herself, others followed.

You want to change someone

How can you tell if you're a Changer? If everyone you meet would be *perfect* if they would just change something—well, that's certainly a heads up, isn't it? Whether you think they need to change jobs, change their looks, or change their attitude, it's really more about you than it is about them. Of course, you *always* think that you have a justifiable reason for wanting the other person to change; Changers always do. Remember, the six most dangerous words in the English language are "I was only trying to help." This is not to say that a healthy part of any relationship isn't helping the other person to improve his or her life. If you're dating someone who, oh, let's say, robs convenience stores for a living and they would sincerely like to cut down on that habit, then by all means, do what you can to help him out. But only if *he* wants to change. If it's *your* need that he change, then you're just wasting your time. Either get out of the relationship (that would be my first suggestion) or buy yourself a ski mask and buckle up because it's going to be a bumpy ride.

Change is hard enough when we're doing it for our own reasons; changing for someone else, even someone you love, is as rare as a unicorn. It just doesn't seem to happen very often, and when it does, it doesn't seem to last very long. There's a famous cartoon that shows two chairs in a marriage counselor's office; above each chair is a large sign that reads: "This is what you get." And it's true. If you're dating someone and there's something about him that really bothers you, then move on. And if you've had a *series* of relationships in which you have tried to change your partner, then you should take that as a sign that, underneath your need to "help," there may be a (hidden) bigger need for you to remain unavailable.

Here are some areas to explore. Do you generally have more dislikes about a person than things that you like? What happens when someone does change for you? Are you satisfied? Or do you simply find another aspect of that person that "needs changing?" No matter how odd or flawed the other person might seem, chances are *you* are what's keeping you from finding love. Any therapist (actually, any Psych. 101 student) will tell you that if you are constantly finding flaws in others, it's because you're not happy with yourself. Maybe you grew up in a painfully critical atmosphere. Maybe underneath all your criticism is a sensitive person who has learned to attack before being attacked. Whatever the reason, the behavior will do a very nice job of keeping you single, no matter how many "flawed" people you date.

Next time you're tempted to mold someone into your version of "acceptable," stop and realize what you're doing. Try to listen to yourself and then try to suffer through the anxious moment that will follow when you *don't* make the criticism that you *feel* you must. Try to identify what it is that's making you reject this person. What are you feeling? Are you afraid of being vulnerable? Do you feel threatened? Or, how about this? Do you find yourself wanting to change the very thing that attracted you to that person so it won't attract others? This is a particularly nasty piece of work that goes on in unhealthy relationships.

Let's look at Tessa. She fell head over heels for Robert, a man she met at a softball game. He was a good-looking man, very athletic, and he looked particularly good when he was on the field. So what did Tessa do once she had won Robert over? She made him quit playing softball. "Made," of course, is not an accurate word to describe what happened. Nobody *made* him quit softball. He chose to acquiesce to her wish that he give up softball. And that was the beginning. Tessa didn't like his friends, so he stopped seeing them. She didn't like his car, so he got another one. She didn't like his job, so he quit. Eventually there wasn't much of Robert left. That's when Tessa "decided" that Robert wasn't very interesting anymore and she left him for her next "project."

Sometimes it starts out in less dramatic ways. For instance, if a man was attracted to a woman who dressed in sexy clothes when he met her, but now wants her to dress conservatively, he should give some real thought to his motives. Control is an illusion. The *attempt to control* is very real and very destructive and will almost certainly keep you single and unavailable well into old age. Just be yourself, and let him be himself, and then see what happens. Sounds simple, but of course it's not.

Sometimes there's a temptation to pretend that you like what he likes, dislike what he dislikes. "Lawn bowling? I *love* lawn bowling. Can't get enough!" That's great if you happen to really love lawn bowling. But don't pull the tired old "bait and switch." It doesn't even work on sitcoms anymore (I know, I write them). Anyway, it's bound to blow up in your face. Isn't it more appealing to find someone with whom you really connect? The guy who is addicted to sports is going to be much happier with a woman who is either wildly enthusiastic about them herself, or couldn't care less if he spends every weekend parked in front of the television. By the same token the woman who wants to dress and feel sexy is going to feel better with a secure man who doesn't need to make her feel wrong for who she is. It's important to recognize that these issues are about control and insecurity. It's much better to work on yourself and get to the roots of your own anxiety. Isn't it better to address what scares you and work on changing "you" than to keep changing partners because they tap into your fears? Whether someone plays softball or not should not be a source of anxiety. If it is, then you're not looking at what's really going on in your life. When you set out to stop another person from being himself, not only are you *not* participating in a real, "available" relationship, you're also creating a never-ending job, first with this partner, then with the next, and with the next. When they eventually move on, you just have to start all over, "changing" someone new. Wouldn't it make more sense to change what's fearful in you? More difficult, more painful, perhaps, but ultimately more satisfying. When we're scared and want to feel better, our first instinct is to want someone *else* to make us feel better. "Mommy or Daddy and a glass of warm milk would be wonderful, but you'll do," is what our hearts say to us sometimes. Sounds great; doesn't work. Feeling better, in the end, comes from the inside, not from another person or from an outside source. You can share "it" (feeling good), you can enhance it, you can nurture it, you can celebrate it with someone else, you can do all kinds of wonderful things with "it," but, if it's real, then it comes from you. The good news is that it's there, inside of you. It's just a matter of getting to it.

5. SOMEONE NOT OVER A PAST LOVE

> *I love Mickey Mouse more than any woman I've ever met.*
> —WALT DISNEY

I'm old enough to have seen a movie (in a theater, not on video) called *A Man and a Woman*, sometime back in the mid-seventies. It's a French film with a famous, romantic music score that you'd recognize in an instant. In this movie the man falls in love with the woman after they meet at the boarding school attended by their children. He's divorced; she's a widow. They spend time together, things go very well indeed and, some months later, the two of them end up together in a charming little hotel somewhere in the South of France. But as they begin to make love, she turns icy cold. She can't go through with it. She finally tells him that she's still not over the death of her husband, even though it's been several years. He died just after they married; he was a stuntman killed by a mistimed explosive. Silently she dresses and leaves. He drives back to Paris alone, in the rain, talking to himself, wishing her husband had lived even a few more years. Then she would have gotten a chance to see a flaw or two. As is it, he says to himself, the husband will always be perfect in her memory. How is he supposed to compete with that? I won't tell you how the film ends. Go rent it. If you don't mind subtitles, you'll be glad you did.

Sometimes we're in love with a fantasy and no one real can ever measure up. Many people find it easier to grieve for someone or something that might have been—or never was—than to risk opening up to something that could be. Whether the loss is due to a breakup, illness, or death, you need to go through the pain and sorrow of your loss and heal it before someone else can get in. There's a law of physics that says that two things cannot occupy the same space at the same time. I suspect that it's no different with our hearts. Not that we can't have place for family, a place for friends, even a place for God and Country while we're at it. But we're talking now about that most special of all places, the place of love and trust and commitment. If you take those three words and multiply them by two, you've got an oxymoron. "I love you, but I still love someone else" isn't a song anyone wants to hear.

As tempting as it is to ease the pain of loss by "losing" yourself in the excitement of a new relationship, you're just postponing the inevitable. Loss is painful. There's just no getting around it. Certainly, make use of friends, family, professionals, support groups; use any tool available to you that might help you through the barrage of difficult emotions that always follow a loss. But diving into a new relationship is not only counterproductive, it's not fair. Not to you, and certainly not to the other person who may actually believe you when you say you're over it. Only you know the images in your mind as your head hits the pillow each night. Only you know when you feel those twinges of pain when you end up at the same restaurant, the same car wash, the same whatever, that you frequented with the partner you're supposedly "over." Sometimes it's the new relationship itself that opens up these wounds. This is, of course, a difficult situation. Maybe you didn't get into the relationship as an escape. Maybe you really *did* think you were over your grief; but now that your heart has been stirred, it opens, or reopens a closet full of feelings that come tumbling out all over the place. That's when it's necessary to be totally honest about what's really going on. Perhaps then, if your new relationship really is a healthy one, and a loving one, you *might* be able to help each other get through this experience together. There was no duplicity in this situation, just the frustrating unfairness of life and the lousy timing of certain emotions.

There's no unfairness in the case of Timothy, only a whole lot of hurry. Timothy is heading into marriage number five as I write this. He's only thirty-eight, so he's gone pretty much from one marriage to the next. Each wife left, saying that Timothy was stuck in the romance of the preceding marriage. He would go back to places they had vacationed, talk about them, tell stories, etc., etc. After wife number four left him he was resolved to stop and really figure out what was going on. He said that he wanted to get to know himself before getting into another doomed relationship. He joined meditation classes, spirituality classes; he begged, borrowed and stole every self-help book he could get his hands on. And six months later he was engaged to be married yet again. Timothy, of course, will tell you that *this* woman is the one; finally, his soul mate at long last. And maybe she is. But it's a pretty safe bet that he will continue his habit of "living in the past," and screwing up the present. The last time I saw Timothy I suggested he get himself a copy of *Madame Bovary* by Gustave Flaubert, and learn something about the perils of choosing romance over reality. Therapy could certainly help. I think Timothy is hiding from something. What he's afraid of may be simple, or it may be quite complex, but it is keeping him very unavailable, regardless of how many times he has been, or will be, married.

CAN'T GET OVER HATING A PAST LOVE

There is another way that not getting over an ex-love can keep you stuck, and that's when the love has been replaced with hate and bitterness. Make no mistake; even though he detests his ex, it doesn't mean his heart is going to be open to you. As a matter of fact, bitterness can keep a relationship (not a healthy, loving relationship, mind you; but a relationship nonetheless) alive for a lot longer than a simple pining for good times lost forever. What you should really be looking for is that he's just plain moved on.

We all know it's rarely just one person in the wrong during

a breakup. Is he calling his ex a [fill in your own expletive] because she's doing better than he is? Does he hate his ex because he has to support (his own) children? Someone full of hate probably has other issues, and feelings which are that strong, and that unresolved, are likely to spill over into other areas of his life, including his relationship with you. (This type is the perfect candidate for a "Rescuer," i.e.; "I'll be the one to calm him down, to prove that we aren't all just a bunch of greedy bitches." Good luck. If he's looking for a greedy bitch, then he'll find one.)

As tempting as it is to jump on board the "Let's slam the ex" train, try to resist. As good as it feels to hear how much better you are than she was, it will ultimately end badly and keep you (and him) unavailable for a real relationship in the meantime. Hatred can be a passionate emotion and, for some couples, it can almost be a turn-on. I've seen relationships that were practically *based* on an outside hatred. Sometimes it's an ex-spouse, sometimes it's the in-laws, sometimes it's a revolving cast of characters including the local school board (those bastards!). Take a good look at the person with whom you're considering a relationship. Do they complain about their work, their boss, their parents, their siblings, friends? Is the world a terribly unfair place to them? Remember my story about the dog that's bitten everyone else in the neighborhood? What makes you think the dog's not going to bite you? Find out what broke up the relationship. How long ago? How many other hated exs are out there? Could you be the next? Will the ex-husband or ex-wife be in your new life together, even if only as a constant complaint? If so, you're looking at an unavailable relationship. One that isn't about the chemistry, or lack of it, between the two of you. It's a relationship about him and someone else. You're only there as coconspirator.

A note here about complaining. I want to stress that there is a big difference between a "complainer" and a "*constant* complainer" or, worse, a constantly bitter person. We all have complaints; it's part of who we are, and finding someone with similar complaints about how the world works, or doesn't work, is one of the ways we determine with whom we're compatible. You could certainly find a complainer with a huge heart and a social conscience who is absolutely available and just perfect for you. Just make sure that there's still room after the complaining for the two of you, and for a love to grow.

6. A DISHONEST PERSON

> *Honesty is the key to a relationship.*
> *If you can fake that, you're in.*
> —RICHARD JENI

That's one of my favorite quotes, but what comedian Richard Jeni didn't add is that faking honesty will guarantee you a fake relationship. When you first meet someone, you probably assume they're telling you the truth. No matter what our background, no matter how untrustworthy our early world, we all have to assume some level of trust in order to get through a day. Telling your story and hearing theirs is how we get to know about each other. But if you sense something is off or you witness a moment of dishonesty, then you may know all you need to know about what to expect from this person in the future. Don't kid yourself that if it's not you he's lying to, it's not your problem—trust me, it will be. If he lies to the boss, lies to a friend, it should be a warning. I've had business dealings with people who lie even when they don't have to. It's like some nervous twitch. I lie, therefore I am. This person is telling you that this is how he deals with situations and conflicts.

I'm not talking about "social lies" or what are sometimes called "little white lies." Everyone has "lied" at some time or another in order to smooth out a social situation, a forgotten dinner invitation, or some such. I'm talking about someone who lies to avoid dealing with a difficult situation that *should* be dealt with honestly.

If you witness dishonest behavior right from the beginning, realize that it will affect you eventually. This is someone who will take the easy way out. Not exactly the kind of person you could depend on in a crisis, emotional or otherwise. Are you willing to chance that? If you're a Rescuer, you might think you'd be the one to change him. Love him enough and he'll change, right? Actually, the exact opposite is true. It's when our behavior costs us love that we find the strength to change. A person who lies is, as a rule, insecure and damaged. If you sense the new person in your life is being less than honest with you, challenge them. What do you have to lose? Of course, the answer to that question is that you may lose the relationship. If you call someone on their lying, or any other behavior that bothers you, then you are setting a boundary and risking loss. It's tricky with liars because they'll just lie about their lying. Go rent the movie *Gaslight* sometime and watch how much fun it is to be with an accomplished liar. Remember that you must pay attention. Listen. Listen to your heart as well as your instincts. You don't have to come off like an investigator to call someone on his inconsistencies. If you feel there's a gray area occurring, politely say you're confused and that you need clarification. If there are just too many things that don't add up, then you probably need to back away. It's not always easy. Liars can be wonderful storytellers, and the world they create is often much more pleasant than the cold, hard truth. But it's not reality; and reality is what you're looking for in a healthy, available relationship.

Review

We've looked at six different scenarios, six different types of "unavailable" situations to avoid. Examine the following statements and highlight the ones that apply to you. This is not a test. There are no right or wrong answers, no scores to add up. The purpose is to help identify the behaviors and beliefs that could be keeping you single and unavailable.

SOMEONE MARRIED

1. He's the only one who's shown an interest in me in a long time.
2. He's the only one I've been interested in for a long time.
3. I know it's not right, but it's better than nothing.
4. It's just until I meet someone else.
5. No one would love me if they really knew me full-time.
6. I like having time to myself.
7. If it weren't for his kids, finances, spouse's health, etc., we'd be together.
8. All the good ones are taken.
9. It's the most passionate and exciting relationship I've ever had.
10. We can tell each other things that we can't tell anyone else.

SOMEONE WHO TELLS YOU THEY'RE UNAVAILABLE

1. I don't feel deserving of someone who is available.
2. I love a challenge.
5. I don't value people or things that come too easily.
6. I need to "win" the approval of an unavailable person.
7. My needs come second to the people in my life.
8. The idea of getting what I want scares me.
9. I believe that if I'm good enough, nice enough, sexy enough, etc., I can change someone's mind eventually.

YOU'RE THE ONE WHO CLAIMS THE UNAVAILABILITY

1. I need to be loved more than I love.
2. I always give a disclaimer at the beginning of a relationship and still I end up misunderstood.

3. I always think there's someone better out there for me.
4. I feel superior to the people I'm involved with.
5. I've never been in a committed relationship.

ALCOHOLICS, WORKAHOLICS, ANY "HOLICS"

1. People are dependent on me, and I like it that way.
2. I believe that I don't deserve a whole, wonderful person.
3. I believe that his illness is somehow my responsibility.
4. If the other person were fixed they wouldn't want/need me.
5. His weakness gives me the power that I feel I need in a relationship.
6. I can use guilt to get my way in the relationship.
7. One or both of my parents had a problem with alcohol or drugs, so I'm familiar with the territory.

THEY WANT TO CHANGE YOU

1. He begins sentences with, "You'd be great if . . ." or "You need to . . ."
2. He corrects me a lot.
3. No matter what I've done, it could've been better.
4. He wants to change something that attracted him to me in the first place.
5. I feel inappropriately dependent on his approval and guidance.
6. I may be repeating past relationships I've had in which I only feel loved if I'm controlled.
7. I feel like I'm being treated like a project that can only improve with his help.

YOU'RE A CHANGER

1. I can see the potential in a person only if he changes something.
2. I really believe I can change the thing I don't like.
3. I grew up feeling as if I couldn't please my parents.
4. If someone actually changes for me, I move on to other areas that need work, or I move on to someone new.
5. I need to be in charge of the relationship.
6. I'm not willing to change.

THEY CAN'T GET OVER A PAST LOVE

1. He told me that he's still in love with an ex, I just don't want to listen.
2. It's been over for more than a year and he's still grieving.
3. There are still tons of pictures and personal items around from the past relationship.
4. He involves me in his grieving.
5. He's let me know, directly or indirectly, that he would leave me if the ex were available.
6. He still wants to be close friends with the ex and it feels as if he's still "involved."
7. He has left my side to come to the aid of the ex.
8. He chooses to continue to share property or something that necessitates contact.
9. He is so bitter about the ex that it interferes with my relationship with him.

YOU'RE NOT OVER A PAST LOVE

1. I still hope for reconciliation.
2. The person I'm seeing is just a substitute.
3. I imagine my ex during sex.
4. I stay in contact with his family or friends.
5. I conjure up excuses for contact with my ex.
6. I've forgotten the bad times and romanticized the good times.
7. I've idealized my ex.
8. I want him to know that I'm doing well.
9. I want him to see me looking good and will go out of my way to make that happen.
10. I'm so obsessed with hating him that I'm not available to anyone new.

THEY'RE DISHONEST

1. I know he tells lies to others but not to me.
2. I know he lies but I don't want to rock the boat.
3. He'll change when he sees how much I love him.

4. I know that I can change him.
5. I don't want to live the truth either, but this way it's not my fault.
6. I get to play the victim, which I secretly enjoy.
7. I want to believe the lies. I need the fantasy world.

YOU'RE DISHONEST

1. I don't tell the lie myself, but I don't correct it.
2. It's not my fault my partner lies.
3. I don't want my life to change.
4. I want to believe the lie.
5. I get to blame someone else for living in a fantasy world.
6. I lie to myself and I feel more comfortable with someone who lies.

Redo

You've looked over the list and underlined the statements that pertain to you. It doesn't matter if your responses are all in one group or sprinkled about; they can reveal beliefs that may be supporting your single and unavailable status. For instance, let's say you've highlighted several statements under the heading "You're a Changer." One might be "I can see the potential in a person only if he changes something." Here's the Redo part. Try writing a new sentence that you'd like to believe instead, such as "I make an effort to accept this person for who he is, not what I want him to be." Or if you picked "No matter what I've done, it could've been better," try treating yourself as you would a good friend and write instead; "I appreciate my efforts" or how about, "Nobody's perfect. Not him, not me, not anybody."

Try coming up with some of your own sentences to Redo. Recognizing your ability to change the pattern is a great place to start. You're ready to move on.

Chapter 2

The Ones to Watch Out For

At first glance, the next group might not seem as risky as the ones described in Chapter 1—and in some ways they aren't. It really depends, on your emotional good health and what you bring to the situation described. For the Single and Unavailable person, the following types of men (and, of course, women) can help you stay that way. And, in some ways, this group can be even more dangerous because they're not always as easy to identify.

1. SOMEONE WHO RUSHES INTO LOVE

When everything is coming your way, you're in the wrong lane.
—STEVEN WRIGHT

When someone needs to rush *into* a relationship, it might be because they don't believe there's time to actually *be in* a relationship. What I mean is, maybe they're hurrying to get in so they can hurry to get out when the thrill is gone. The initial excitement, of course, can be intense. Everything about it is accelerated and thrilling—just like in the movies; your eyes meet and lock, you feel a shiver through your body, and then it's—lower the lights and pass the popcorn—you're in love! It's fun, it's flattering, and it's a real ego boost—guaranteed to make you feel alive, at least temporarily. It's everything a strong drug ought to be, and it's even legal! But it's dangerous. I know a man who spent twenty years of his life flying jets for the Air Force. He told me that, for him, falling in love was like putting an F-15 fighter jet through its paces at top speed; loop the loops, dives, pull outs, and all the rest of it. The only difference, he noted, was that, unlike love, he could safely land the F-15 *before* the plane ran out of fuel.

The problem is that many healthy, solid relationships begin with what is commonly referred to as "chemistry." It can be an important ingredient in recognizing one's attraction to another person. We all need to listen to that little voice that "draws" us to someone who interests us. The difficulties begin when we *trust* that voice as if it had qualities like wisdom, foresight, and knowledge. It's just a voice and it could be your heart talking, or your hormones, or just deep loneliness. You should listen to that voice, but you must also question it, examine it, and monitor it as you find yourself getting deeper into a relationship, especially a relationship that doesn't feel complete and healthy. Even though every fiber of your being is telling you to rush towards the pleasure you're feeling with this other person, try to move slowly. If it's real, the love will still be there. If it's not real, if it's just a transitory "voice" speaking, then you will have saved yourself a lot of hurt and a lot of time by recognizing *early* that you are beginning an "unavailable" relationship.

What makes it go from being a normal dating situation to something you should watch out for is the pacing and the intensity. When you're with someone who moves very fast (I call them "Rushers"), they will tell you absolutely everything you want to hear from an "available" person; they just say it *way* too soon. I'm sure you are a wonderful, dynamic, smart, gorgeous, and sexy person, but if someone tells you all these things, and maybe even that they're falling in love with you, all on a first date—you're probably out with a Rusher. If he's cooking dinner for you on the second date, or calling you twenty times a day right from the start, or he's saying "I love you" almost from the first night, then you're dealing with a Rusher.

When you hear the phrase "I've never known anyone like you" on your first meeting, bear in mind that he doesn't know *you* either! If you've done some of the exercises in Chapter 1, then you are hopefully becoming a better listener and somewhat more alert to the warning signs that someone may be unavailable. As you become more secure and truly more available, you will process, and then react to, this information differently. It's flattering to feel irresistible, but someone who tells you too much, too soon, isn't really complimenting you so much as he's trying to "close a sale." If you really think there's relationship potential, then ask him to slow down. Do it gently, do it with tact, but do it; and then see if he can put on the brakes and really get to know you. If he can, then it just means he was a little nervous, or that he was so excited to feel all those wonderful things that he just had to tell you. However, if he can't slow down, then you're dating someone who's not available. If you want to meet someone who loves the "real" you, you're going to have to let them get to know you. And that takes time. Real love doesn't usually arrive, as if sent from the heavens. It grows.

Some people are more vulnerable than others to a Rusher type of relationship. If you're currently in an unsatisfying relationship, or you're overly anxious just to *be* in a relationship, then you may be especially vulnerable to a Rusher. Let's face it, it feels good to be adored. Who wouldn't want that feeling of being *so* important to someone? He's *saying* it's love, and it sure feels good to hear the words.

But it's not love—and no matter how flattering it seems, it really isn't—because it's not about you. It's about *him* and *his* need to say the words. Almost anyone could play your part. There's a reason that the phrase "Love is blind" remains such a top-ten hit through the decades. Many kinds of love *only* work if we remain "blind" to what is really going on.

If you've been going through a particularly stressful time in your life and you've been feeling deeply lonely, then it can be very easy to let your guard down and jump right into the fantasy of a love, whether it's real or not. We've all had times in our lives when we don't really care if it's real or not; we just need to feel good. We're not usually thinking very clearly at such times and we can make some pretty horrendous choices, choices that can keep us stuck in unavailable relationships for months or even years of our lives. *Then*, when some time has gone by, there is a tendency to find ways to justify the investment, long after the good feelings have gone away. This is why a slower pace is so helpful. You won't get in so deep so quickly and, if you begin to realize that the feelings aren't genuine, it will be easier to step back, see the relationship for what it really is, and then find the strength to move away from it. As I mentioned earlier, *sometimes* a Rusher relationship can *lead* to real love, but only if you slow things down. This will usually weed out a Rusher. He doesn't have time to linger. Once the newness wears off, he'll be gone, off to the next conquest.

Think of the friends you have in your life and how those relationships evolved over time. You learn a little more about them as time goes on. This is how a relationship should unfold. You should be concerned if, by the end of the first date, you know the person's entire financial situation, their medical history, every date they've ever had, and every dream they've ever dreamed. If it sounds as if they're letting you know just how much they "really, really want a relationship," then make sure that you aren't simply in the wrong place at the right time. It may *sound* as though they like you so damn much that they want to "make this relationship work," but the truth is that you have very little to do with their plan. They're giving you the information it would normally take months to learn and because of that you can end up feeling a false sense of closeness. A person who wants to integrate you into their lives immediately may be showing potentially unstable behavior. As important as a healthy relationship is in our lives, I would be the first person to warn against someone who thought a relationship could "save" them. Nothing "saves" us but ourselves. And, as we've discussed earlier, a relationship doesn't just *happen*; it's built, over time, with care and effort and love and trust. If you try to "make it happen," you're trying to build something strong on a weak foundation. If you're the type of person who is looking for validation by rescuing or saving people, this could seem ideal at first. But when you start out with that degree of neediness, it can only end badly when you realize how weak the foundation really is.

Wes is an example of someone trying to rush into a relationship. Wes's wife, Amanda, ran off with their contractor and left him with two kids and an unfinished house. Wes was devastated. He had been very much in love with his wife, not to mention the house, and had no idea there was trouble in the marriage. His way of dealing with the loss of his wife was to try to replace her without missing a beat. Being a good-looking guy, Wes had no trouble meeting and dating women. His routine for a first date was pretty impressive. He would show up with two dozen roses, treat the lady to an incredibly romantic meal at a restaurant overlooking the ocean. They would enjoy a candlelight dinner, take a stroll along the beach, dance under the stars, and all the time he would grace her with a steady stream of sweet compliments. What woman could resist? This fairy-tale romance would continue for a few dates, or until he felt as if he had captured her heart, and then it would come to an abrupt halt and the poor woman never knew what hit her. What happened to the flowers? The dinners? The sweet nothings (maybe they're called "sweet nothings" for a reason!)? The relationship, or whatever it was, would end (badly, I might add, with hurt feelings of betrayal) and then Wes would start all over again with someone new. Same restaurant, same two dozen red roses, same wonderful words; then, when the "rush" was over and the thrill was gone, it was adios and on to the next.

What Wes was looking for wasn't a new love. Wes was trying to replicate the love he had with his wife. He took all these women to the same restaurants he had taken his wife to, said the same things, all in the hopes that he could recreate a relationship that was now gone. It wasn't real. It wasn't organic, so he rushed into it, hoping to force it to happen by the sheer speed of his courtship. Then, when the inevitable happened, when the "new love" didn't match up, he would just break it off and start over with a new victim. I use the term "victim" because these weren't really candidates for a relationship for Wes. He had his scenario written and he just plugged in a woman. Each and every one of whom was disappointed in the end. Including Wes.

If Wes ever does want to be in a real relationship again, he's going to have to deal with the grief, loss, and (probably) anger over Amanda leaving him. Until then there's not really room in his heart for someone else. In addition, Wes might want to rethink his belief that Amanda left a "perfect" marriage and be willing to look at his part in her departure.

It's a good idea to step outside the good feelings that accompany the thrill of being "rushed," and evaluate the situation and ask questions. Find out his relationship history. How long ago was the last relationship? How long did it last? Why did it end? Is there a pattern? Of course, these questions need to be asked in an appropriate way. If you start grilling your date with relationship questions too soon, you're the one who's going to come across like a Rusher. However, when a person declares his love for you on the first date, he has taken the lead and this gives you permission to question his intentions, patterns, and history. Because communication is only seven percent verbal, you must learn to listen with more than just your ears. Ninety-three percent, that's right, ninety-three percent of what you're going to learn about someone else and what you're going to reveal about yourself will be done without words. Ninety-three percent of your interaction will be done with visual cues, body language, and attitude.

YOU'RE THE RUSHER

If you're the one who's looking for love on the first date, you might be a Rusher and, possibly, unavailable for a real relationship. As I'm sure you realize, most people don't think *they're* a Rusher. Even the most blatant Rusher usually believes that he or she is simply following the force of nature that has filled his or her heart with these feelings of passion, desire, and love. You *think* it's love every single (exciting, thrilling, lousy) time, but, guess what? It's not. It's great to be optimistic when first getting to know someone. The whole point of this book is to help you *stop* wasting your time on "unavailable" relationships so you can *start* spending time in an "available" (healthy, loving, supportive, fun, passionate) relationship. You could be helping to perpetuate your singleness by looking for love at first sight. It takes time and trust for a real relationship to develop, and an available person knows that. By adopting an "Owner Must Sell" approach, you may be scaring off someone who just might fall in love with you, if you could just give him or her the chance.

It's true you could meet your soul mate at the dry cleaners, he could be picking up a prescription at the same pharmacy, or he could be behind you in line at the bank. It's absolutely possible. You have to meet the love of your life somehow, someday, in some way. Why not today? Why not at the car wash? The problem is not in hoping for a chance meeting with a person who will be your true love; it's in feeling desperate about wanting it. It's a little like going grocery shopping when you're hungry, which is *never* a good idea. You buy tons of stuff that isn't good for you. If you're feeling vulnerable because you're feeling lonely, then try (I know it's not easy, hence the word "try") to ease that loneliness with something that will soothe your soul and ease your heart. Double up on time spent with good friends, go deeper into a hobby that brings you a feeling of satisfaction, take on that project at work. I'm not saying that any of these activities will take the place of love in your life, but they may ease the aching loneliness that we all can feel from time to time. Then, when you do meet someone, you're not ravenous. You're not "grocery shopping when you're too hungry." When you have desperation in your soul, it can cause you to *create* a person to fit your needs.

I once heard someone define romantic love as "being someone you aren't for someone who doesn't exist." Personally, I think romantic love *can be* a magnificent, energizing force in our lives, but I know it can also be a fantasy that can cause great pain. Let's work on making it wonderful and possible.

If people took the creative energy they put into manufacturing the *fantasy* of a relationship, and they put that energy into, oh, say . . . medical research, or environmental studies, or anything at all worthwhile, we might have a much different world. And if you put that energy into a healthy relationship, then what you might get, most times, is a really great, energizing, life-enhancing partnership with someone whom you love and who loves you.

If you approach someone with an "It's gotta be you, it's gotta be now, I only have twenty-four hours to live" type of energy, it's bound to scare off a normal, healthy, available person. If you've met someone who *responds* to that approach, then you need to take a second, more discerning look.

Another danger is presenting yourself as half a person looking for another half to complete you. Love should be shared, not negotiated. In a "you complete me" frame of mind, you are vulnerable to turning anyone who shows interest into the love of your life. When your need for attention and reciprocation is that extreme, you can expect to attract other insecure people.

In addition, you're more vulnerable to entering what is called a state of "limerance," a state much like infatuation but much more extreme, where the longing for love is intense and unrealistic. The term limerance was coined by Dorothy Tennov in her 1979 book, *The Experience of Being in Love*. One aspect of limerance is a desperate longing for love even before it has been directed at a particular person. Remember that being in love with the *idea* of love is very different than being in love. It's characterized by an acute longing for reciprocation and can be so extreme that when you're in it, you are able to create a feeling of being loved just because you imagine it and want it so badly. For example, you might hear a song and think the other person, your "limerant object," must be hearing this and thinking of you, simply because you have imagined it. You experience the feelings of being loved and thought about, regardless of the reality of the situation.

I know a woman who was married to a singer for many years. She had rushed into the marriage after knowing him for only a couple of months, and had worked very hard to create the illusion of relationship where one didn't really exist. No matter how hard she worked to please him, she never felt as though her husband connected with her in an intimate way. His first, and only, love was his work. But she soldiered on in the sincere belief (a form of limerance) that if she continued to be nice, and sweet, and supportive, that he would one day wake up and actually notice that she existed. She was waiting for the reality to catch up to the fantasy she had created and rushed into. One night she was in the front row of the audience during a performance when, for the very first time, he sang a love song directly to her. It was one of her very favorite songs and she was absolutely thrilled that he would sing it so lovingly to her. And, to make it even more meaningful, he had tears in his eyes as he sang it. Tears were in *her* eyes when she went backstage after the show. She waited for all the fans and hangers-on to leave the room, and then she put her arms around him. She was just about to thank him for the beautiful song, when he said, "Oh, I didn't know you came tonight." He had no idea to whom he was singing the song. The stage lights blinded him and the tears were . . . well, that's why they're called performers. My friend was devastated. This was such a symbol for her entire marriage. She had rushed into a marriage that wasn't real; she'd *made up* an entire relationship that didn't exist, and probably never had.

When you're serious about becoming available, be willing to take your time. Certainly you should be willing to date—that's what this book is all about—but also be willing *not* to date. If your life is on overload, if you are looking at a full plate of emotional issues, then maybe now is the time to be with yourself or with friends. Don't look at this period as unimportant or second best. Treat all time as valuable—because it is. As the saying goes, "Life is not a dress rehearsal." Every minute of your life counts. And when you do begin to date again, be willing to accept that each encounter might not lead to marriage (or even a second date)! Try to look at time alone as an opportunity to have fun and relax. If your "alone time" is full of anxiety and fears, then look at that and take it as a sign that you have some work to do. Get help if you need it, and, by the way, most of us do. Anxiety, by its very definition, puts us into overload. And overload is not a good place from which to make smart decisions regarding our lives, especially our hearts. Instead, take a look at the anxiety and make a plan to deal with it.

Again, this is easy to write about, but very difficult to do in real life. If you are from a family, or a community, that has a judgment about therapy, then I suggest you take a good look at the cost of that judgment in terms of lives, in terms of the quality of relationships, in terms of plain old happiness.

Start thinking about what *you* want in a relationship; the kind of person and the kind of experience you want. Then narrow the field, from every possible person you see to a real, select few who meet your new criteria. Of course, when you narrow the field, you may, at first at least, have fewer dates. Chances are you have been meeting people due to certain circumstances or certain choices. When your "wish list" changes, then it's quite possible that those circumstances and choices will change as well. It will take some time before you create new choices for yourself. Don't panic. Take a deep breath and, as I mentioned earlier, find a way to enjoy the time alone or with friends. Ironically, these are the things that will likely *lead* you to new areas where you can meet new people. Terms like "hobbies" and "outside interests" have taken on a less-than-hip connotation, but hobbies and outside interests are not only the things that will make you an interesting person (to yourself as well as to someone else). They also lead to the very situations where you're likely to meet someone new.

And when you *do* start dating (the kind of person on your *new* wish list, that is), remember that Rome wasn't built in a day. Instead of thinking of the dates that don't work out as failures, reframe the experience and look at them as just, well . . . dating. Dating can be a valuable and solid practice in leading you to the right person. But if you put every date into a "pass/fail" framework, then you're setting yourself up for hurt feelings. You're just meeting someone. They're just meeting you. With more than five billion people on the planet, I think it's safe to say you'll have other opportunities if this one doesn't work out.

I happen to love the sport of people watching. It's satisfying, and requires no warm-up exercises and very little equipment. The cost is low (a cup of coffee) and there's great fun to be had as well as lots to learn from watching people as they make their way up and down a boulevard. Part of dating is learning about people, and learning about yourself. If you can put it into that context, then I think you've got a better chance of enjoying the rough spots that come with change of any kind.

The day I filed for divorce I was driving home after signing the papers. I was on the freeway in bumper-to-bumper traffic. I looked over and, driving next to me, was a very attractive man. He rolled down his window, said something quite charming, and then asked if I was married. I started to answer "yes" out of habit— but then I caught sight of the divorce papers sitting on the front seat. At that moment I made a decision, maybe not the smartest move, but I wanted to meet someone new and this seemed like a decent guy. I gave him my phone number. We ended up going out for a while and, even though this wasn't the man of my dreams, he was interesting, and kind, and fun. The important thing was that I *knew* I didn't want a relationship. I wanted a date. I wanted to go out and meet people and have fun, and do all the things a newly single person might want to do. And although this book is about doing the work necessary to make yourself available for a real, healthy relationship, I also understand that there is a time in our lives for dating. I was *much* younger when this happened and, as I said, I had been married from a very early age, so I had missed a lot of the pure, simple *dating* that a lot of girls/women get to experience in their teens and their twenties. They were fun times and I wouldn't trade them for anything. But they were *not* about looking for a relationship. They were about meeting people and learning about them. They were about learning about myself. It was practice. It was dating.

2. SOMEONE JUST OUT OF A RELATIONSHIP

> *The heart is the only broken instrument that works.*
> —T. E. KALEM

You've just met the most wonderful person. You can't believe someone so fabulous is so available. He just broke up a relationship two days ago and wants to get on with his life. He's already telling you how wonderful and special you are. You can feel the intense chemistry right from the beginning and it feels great; but beware, there might be some unfinished business from the old relationship. If you really want to start something with this person, understand that he may need time to heal before he can really commit to you.

This is a tricky category because sometimes a relationship is truly over when it's over. And other times it's not. And it's not always easy to tell the difference between the two. Sometimes a couple has been through so much heartache, has tried for so long to make things work, has so completely exhausted their ability to repair the relationship, that, when it ends, it is truly a relief for both of them. This is one of the advantages of really trying to work on a relationship when it's ailing. Even if you don't find a way to make it work, at least you know that you left no stone unturned in your efforts to make things right. But the truth of the matter is that most people quit a relationship in anger or frustration, and those are feelings that can linger on and grow, even in the absence of the other person. Long after the relationship is officially "over," the *connection* is still as strong as ever. As a friend of mine used to say, "The song is over, but the *malady* lingers on."

By the time two people actually break up there's frequently been some major ego damage to both parties. Only rarely do relationships just peter out until there're no feelings left. Couples don't tend to fall out of love fairly, equally, or at the same rate. Many times a problem in a relationship or a marriage is like a service call for an appliance; it may require more than one attempt to fix it before you agree that it's worth working on, or that it's beyond repair.

Some people have a hard time calling it quits. They need a reason to leave and that reason could be you. Make sure it's not your love, your joy, and your caring that is serving as the catalyst, enabling him to find the courage to step away from a difficult relationship. It's not your job to be the one who provides the incentive to get him over the hard part. Not only isn't it your job, it's not the job of any relationship to "finish off" a previous relationship. If that's what's happening, then guess what happens once the previous relationship really *is* history? Then the new relationship (i.e., the one involving *you, your* heart, *your* time, *your* life) has now served its purpose and you'll be heading into some pretty rough waters.

Not that it's easy, of course. Nobody wants to be the one to say: "Call me when you're *really* over your ex-wife or girlfriend." If you really think there could be something wonderful happening with someone new in your life, then allow him to go through the grieving period he needs to be finished. Don't shortcut the process. If this is the right person you'll have a lifetime together.

THE FLIP SIDE

If you're the one who's just left a relationship, the same caution is called for. If it was a significant relationship, even if it wasn't a healthy one, then you will have a hole in your heart that will beg to be filled. It's perfectly natural to be drawn to the "high" of a new love affair. Just know that a "high" is not necessarily the real thing. It may just be an escape from the pain. Sometimes that's okay, but every time you choose a short-term "fix" over a long-range plan, every time you choose "good" over "great," you are strengthening a pattern that becomes that much harder to break. There is a relatively new branch of neurology that suggests that our actions, when repeated over a long enough period of time, actually form a groove in our neural pathways. If true, then that means that a habit isn't only a pattern of behavior, it's also a physical "rut" that we create when we cause certain combinations of neurons to fire in a particular sequence. Every time you make an unhealthy choice, every time you choose to be unavailable to a real relationship, you make it that much harder to get yourself back on a path to a meaningful life. This is perhaps why it's so difficult to break habits that we *know* we should break.

The good news, however, is that if these harmful "grooves" can be made by choices, then positive, healthy "grooves" can also be made, if we just take the first step and consciously change our behavior. It's like getting your bicycle wheel out of a rut in the road; it may not be easy, but once it's free, then you have full control over where you want to go.

Try to remember that if you're just out of a relationship, you're not really emotionally available—you're just "interested." Understanding this fact is a good beginning. Also understand that any choices you make in this condition may not be good ones. If you really want a lasting relationship, make sure you're a whole person meeting another whole person. Once again, it's a good idea to give yourself a period to be alone. Take some time to feel all that you've gone through. This will probably happen in waves, not all at once. Assess where you are and what you want to do next. If you have anger, hurt, or confusion from your last partner, it's still in there. Deal with it. Get it out.

When you're feeling vulnerable after a breakup, it feels good to have someone show interest in you. But there's a risk in putting too much importance on another person's ability to validate you or make you feel better. If you give him the power to make you feel better, then he also has the power to take it all away. You're giving his opinion more weight than your own. His response is controlling your belief in yourself. And, in all likelihood, it's a lack of belief in yourself that got you into trouble in the first place. Spend some time answering those inventory questions: Who am I? What do I want? What do I think I deserve? before plunging into another "unavailable" relationship.

You will have hard times in your life. We all do. When you're going through a rough patch it's easy to feel better when something good *happens* to you. Meeting someone you think is your soul mate, getting a great new job, winning the lottery; these are damn sure going to make you feel better. However, the real and true power comes when you are able to make yourself feel happier and more hopeful without anything new *happening* to you. When you can feel better about your life just by making the decision to *look* at your life . . . really look at it, and be happy with who you are and what you want to do with that life, then you can know true happiness. It's not about outside forces, it's not about money, or status, or having a perfect body, or even about finding Mr. Right, it's truly about a power within you. It's just a matter believing it, nurturing it, and making it part of everything you do.

Many times it feels as if we don't even know who we are without another person's definition of us. I think this is especially true for those who marry young. At least that was my experience. When I first left my parents' home to strike out on my own, I saw it as, first, an escape, and second, an opportunity to learn about myself and make my own rules. If you are one of these "escapees," then you know that it takes a while to get the hang of things without someone else's rules and regulations. At first many people rebel and do the exact opposite of everything they've been taught. With time, though, some will adopt many of the habits they were raised with. But that time of rebelling or pushing the limits is necessary to discover who you are. Even if you're making one mistake after another, at least you're learning. But you don't get that time, or the chance to learn, if you just move on from one relationship to the next, each one with its own new set of rules. None of them your own. You become very adept at learning rules (someone else's). It's like doing something for a living that you didn't choose and you don't really like, but you know how to do it, so you keep doing it. Why? Because it's all you know. The problem is, of course, that few of us *know* that we are stuck in this situation while we're in it. Usually it takes a jolt, or perhaps a book like this one, for us to see that we *do* have a choice. It's just a matter of making it, then living through the anxiety that comes with making *any* change in our life.

This is one of those times when solitude becomes a powerful tool for change. So many people never give themselves time alone—I mean, without a relationship alone. Alone, of course, doesn't have to mean lonely. I've heard many women, and men, say that they were never lonelier than when they were unhappily married or in a relationship that didn't work. We've all been lonely even when we weren't technically alone. Ironically, it's when we don't know how to be alone that we are most likely to be lonely. Perhaps that's why so many people have a replacement mate before they even leave the old one. Those people don't want to be "alone" because they're afraid of being "lonely." I know. I was one of those people for many years.

Have you ever seen a baby monkey hold on to his mommy? He seems to hang on until he has another monkey to grab onto. Maybe it's their instinct. And maybe it's ours as well. But it doesn't serve us as adults who want to make healthy choices for our lives. So strike a blow for evolution. Learn to spend time alone, just being you with yourself. If it's not something you've done a lot of, then think of it as an adventure. You will discover things you never knew existed in your heart, in your mind, in your imagination, and in your future.

3. SOMEONE WHO DOESN'T SHARE YOUR FUNDAMENTAL BELIEFS

> *If a woman has to choose between catching a fly ball and saving an infant's life, she will choose to save the infant's life without even considering if there is a man on base.*
>
> DAVE BARRY

Many times we're attracted to people who are exactly the opposite of us. Why? Well, sometimes it's *because* they are so different. And, sometimes, it can even work out beautifully. For instance, if you're an introvert, matching up with an extrovert could be the perfect complement to you. The shy one gets to come out of his shell a little and the outgoing person gets an appreciative audience. It can be a nice contrast. Or at least that's how it looks on paper. It's what I call the "osmosis" theory of relationships and while it can boast its success stories, it also has tremendous pitfalls. Just by dating someone, we can't usually take on their characteristics, no matter how much we admire them. If someone is truly interested in becoming more of an extrovert, dating, or even marrying, one isn't going to do the trick. If you're an introvert, there's a reason for it. The changes that would lead you to have a more outgoing personality need to be made at a core level. When you see an extrovert, you're seeing a personality, not the roots of that personality. If you try to paste an extrovert's personality onto an introvert's soul, you'll only create a very uncomfortable introvert.

And this discomfort doesn't do wonderful things for the relationship between the two people involved. This is not to say that we can't appreciate or *learn* from the other person in our relationships. Learning is one of the primary functions of a healthy relationship; learning about others and, more often, learning about ourselves. That's what people are talking about when they say they learned a lot from their relationship. But "learning," and even changing some personality traits, are one thing; "becoming" a different person is something entirely different. It's asking too much of a relationship and it puts a strain on many otherwise healthy partnerships.

Over the course of a successful relationship there will be countless situations in which you'll be required to discuss, bargain, or compromise with your partner. You're not going to agree on everything and so there will be what my uncle used to call "frank exchanges of views." That's called a partnership. Couples negotiate on things like where they want to live, how they want to spend vacations, raise their children, and spend their money. The ingredients that will make for successful negotiations (instead of constant and debilitating fights) are a shared value system. This is different from borrowing personality traits, or learning how to get to the gym on a regular basis by watching your husband do it. These are core beliefs that shape your view of the world. If you and someone you're seriously dating have different values, then you can share all the personality traits in the world and there's still bound to be trouble.

If you know up front that you have an unshakeable view or expectation about a particular area of your life, and your partner doesn't share this view, you are deluding yourself if you think that they're going to change or that you can simply ignore it. Oh, maybe for a week or even a couple of months, but not for a lifetime. It just doesn't work that way. No matter how gingerly you tiptoe around each other, the day will come when your opposite views collide. He sees the world one way and you see it another, and we're talking fundamentals here. He wants one set of things from life and you want another. If you're seeing someone who wants children and you absolutely know you don't—ever!—that's non-negotiable. It can't work. It's not fair to agree to something and then hope the other person will change their mind later down the road. The one who gives in is going to feel angry and resentful about their decision. Having children is not the kind of topic you can toss a coin to decide. If you put off confronting an important issue or fundamental difference because you don't want to deal with it now, you *will* deal with it later! Pay now or pay later, the saying goes. And it's never been truer than in circumstances such as this.

Take Allen for example. Allen is Jewish. He is adamant about wanting to marry a Jewish girl. The problem is, Allen doesn't date Jewish women. He *only* dates Catholic women. So what the heck is Allen doing but keeping himself unavailable and wasting a lot of Catholic girls' time. It's not that Allen is feigning his affection; he really likes these women. But Allen keeps falling for women he absolutely *knows* he will not marry. Talk about unavailable. And, worse, Allen doesn't find it necessary to *share* this prerequisite with the women he dates. They have no idea that their time is being wasted. One of two things has to happen if Allen really wants to be available for a relationship. He can go out only with women of his faith from now on, or he could explore the possibility of seeing a woman who's willing to convert to Judaism. The bottom line is that right now Allen's not available to the women he's dating *or* to the women he'd like to date.

Think about your own fundamental beliefs. Make a list of things that are most important to you in a mate. Look over the list carefully and ask yourself some questions. First of all, consider the difference between personality traits and values. Then, further note those values that are core values (this is to say nonnegotiable, e.g., I would never cheat, I try to do the things I say I'm going to do, I see the world as a good and decent place, etc.) And noncore values (less important, negotiable areas of your moral structure, whatever that may be for you). It's important to give thought to such issues, if only so you have some idea of what you're looking for in a potentially healthy, available relationship. It's also a way to get to know yourself on a level not usually encouraged in our media-driven, MTV-generation world. I don't see that many prime-time shows dealing with values and what they mean to our lives. If you are in a relationship with someone who has very different core values, but you're still very attracted to him, then maybe you're using the drama of this relationship to stay unavailable. There is no better ongoing battle than a battle of values. They live in the deepest parts of our souls and our minds and they are a *huge* part of who we are. If they are challenged . . . well, then, it's going to be a long battle that won't be pretty but will serve quite well for someone who is looking to avoid the potential discomfort of a *real* relationship. Often, unavailable people stay in an impossible situation simply because it takes up *all* their time (Lord, they're exhausting), keeps them single, and yet gives the *appearance* that they're in a relationship. If you have a history of breakups over nonnegotiable issues, maybe you haven't made your "list." Maybe you haven't given enough thought to these issues. If that's the case, then do some work in this area. This is part of that inventory I keep talking about. The first question is always, "Who am I?" It may sound a bit too heavy to tackle, but it's an important question and the answer will give you an incredible amount of strength to take on the challenges of finding a healthy partner. If you *have* made a "values list," then don't wait so long to talk about it in a new relationship. If you have "deal breakers," then find a way to bring them up early on. I'm not talking about some angst-ridden speech about moral ambiguity and philosophical quandaries. There are ways and there are ways, to talk about who you are and the things that matter to you in a person. And *then* pay attention to the answers you get. People almost always reveal who they are, one way or another. But you must listen, with your mind and your heart, not just your hormones. If he's wrong for you, discover it sooner rather than later, then move on to someone available.

Having said all that, I must say a word about keeping the list real and using its powers for good. By this I mean that the whole idea behind the list is to learn more about yourself and to find someone wonderful and available with whom to share your life.

Don't construct a list that is so dogmatic that a mere human need not apply. We're all flawed. We're all struggling to find our way in this world. Like all the "warnings" and "types" mentioned in this book, the list should be thought of as a way to bring someone *into* your life; but the right someone, the someone who won't steal your time and damage your heart. I do believe that he or she is out there and that you can develop the tools to find him or her. It took me until I was fifty to find the right person, but I did. As I mentioned in my introduction, I'm not a therapist or a doctor. This book is a collection of words and stories of my experience and the experiences of others. There are many warnings and many caveats listed, but the bottom line is my belief that if I can do it, then you can do it as well.

What happens if you've spent some weeks or months with someone and things are going extremely well? He seems available; you're available to his being available. All God's children appear to be available and then, suddenly, there's a "deal breaker" that rears its ugly head. You see him treat a friend in a way that is really at odds with who you want to be and who you want to be *with*? Don't pull the ripcord immediately. Talk to him about it. See if there's any wiggle room. More importantly, see if he knows what he did and how he feels about it. When I said earlier that you were deluding yourself if you thought you could change someone—the next part of the sentence was (and this is key), "if he doesn't want to change." See if this is something that he truly wants to work on. That's a whole different situation than trying to change someone who has no desire to change. *That's* (with rare exceptions) a losing proposition custom made for people who are determined to remain unavailable for a real relationship.

The flip side

If you find yourself *continually* involved with people who disagree with your most essential views, what are you doing about it? Are you trying to change their minds? Is it your mission to win them over to your way of thinking? If so, then why? Is it the ongoing, never-ending, never-*going*-to-end battle that turns you on? Does lack of conflict bore you? Do you tend to have the same kind of opposing relationships with friends? Do you use differences to keep people from getting too close to you? Are you meeting people who you're not right for simply (or not so simply) to keep you safe?

This is different from a difference of opinion. This is *looking* for a difference of opinion. Both will keep you single and unavailable if you don't address them. Again, I mention the inventory list because it's a good way to recognize your motives. If you have a clear set of values that you're comfortable with and you are just choosing people with different values, then that's one scenario. But if you find that you are *changing* that list in order to do battle, then you're simply using the issue of values to pick a fight. Why would you do that? There are dozens of possible answers, many of them discussed in various sections of this book. But for the purposes of this chapter, let's just say that you're doing your best to stay single and unavailable.

4. Major differences in age, intelligence, or status.

> *The play itself was a profound success.*
> *But the audience was a profound failure.*
> —OSCAR WILDE

Sometimes you don't care about the differences in the beginning. My girlfriend, Jill, and I were enjoying a nice long weekend in Rosarito Beach, Mexico. It was a party atmosphere and we were there for fun. Jill was sitting at the bar when this handsome young guy (really young) offered to buy her a drink. They ended up talking, dancing, and having just a fabulous time. It was a different decade, a different era, and she was away from home and feeling young and free.

At this point in her career she had a good job with a good salary. But this twenty-two-year-old didn't know that. He just thought she was attractive and fun. She didn't look or feel her thirty-five years. They danced on the beach until three in the morning. It was such a liberating feeling after a dry spell that she developed a huge crush. As we drove back to LA, we giggled about our crazy weekend. And that was that.

Until a month later when Dave called and said he was going to be in Los Angeles and wanted to visit Jill. She hesitated because now it was her neighborhood, her home, and her life. But she said okay. When he arrived she was shocked. In the harsh light of day, he looked twelve (and she looked and felt one hundred and twelve). She got over it. He was even sweeter and more handsome than she remembered.

And so it began. One weekend a month they were in their own little world at her house. During the week they talked on the phone. She didn't know about what. It was a fling. Surely it would've burned itself out if they had lived in the same city, but then Jill did a crazy thing; she invited him to move in with her.

Jill now says, "If only we had broken up within the first three months, he could've been the love of my life." What should have been a few wild, memorable, sweet weekends turned into a relationship that wasn't meant to be. The truth is that she had no idea how starved she was for "nice."

Dave was a *sometime* carpenter by trade and pretty much a *full-time* underachiever. He was one of the sweetest people she had ever met—but completely unmotivated. One of his claims to fame was that he knew all the words to the movie *Top Gun*. She thought that was *so* cute. Of course, she thought he was kidding. Or at least exaggerating. Nope. Every . . . single . . . word. (Free piece of advice you won't get anywhere but here: If someone you're dating says he knows *every word* to *any* movie, but especially any movie that includes dialogue such as, "Incoming at two o'clock, Iceman!" run, do not walk, to the nearest church, temple, synagogue or ashram and offer a prayer for your own salvation.) Needless to say, it was soon apparent to Jill that this was a dreadful mistake.

Unfortunately, I'm sorry to report that Jill allowed this "relationship" to go on for two years. I wish I could tell you that someone held a gun to her head and forced her to stay, but that would be a lie. The truth is that her own "stuff," her own issues of self-worth, were such that she didn't know she *could* get out of it. She didn't know that the decision was hers to make. Her friends tried to show her the light. "He seems nice . . . but," and then they would try, tactfully, to list the million and one reasons why he wasn't even remotely right for her. Even her kids teased her. She even made jokes at her own expense. But the sad truth was that she didn't know how to end the relationship with Dave. If he had been a liar or a cheater, it would have been easier for her to end it. Dave actually did her a huge favor when he started using drugs. This gave her a concrete reason for ending it. But the drugs were just part of it. She *should* have been able to end it for the reason that she wasn't happy. But she knows now that she wasn't *ready* to be available for a real relationship. She stayed because a part of her wanted to stay. That was a tough thing for Jill to admit, but it was the truth. The good news is that Jill has been able to look at the reasons *why* she wanted to stay unavailable (fear, mistrust, etc.) and she's faced them down.

She says the saddest part is that when Dave left after two years, nothing was different. He brought nothing and took nothing. He hadn't really affected her life. She knows now that her time with Dave served another purpose, which was to keep her unavailable for a real relationship. I'm not saying that a big age difference in a relationship can't work; it can. Anything *can* work; that's why this relationship stuff is so difficult. Ultimately it's up to you to take a good look at the dynamics between you and your partner and determine whether or not you're in an available relationship that may *look* like it couldn't work, but *does* . . . or if you're in a relationship that looks like it doesn't work because, in fact, it *doesn't work*. Major differences in age, etc., like all the warnings in this book, are offered as dynamics to be examined by you. Only you know what you're getting out of a relationship and how you feel when you're with this person. All I'm saying is; look *honestly* at those feelings and look for the strength to hold out for a healthy, available relationship in your life. If Jill had known what to look for all those years ago, if she had known about lists, and listening, and about how much time could go by, she might *still* have spent time with Dave. But surely she wouldn't have spent two years of her life trying to make something real out of a fun weekend in Mexico.

THE FLIP SIDE

Let's talk about the other person in that relationship, the one who's on the other end of the big gap. The one who is, or at least appears to be, the less advantaged one in the relationship. I'm sure some people are very happy in that role. If you're one of them, and you *know* that you're just in it for the fun and for the learning, then you needn't read the rest of this paragraph. But if you're in what I like to call a "Teacher/Pupil" relationship, and you *think* it's a real, available relationship, then stick around for a sentence or two. You may be genuinely attracted to a person who's significantly older, wealthier, or perhaps just more experienced than you, but isn't it possible that you're attracted to the situation and the learning more than you are to the person? As I said, if it's just a casual thing, then why not? We *all* learn from others. Dating is one way that we learn about the world, about people and, of course, about relationships. If you spend some time with someone much more experienced than yourself, then you will be exposed to things and ideas that you might not encounter on your own. Just know this is but one aspect of a healthy relationship. If it becomes the main focus, then you run the risk of it becoming a "hierarchical" relationship, that is to say, a relationship in which one person is *established* in a position of strength and power and the other person is established in the weaker position. These relationships can work for a while, and certainly there are many hierarchical relationships that last a lifetime. But sometimes an element of resentment *can* creep in and sour whatever love, respect, and admiration were there at the beginning of the union. There has to be some form of equality for a relationship to work. Even if one person's power is hidden from the outside world—perhaps it's intellectual or emotional, perhaps it's sexual—whatever it is, there is usually a struggle for parity. If you *start out* with an imbalance, then you are setting yourself up for an unavailable relationship.

When you choose to be in a relationship with someone of greater status, wealth, or age, because you hope being with them will make you feel better about yourself, you're asking more from a relationship than you should. True feelings of love and self-esteem don't come from outside of you. We all look to enhance our lives via our relationships—*all* our relationships; friendships, business relationships, family relationships—but there are still many qualities of life for which we alone must take responsibility. When we ask another person to provide these things, *that's* when the resentment begins to appear and the relationship begins to deteriorate. I talked to many single people who spoke of past relationships or marriages in which this had happened. Relationships in which an older or more experienced partner had begun to resent his or her role. Sometimes the resentment revealed itself as a lack of respect, sometimes there was a control that was stifling. "Nobody would put up with you and your . . ." Fill in the blank; ineptness, immaturity, stupidity, etc. One way or another, you should be looking for some form of equal status within the relationships in your life. If you're not, then perhaps you're keeping yourself unavailable to a balanced relationship by looking for a hierarchical, "Teacher/Pupil" relationship.

Some people are lucky enough to connect on a level in which age and status have no meaning. They feel no gap in their worlds. That is the goal of any solid union. They feel equal in their world. It's hard to really love someone whom you feel is better than you— or not as good as you. You're separated by virtue of those feelings. You're unavailable to an equal relationship and so is your partner.

5. A PERSON WHO IS TOO JEALOUS, OR INTO DRAMA

> *Love is a fire. But whether it's going to warm your heart or burn your house, you can never tell.*
>
> —JOAN CRAWFORD

A lot of people thrive on relationship drama. Their relationships rarely run smoothly for very long. And they seem to like it that way. Oh, they would never admit as much, but look at their histories. They're either in a crisis with their partner or just coming off of one. They are used to extreme highs and deep lows. And if you think you're going to be the one to "smooth" them out, then think again. And after you do that, then think again, again. If someone is addicted to drama then, trust me, you're not *in* a relationship with him, you are simply a *player* in that drama. If that's okay with you, then, by all means, knock yourself out. Just know that what you are in is *not* an available relationship. Someone who is that into drama isn't *available* for or open to the normal range of emotions. And while their high highs and low lows can be very exciting at first, they are usually, ultimately debilitating and, finally, boring. Just ask someone who has spent a few years with one of these emotional yo-yos.

Mikki is a perfect example; she's hopelessly addicted to drama. She can't remember a time when she wasn't filled with jealousy of one sort or another. She blames it on her first boyfriend. He lied and cheated on her the entire time they were together. That was more than twelve years ago. Since then she's had at least five men in her life—and not one of them has lied or been unfaithful. But she's sure it's going to happen again and she's not about to relax her vigil. She has tortured every one of these men with her insane distrust. She's either in the middle of a jealous rage or she's doing her very best to cause one. Anything less than that off balance feeling doesn't feel like love to her. She calls it "being passionate." (So was the Inquisition.) Anyone healthy would call it dysfunction or just plain meanness. If someone you're dating or thinking about dating is *looking* for drama, believe me, he'll find it. And if the drama at first has nothing to do with you, then, believe me again, it will. That's how these people work. They reveal to you what appear to be their real emotions. They seem to be vulnerable when they share their anger and their jealousies with you. This brings you closer and, of course, you're tempted to become vulnerable with them as well. They showed you theirs, so you should show them yours, right? But the difference is that while you're showing them real emotions, they're most likely revealing their neurosis born out of their addiction.

Maybe Mikki's afraid that she'll be boring—or bored—without the histrionics. Surely that's what she tells herself. But Mikki's rage and her jealousy have very little to do with her first boyfriend. We've all, most of us, been lied to by someone. It hurts. We learn a bit about watching what people do, not just what they say. And then we get over it. If we can't, and we really want to be in a healthy relationship, then we go get some help. Mikki's done just the opposite. She's set up her life in such a way that she spends all her energy looking for betrayal and trying desperately to control the environment that her current partner lives in. If she can limit his access to even viewing other women, then maybe she can rest.

The biggest flaw in Mikki's plan is that by the time she has succeeded in training her man to report his every move to her, by the time she has gotten him to give up all undesirable activities, (i.e., anything that doesn't include her), by the time she has him wearing a pager, he's a broken spirit. And then, of course, she's about done with him. Who wants a broken spirit? Now he's boring and uninteresting, and totally lacking in the drama and anxiety he provided. Pretty sad, huh? Well, it happens all the time. And the really tough part is that all that drama makes it extremely difficult to see what the hell is going on. Both partners go from one battle to another, and it's almost impossible to step back long enough to see the big picture and ask the really pertinent question, which is: "What the hell am I doing this for?" Unless you're a committed masochist and you *need* this kind of drama and abuse, then you would be wise to take a deep breath and run a check on what you've gotten yourself into or what you're thinking of getting into. This much is for certain; a relationship with this kind of a person is *not* a relationship with someone available.

A better plan for Mikki, if she decided she wanted to get off this emotional merry-go-round, would be to concentrate on the part of her that feels the insecurity and work on that. It would be a lot more effective than putting her mate through spirit-breaking boot camp every few years.

The very thing Mikki says she wants—an open, loving, and trusting relationship—is not a possibility for her because she isn't open or loving or trusting. Being suspicious and mistrustful is a good way to keep anyone from getting too close to you—and it keeps you unavailable for real intimacy.

It's interesting to note that Mikki hasn't always been faithful or honest with her partners, either. One of the reasons I believe some people are so distrusting is that they themselves are not trustworthy. Because Mikki is duplicitous herself, she anticipates it in others.

Someone who is this jealous without cause needs to look deeper to find the root of her insecurities and anger. In Mikki's case she's had enough therapy and read enough books to know the roots of her insecurity. But *knowing* about a problem and *doing* something about it are two different things. As much as I have stressed in this book the need to learn about the roots of your behavior in order to become healthier, I must also stress that knowing about something intellectually is very different from doing the hard emotional work necessary to facilitate change. Mikki knew that she had an ex-boyfriend who cheated on her and that her father had ignored her completely once her little sister was born. She's felt gripping fear about being replaced by another woman and it's made her distrustful of men ever since. Those feelings are real— but they no longer serve her, and they no longer apply to her life today. It's not easy to let go of a pattern that is ingrained in our view of the world. But if she doesn't do the work to make those fundamental changes, then she'll just keep repeating the same scenarios over and over again. The more she does it, the more familiar it feels, and the tougher it is to get out of that groove. And all the while she, and the men with whom she's involved, will be unavailable for a real relationship.

THE FLIP SIDE

What if you have found someone who is truly your mate in many ways but, for reasons of his own, he finds it impossible to trust you? The truth of the matter is that, in this situation, you have some difficult choices to make. If the jealousy is all-consuming and totally without basis, then you are dealing with someone who is deeply damaged, no matter how "wonderful" they might be otherwise. But many times the jealousies aren't so black and white; they often live in the gray area of a relationship and tend to make the recipient feel more uncomfortable than attacked. But "uncomfortable" and "not trusted" aren't the kinds of characteristics that one associates with a long-term, healthy relationship. Adding to the problem is that jealous people frequently *deny* being jealous. "No, I'm not jealous, I just care about you and I'd like to know where you're going to be—every ten minutes." Mind you, if you're *comfortable* being checked up on every ten minutes, if it makes you feel loved, then you might be in the right place. Your needs may be in sync. Most people, though, would agree that a good relationship allows both partners to breathe without being constantly monitored by the other person. For some, being involved with a jealous person, being the recipient of all that "passionate" attention, can make them feel important and loved—in the beginning at least. But it's a vicious cycle. You can begin to need that jealous response in order to validate your own importance, even your own existence.

Often, being accused of wrongdoing over and over can end up being a self-fulfilling prophecy. Ironically, it can drive you to do what you're repeatedly accused of doing. It's a dynamic that frequently occurs between parents and their teenaged children. After a while, the teenager figures out that as long as he's being punished for doing something, then he might as well *do* it. Well, it can work the same way in a jealous, dysfunctional relationship. At least the teenager has the good sense to be angry about the false accusations. When we "grow up," some of us mistake that faux attention for love and bring it into our lives *voluntarily*. Worst of all, it can make us overlook the people who don't push those fear buttons or put us off balance; in other words, the people who are available for a real relationship.

When you meet someone new, pay attention to how he describes his life. Is it full of drama, crisis? Is there one emergency after another? Is there an air of hypervigilance that seems inappropriate? This could be an indication of the way they function. They may draw misfortune and hardship to them, whether real or imagined. Listen carefully; it doesn't have to be about relationships to be a clue. It can be about something concerning the job, the home, the family, finances, or health. Whatever. But beware of people who don't seem to trust their boss, their landlord, the car salesman—okay, the car salesman is worth the worry, but you get the idea. If this person thinks everyone is dishonest, chances are they need to "medicate" themselves with drama, or they simply have a problem with honesty themselves.

If you find yourself attracted to people who are consumed with jealousy, maybe you're looking for the false validation that comes with being in the middle of a drama. Remember that it's someone else's drama, not yours. And that means that you're not available for the real, healthy drama that comes with living your own life, taking your own chances on love, and allowing yourself to be vulnerable to another person for all the right reasons. It would be much more effective to work on your own issues, and look at the reasons why you "lose yourself" in this kind of drama. Obsession isn't love. Someone who doesn't trust you doesn't love you. If you're repeatedly attracted to a drama addict, maybe you're looking for entertainment. In that case, you could see a film. It's cheaper and it's over in two hours. And if you find you miss the excitement of being called at all hours or someone hounding you, then perhaps you should take the advice of comedian Steven Wright when he says, "If you think nobody cares about you, try missing a couple of payments!" Seriously though, perhaps you could take a look at your need to be needed and put it to good use by using your time and energy to help someone else. You could volunteer at a hospital, become a Big Brother or Sister to a child, foster an animal, or any number of "giving" choices.

6. SOMEONE WHO CROSSES YOUR SEXUAL BOUNDARIES

It's been so long since I made love,
I can't even remember who gets tied up.
　　　　　—JOAN RIVERS

Lurking in the shadows of any discussion regarding love and relationships is the word "vulnerability." When we open ourselves up to love, or to a relationship that may lead to love, then we are making ourselves vulnerable. Very few of us have had a childhood that was free from pain or betrayal of some kind, and so the idea of making ourselves vulnerable to the possibility of pain and betrayal, and doing so *voluntarily*, is understandably frightening.

One of the most vulnerable human experiences, potentially, is that of sex. When we talk about sex we are talking about an act that can be everything from purely physical, to deeply emotional, to combinations of both. The potential for pleasure is famous; the potential for pain is less well publicized, but enormous all the same.

This is not a book about moral judgments of any kind, and certainly not in the area of what two consenting adults decide to share in the privacy of their bedroom. But I do believe that it takes time to get to a place where you're comfortable enough with another person to share your private personal desires. It has to feel safe for both of you and it's not always easy to know when things are "safe."

Years ago Eve dated a gynecologist. After a few dates she accompanied him back to his home. It was the 1980s. She was young and he was handsome, attractive, and single. One thing led to another and they ended up in his bedroom. Right in the middle of the room was an examining table—stirrups and all. She didn't really question it. He was a doctor, for God's sake. He led her to the table where they started to kiss. The next thing she knew she felt something warm and wet all down the front of her. It happened so fast, it took her a minute to realize he had actually relieved himself on her. Right on his examining table. Right in the middle of his bedroom. On her first trip to his house. Eve says, being extremely codependent back then, her first thought was, "Gee, I hope he doesn't think I did that." Then again she thought, "He's a doctor for God's sake. He must know what he's doing." She was so freaked out she couldn't speak. He had just given her a breast exam and a urine test. Her breast—his urine. Then he asked her, cool, calm and *after the fact*—if she liked what he had done. She was barely able to say she didn't think so.

She never saw him again. (She never went to a male gynecologist again either, by the way. She acknowledges that certainly there are plenty of wonderful, reputable male gynecologists, but she just couldn't face one again.) The fact that the good doctor took his work home with him and was into what are referred to as "golden showers" wasn't the biggest problem here. Besides the shock value, Eve was feeling numb at how impersonal the whole thing was. This man had a preprogrammed fantasy and could plug any woman into it. It had nothing to do with her. All he needed was his examining table, a woman lacking self-esteem, and a full bladder. She says the whole experience was just too much . . . too soon . . . too wet.

However easy it is to poke fun at what happened, it was a violation of Eve's sexual boundaries. It's different when two people have been together long enough to trust each other. It can be exciting and fun to experiment with fantasies. The trust is what enhances the intimacy between the two of you. My friend Bob Griffard has a saying that, "Lust plus trust equals great sex." The lust ingredient is in plentiful supply most everywhere you look. Trust, however, is a rarer bird. Trust, in a way, is what I've been talking about in all the preceding chapters. Trust is what we *don't* have when we are, in some fashion, involved in an unavailable relationship.

When someone's sexuality feels so far removed from anything emotional, take it as a sign that the person may be more comfortable dealing in fantasy and fetish than in sex as a healthy part of intimacy. And while an exploration of sex and a mutual decision to push sexual boundaries can be a wonderful part of a good relationship, understand that you are well within your rights to set a pace for these explorations, a pace with which you are comfortable. Some people are perfectly comfortable with their—how shall I say—nontraditional sexual habits. Look at the doctor, he had no problem "sharing." But for many others, having unusual desires may make you feel separate and secretive. It's difficult enough to connect with another person on this planet, but when you're carrying around a five-hundred-pound secret—it's damn near impossible.

Revealing this secret can be a delicate matter. It's hard to find the right time to share. But if you get to the point where you think this might be the person you want to spend your life with, you'd better find the time. Or it might be chosen for you.

Sandy found out after she was married for six years that her husband, Jeffery, wore lingerie under his Hugo Boss suits. She learned this news in the worst way. After he had been injured in a car accident and taken to the hospital, his secret was discovered. Instead of having a conversation in which, perhaps, Sandy might have had at least a chance to understand the history of her husband's fetish, Sandy was forced to take in this information in the middle of an already anxious moment. It was humiliating for both of them. Jeffrey had lived with the fear of discovery throughout the marriage, burdened with guilt and shame. He really should have told her before they got married. That, or driven more safely.

Sandy was understandably shocked when she found out that her big, burly husband wore women's underwear on a regular basis. But shocked and appalled she could have dealt with. The part she found most difficult was the feeling of betrayal. She couldn't believe that the person she considered the closest to her in the world had a secret life that she knew nothing about. They are currently in therapy and trying to work it out, but they have a long road back to trusting each other. Nobody (certainly not me) is saying that this would have been an easy conversation for Jeffrey to have. But the point of a relationship, a real relationship anyway, is to have a safe place within which to share who you *really* are. I know that Sandy and Jeff are married, so technically it's not a Still Single story, but *anytime* you are keeping a big secret from your mate, you are not really available for a true, intimate relationship. Even if you think that you've gotten close to that person, you really haven't. There will always be this "secret self" that is unavailable to you. Withholding his big secret caused more damage to Jeffrey and Sandy's marriage than his sexual expression.

Not that being honest about your propensity is a guarantee that you'll live happily ever after. In researching this subject I interviewed another couple in which the husband was a cross-dresser. After Ned and Deena had dated for six months, Ned bravely shared his secret desire to wear lingerie with Deena. Though she wasn't thrilled about it, she didn't cancel the wedding either. That was twenty-six years ago and Deena hasn't stopped punishing Ned. She reminds him as often as she can that no one other than she could ever love such a "depraved" person. (If you want to call a lifetime of abuse "love.") It's the worst kind of emotional blackmail. And Ned takes it. Deena gave Ned the worst kind of mixed message all those years ago; she *told* Ned that she could handle his fetish, but she failed to mention that the *way* she planned on handling it was to shame him every chance she got. Ned may have *thought* that he was picking someone who was "available" to him, even with his "peculiarities," but he wasn't. After twenty-six years I think it's safe to say that Ned has some boundary issues. Actually, I don't think I'm going out on a limb to say that Ned might have his own not-so-secret agenda in which he "transfers" his own punishing voice onto Deena. Maybe they both have exactly the kind of relationship they desire, but it's not one I would want, and I'm hoping it's not one you would want either. When the words "shame," "abuse," "punishment," and "betrayal" are log lines to a marriage, the word "available" is usually absent.

THE FLIP SIDE

If you're the one with the (legal, consenting) sexual preference, and you're happy with it, then your issue isn't about sex, it's about courage and honesty.

Having an unusual sex life doesn't mean you don't deserve a happy, healthy, normal relationship. If you think you're unacceptable, unlovable, or unforgivable because you're acting out a particular fantasy (providing that fantasy violates no one else's boundaries) then you may be buying into the same prejudices that forced you into hiding in the first place. If it's sex between two consenting adults, then it's nobody's business but your own and your partner's. I've seen too many people allow themselves to be damaged by a set of rules they had no voice in writing. I would much rather have a world in which people were allowed to express themselves as they wished, in a manner they and their partner deemed loving, than live with the self-righteous condemnation that permeates our society today.

7. SOMEONE TOO MISERLY

I'll share your toys, I'll share your money, I'll share your toast,
I'll share your honey; I'll share your milk and cookies too.
The hard part's sharing mine with you.

—SHEL SILVERSTEIN

"So many types of unavailable people, so little time," soooo . . . pay attention! People usually reveal who they are sooner than you'd think. It's just that we're so distracted by the "chemistry" we're feeling that we ignore the signs. Making things even more difficult is the fact that lines can get very blurry. For instance, frugality. When does someone stop being frugal and start being miserly? The first can be a wonderful attribute; the second usually comes from a poverty of spirit and can lead to misery. Relationship counselor Mary Padlak gives this advice, "If someone is miserly or cheap with money, chances are they'll be cheap with affection and quality time."

Being miserly has very little to do with how much money someone has. You can have money issues whether you're rich or poor. There's a big difference between being cautious with money and being a paranoid penny-pincher. The goal is to identify the emotionally bankrupt candidate before you lose your heart to him.

When you're attracted to someone who is tight with money you don't have to run screaming from the building. Maybe they're going through a rough patch. If they recently divorced, downsized, or invested badly, these are good reasons for them to be watching their money closely. There are other areas of their life that can help reveal their character. For instance, are they generous with their time? Someone who donates his time to a charity is probably not a miserly person. Someone who is connected to and spends quality time with children is probably not a miserly person. Remember that these are just guideposts. Someone can be wonderful with animals and terrible with people. Someone can feel *safe* with his family, but insecure and secretive in a romantic relationship. What we're looking at are "indicators," not Gospel. These are qualities to look at and consider when trying to determine if someone is really as available as they say they are. If you've never seen Moliere's *The Family Miser*, I urge you to treat yourself. It's a wonderful farce as well as a serious lesson in human behavior.

If you choose to be with someone whom you believe to be miserly, don't expect to change him. This could be the type of person who will withhold love or material things to punish you. Often they deny these things even to themselves. And why wouldn't they? They commonly believe that the world is a place of scarcity, so resources (i.e., love, money, etc.) must be watched carefully and doled out only when absolutely necessary. This is their deeply held view, so don't think that you alone can change them. The sad truth is that, in most cases, you can never give this person enough and they always make you feel as though they've given you more than you deserve.

A dead giveaway to this type is their general mistrust of other people. Often this is because they themselves are not to be trusted. They're exceedingly proud of their wealth and value it the way most people would value hearth and home. The married man with whom I had an affair was a bit of a miser. He once gave me a gift that he found at a collector's show. It was a "tough-to-find" item and when I said that it must have cost a fortune, his reply was, "You don't want to know." The implication, of course, was that he had spent a lot of money. I had recently broken things off and the last thing I wanted from him was an expensive gift. I intended to reimburse him and I asked a friend to find out the cost of the item. My friend purchased the same thing for $12.00. Now, I don't happen to care much about gifts, expensive or otherwise, and I don't know exactly what he paid for the gift. I'm telling this story because David, even though he was worth millions, couldn't manage to give me a gift without finding a way to make me feel as though he had gone to enormous expense. Such are the ways of the miser.

Because their fear is that there's not enough of something, they don't see loving another human being as *getting* something, they see it rather as *giving* something up—having to share their "stuff." They don't like that. Make sure someone who's saving for a rainy day doesn't live in an emotional desert.

THE FLIP SIDE

Let's say you're the "thrifty" one. (No one actually *admits* to being a miser.) How could this be a trait that's keeping you out of love? Understand that being selfish is a sign of insecurity. It's hard to be open to love when you don't trust yourself or other people. It's hard to be open to love when you think people are out to steal from you. Somewhere there's a fear that you won't have enough. Even though the *feeling* is that you won't have enough money, the *real* fear probably has little to do with finances. The real fear lives somewhere much deeper in your soul. If you don't think this is true, then ask yourself: Does having more money change anything? The answer is, of course, no. More money, even *much* more money, rarely changes someone who's miserly. The more you have, the more you worry about the people or the forces that want to take it away from you. This is not anyone's idea of a welcoming position. These feelings of suspicion and paranoia keep you available only to your fears; "prisoner" is a better word. The only person you're going to attract is a mirror of you. Either it will be a fellow miser or someone whom you really shouldn't trust. Like many fears, they can create self-fulfilling prophecies.

I want to introduce you to two extreme examples of how a money situation affects people differently. One man, Ted, is a very successful restaurateur. He pays his ex-wife, Louise, $10,000.00 a month in child support and alimony. Louise lives with Ted's ex-best friend, Ron. They have no intention of marrying because Louise would lose the alimony. And you know how Ted feels about it? Just fine. He says, "It's worth it! It's only money and now I have my life back." He spent twenty miserable years with Louise and now he's feeling alive and creative again for the first time in years. He's back to work again and has ended up making more money than he ever dreamed possible. Ironically, when he was married, he was frequently worried about money. Perhaps Ted was transferring his anxiety about how unhappy he was in his marriage onto his financial situation, which was always pretty rosy. Now that he's happy, he looks at money in a whole new way. He's not careless; he just knows how important and unimportant it really is.

Now the opposite is true for Ralph. Ralph and his ex-wife Laura had a horrible divorce. Five years later Ralph is still so bitter that he refuses to work because he doesn't want "that bitch" to get a penny of his money. Ralph and Laura have two kids who are stuck in the middle. Ralph *says* he loves his kids, but his heart is so full of hate for his ex-wife that he's willing to withhold support and fail to provide his children with a better life. Not only is this inexcusable behavior regarding his children, Ralph is also destroying his own life for the sake of his revenge. He'll never be able to meet another woman and fall in love until he gets past his hatred. There's no room for love in there. Unbelievably, his parents contribute to this tragedy. They bought him a home and a car so he can perpetuate this ridiculous vendetta. It's such a sad choice, for everybody. (See also: Chapter 1, Someone not over a past love.)

8. SOMEONE TOO NEGATIVE OR DEPRESSED

In the province of the mind what one believes to be true either is true or becomes true.

—JOHN LILLY

Depression, a therapist once told me, is one of the most mis-used words in the English language. Everybody gets depressed occasionally. That's life. But Depression (with a capital *D*) is a very different condition. Depression, as opposed to the mood swings that we all experience during the course of a day or a week, is a terrible, debilitating disease that can be extremely difficult to treat. Advances in antidepressant medication during the past twenty years have brought great relief to millions of sufferers, but there are millions more who are struggling to see some light in their lives.

When I talk about "real, healthy, available relationships" I'm talking about two people who have no burning secrets from each other, two people who have looked at their own lives and decided that they are now ready and available to attempt a loving rela-tionship. This means accepting the fact that all of us struggle in our life, all of us come up against obstacles that seem to overwhelm us, all of us will struggle with dark places in our soul that take time and courage to confront. These are all parts of any good re-lationship. When we meet another person who feels right for us, we can't pick the moment of his life in which to meet. He might be a good person going through a particularly bad time in his life. The man in my life met me just as his younger brother was di-agnosed with terminal cancer. The next six months of his life were extremely difficult, and while I got a chance to see how he dealt with tough times, I also knew that this was not a "normal" situ-ation. You might meet someone suffering a career crisis, a personal loss, or an illness. But difficult or "depressing" times are different from clinical Depression. If you meet someone who is struggling with this disease, then know that you are taking on a lot. The most difficult scenario is being with someone who's suffering from Depression and doesn't know it and/or refuses to deal with it. Complicating matters even further is the fact that people suffering from Depression are frequently highly intelligent, very interesting people. But their disease is very powerful and should be treated by a professional. Not that anything about Depression is a joking matter, but a psychiatrist once shared with me that he wished he could send out a bulletin to everyone trying to help their husband or wife treat Depression; the bulletin would read, "Don't try this at home!" There is a huge difference between loving someone and treating them. Depression needs treatment. A loving environment and a supportive partner are, of course, significant factors in recovery. But don't confuse these things with treatment and proper medication. If someone is suffering from clinical Depression, and they're not dealing with it or not getting treatment, they are probably *not* available for a relationship. No matter how interesting, witty (yes, witty; Oscar Levant was one of the wittiest men in the world and he suffered terribly from Depression), compassionate, or decent they might be, please know what you're up against when you try to deal with Depression from within a relationship. Once the Depression has been recognized, monitored, and brought under control, you'll have a much better chance at having a relationship. Without the shadow of the disease, you both may find yourselves available in ways you never imagined.

There's clinical Depression, and then there are people who just seem to be constitutionally incapable of optimism. No matter what. Double their salary and they're upset about being in a new tax bracket. Send them to Europe and they're frantic because the toilet paper isn't six-ply. Introduce them to a wonderful, interesting person and, trust me, they'll be too young, too old, too tall, or too short. There will be a problem. There could be a million "reasons" for their murky outlook, but for the purposes of this book, let's just examine what this person could mean for you and your "availability." First of all, if you're involved with, or considering being involved with, someone who fits the preceding description, know that this relationship is going to be a *lot* of work.

These people secretly, or not so secretly, are looking for you to be their antidepressant. If you're basically an optimist, then you are going to be pressed into service as a constant "upper" for them. And, in all likelihood, you *will* be! For a while, anyway. Then they'll "crash," which is to say that they will return to their reset personality, which is pessimism. It's a roller-coaster ride, not a relationship. Oh, it's a position of great power for the "upper," but it can be very frustrating and extremely exhausting after a few months or years. But maybe this is how you were raised. If your job in the family was trying to make an unhappy Mom or Dad happy, then you may feel it's your job to make the other person in a relationship happy as well. Your relationship may look and feel like new, but it's not. If you're "remastering" your family dynamic, then it's actually a very old relationship that you won't let go of. Perhaps you've chosen someone who simply can't be pleased. You can try, try, and try again to please him, just as you did when you were a child. If this is the case, then get thee to a therapist. You must *finish* that old relationship before you're even *close* to being available for a truly new relationship

If you are a Rescuer or a people pleaser, then a negative, whiny person is right up your alley. Your work will never be done nor will it ever be enough. You won't change the behavior of a cranky, whiny person unless they want to change. If your desire is to be in an equal partnership, it's time to bring in someone who has some sense of who they are, some ability to find some happiness in this life.

How do you know if the person you're getting to know is just in a slump or has a chronically dreary outlook? Time and knowledge of their history will reveal this to you. Are they content in their irritability? Are they just having a bad day, or is this how they see the world? Is the traffic *really* particularly horrible today or does it seem as if the traffic is *always* horrible when they're behind the wheel? I live in Los Angeles, I was born here, and I'm always amazed when I'm driving with someone who has lived here any length of time and still lets the congestion annoy him. It's Los Angeles! There's traffic! Either put together a plan to help get rid of it, or shut up and quit complaining. What? Does it come as some huge *surprise* that the freeway is congested at five o'clock on Friday afternoon?

If you're with someone who is choosing to be upset and aggravated by life, then know you are choosing his or her drama over yours. Sometimes what's going on is that the negative person is serving as your mouthpiece. Maybe you're not comfortable being the "bad guy" and so, by choosing a cranky partner, you've found a way to express your negative views *through* them.

Emma's husband Clay was known for his irritable disposition. He was absolutely paranoid about the order of things in his home; everything had to be perfect. His lack of cordiality was always a real source of conflict between them. Their home was beautiful, but they never had anyone over because Clay couldn't bear to get it messed up. Occasionally the unavoidable would happen and someone would visit, and then he would just moan and complain and generally make Emma's life miserable. Emma finally had enough and left Clay. She got her very own place, eager to begin her new "socially active" life. But then, the oddest thing happened; Emma realized that she didn't feel comfortable with people either. She had always thought that she was a sociable and welcoming person who just had the misfortune of choosing an unsociable, unavailable man to marry. But once she was on her own, she shut out the world just as Clay had. She realized that she had chosen Clay to be the "bad guy" who would serve to enforce her own wishes. She had been *using* her relationship with Clay to stay unavailable, not only to Clay but also to the outside world. So even though she was single again, she was still unavailable to any kind of intimate relationship.

The message is, pay attention to the people who attract you. If you find yourself drawn to pessimistic, negative, or controlling people—ask yourself if you're using them to say or do something you don't feel entitled to say or do yourself.

Review

In this chapter we've covered some relationship areas to avoid. I want to stress, once again, the reason for all the warnings. It's not that everybody out there is somebody to flee from. Quite the opposite. It's by *learning* about the ones to avoid that we make ourselves available for a relationship with the ones to welcome. The ones who have had the courage to look at their lives, the ones who are done with keeping secrets, the ones who are "available" to be in a relationship with you. I wouldn't be writing this book if I didn't think it was possible to find lasting happiness. I just know how easy it is to waste precious time on people who aren't offering what you're looking for. As I've said several times in this book, dating is a process, a learning process, for *all* of us. The goal here is for you to enter into the best, the most loving, lasting relationship you could possibly have. I was in my late forties before I realized I was the one who was "unavailable" for a relationship, and fifty before I met the man of my dreams, with whom I'm truly happy. And although he was well worth the wait, I don't want you to have to wait that long.

So, go over the following statements and see if you can identify any behavior that has been keeping you single and unavailable.

SOMEONE WHO RUSHES INTO LOVE
1. He declares his love immediately.
2. He wants to see you every day right from the start.
3. Talk of marriage is mentioned on the first few dates.
4. He doesn't want to slow down the pace.

YOU'RE THE RUSHER
1. I believe in love at first sight.
2. I feel like I'm running out of time to fall in love.
3. I'm constantly waiting for love to happen to me.
4. I feel capable of falling for almost anyone who shows an interest in me.
5. I need to know where a relationship is going right away.

SOMEONE JUST OUT OF A RELATIONSHIP
1. I'm helping him recover from his breakup.
2. He's not completely out of the relationship.
3. It's over, but he still lives with the ex because of the kids, or for some other reason.
4. He doesn't want to be alone.

YOU'RE THE ONE JUST OUT OF A RELATIONSHIP
1. I don't want to be alone.
2. I'm afraid to feel the pain of my breakup.
3. I've always been in a relationship.
4. I feel safe in a relationship.
5. I tend to take on each new person's agenda.

YOU DON'T SHARE FUNDAMENTAL BELIEFS
1. I'm attracted to opposites.
2. Many times the thing that attracted me in the beginning ends up being a cause of conflict.
3. I'm hoping he'll change his mind about a big issue.
4. He's hoping I'll change my mind about a big issue.
5. I love a challenge.
6. My friendships tend to be difficult as well.

MAJOR DIFFERENCES IN AGE, INTELLIGENCE, OR STATUS
1. I consistently date younger/older people.
2. I'm always the one with the money, the power, the bigger job.
3. I'm in control.
4. I'm never in control.
5. Most of my friends are significantly younger/older than me.
6. I have a lot to teach/learn.

SOMEONE WHO IS TOO JEALOUS, OR INTO DRAMA
1. He doesn't trust people.
2. He anticipates the worst in people.

3. He's had a history of cheating partners.
4. He claims it's his concern for you that makes him jealous.
5. He needs to know where you are at all times.
6. He discourages you or forbids you from an activity.
7. He wants you to change friends, or your job.

YOU'RE THE JEALOUS ONE
1. I don't trust people easily.
2. I'm insecure about my looks.
3. Previous partners have lied or cheated.
4. I create drama to keep the attention on me.
5. I never relax.
6. I want to control his environment.
7. I've been duplicitous.
8. I hate myself for being jealous.

SOMEONE WHO CROSSES YOUR SEXUAL BOUNDARIES
1. He makes me feel shame about our relationship.
2. I'm not comfortable talking about our relationship.
3. I lie about our relationship.
4. If I didn't participate with him, he would leave me.
5. I have low self-esteem.
6. I don't feel safe.
7. I'm not comfortable with my participation sexually.
8. I have felt emotionally blackmailed at times.

SOMEONE TOO MISERLY
1. He doesn't trust people.
2. He makes me feel cheap.
3. He makes me feel petty.
4. I'm embarrassed by his miserly behavior.
5. He is stingy with kindness.
6. He doesn't trust most people.
7. He makes me feel indebted to him.
8. He is jealous of others' success.

YOU'RE THE MISER

1. I'm afraid there's not enough for me.
2. I don't trust people.
3. I don't feel kindness easily.
4. I keep track of all I do for others.
5. I am jealous of others' success.
6. I don't feel safe.

SOMEONE TOO NEGATIVE OR DEPRESSED

1. I spend all my time calming down or cheering up this person.
2. I can make it better.
3. It reminds me of my childhood.
4. I secretly think he's right, but I don't want to be the bad guy. He fights my battles for me.
5. It's my fault.

Redo

Now that you've looked over the list of statements, what can it tell you? Let's say the section on major differences in age, intelligence, or status is one you related to. It can have an impact to see several highlighted sentences that point out how inequitable the relationships in your life are, or have been. Maybe you can take a look at the people and situations you're bringing into your life and pause for reflection before adding someone new who fits that category.

If you're currently involved in any of the described situations, make a list of the pros and cons. Does it add to or subtract from your life as you wish it to be? What would it take for this to be a great relationship? If you don't know or can't articulate it, you probably can't have it. So spend the time you need to come up with some answers. If it takes an hour, fine. If it takes a week, then let it. This is where the work begins, with the answers to the question: "What do I want?"

What's good? What's missing? What are you willing to compromise on? Go over the list and spend some time with the results. Only by letting go of the bad (or even the good) can you make room for the great.

Chapter 3

Behaviors and Beliefs That Can Keep You Unavailable

Why do you think you're single? I'll bet that it has more to do with the way you're thinking than with the way things really are. I've talked a lot about lists and about visualizing the relationship you want. What follows are some of the roadblocks, real or imagined, that can get in the way of that visualization. Take a look at the following situations and see how many apply to you.

1. YOU HAVE TOO MANY OBSTACLES IN YOUR LIFE

> *Life begins when the kids leave home and the dog dies.*
> —ANONYMOUS

Seasons. Mother Earth has them and so do we. Not every season of our lives is a season to go in search of that rare beauty, the lasting relationship. Everyone experiences periods in their lives in which they are too busy or too obligated to think about dating and falling in love. We all have priorities and responsibilities that sometimes rule out the time and commitment it takes to nurture a partnership. It's a normal part of life to be temporarily unavailable. But some people use these obstacles, and even create them, in order to keep from being in a relationship. And they don't even know they're doing it!

There are real situations, like caring for a sick parent, raising children, and meeting work deadlines that make it difficult to find the time for love, but if this has been your excuse or "reason" month after month, year after year, then something else is going on. People fall in love in the middle of ground wars (my parents did); they fall in love during natural disasters (I know one couple who met during the aftermath of the LA earthquake). I guarantee you that, if you want a relationship, if you're available for one, then you will find the time for one. A friend of mine met her husband when she was on her cell phone driving and was so engrossed in her conversation that she rammed into the back of his car. Putting aside your (completely justified) anger at people who drive and talk on cell phones, I'm just saying that even busy, distracted people have time to meet someone. I once dated a doctor I met while he was delivering my dear friend's baby. In between her labor pains he asked for my number. Now come on—he was busy!

Some people use their goals as obstacles. It's a great thing to have goals, but it's just as important to remember that we are capable of reaching goals *and* having a life at the same time. The two don't have to be mutually exclusive. Truly, the purpose of goals is to make your life a richer and fuller experience. When the goals become an end unto themselves, then you've got the cart before the horse, so to speak. If you keep putting off your life because you think you need to focus your energies on accomplishing such and such a goal, you're missing the point. You're also missing the chance to make yourself available for a relationship. Remember John Lennon's lyric: "Life is what happens while we're busy making other plans." Your biggest goal should be to live your life.

It's a lesson that Luke never learned. He wants to have his life in perfect order before he can start living it. He and Kim dated for four years. Luke wanted to wait until after he finished college to get married and start a family. Kim hung in there. Then he wanted to wait until he graduated law school. Kim hung in there some more. He told Kim they'd get married after he got his law practice up and running. Kim left. Mandy entered. By then the law practice was doing great. In fact Luke told Mandy that they would marry as soon as the practice slowed down; he was too backed up with court cases. That was eighteen years ago and Luke's still too busy to start his life. Mandy left a long time ago. Now it's Kate who's "hanging in there." Luke may *think* he's waiting for the proverbial "right time," but he sure looks like he's determined to stay unavailable. If Luke really does want a relationship, then he had better make some changes in his thinking because there's no such thing as getting your life perfect first. Why? Because there's no such thing as getting your life perfect at all; first, second, last, ever! Luke has had at least three wonderful women in his life. With each one he claimed to be madly in love—it just wasn't the right time. He's now fifty-three and still waiting.

Sometimes busy or goal-oriented people tend to equate time management with relationship management. "I can't be in a relationship because I just don't have the time." In my opinion, it's only true if you want it to be true. Two very busy people can have just as meaningful a relationship as two people who have decided to, or can afford to, take life a lot easier and have a lot more time to devote to each other. The term "quality time" has been overused and cheapened in the last decade or so, but it's not a bad way of explaining the "relativity" of time spent together. If you're an A type personality, always moving, always busy, and you're in a satisfying relationship with another A type personality, then you probably don't have hours and hours to take long walks along the beach. That doesn't mean you don't have a good connection. Don't buy into the TV ads that portray love as something that has to be slow and lingering. If slow and lingering works for you and your partner, then fine. But don't think that if you lead a busy lifestyle it necessarily means you're not available for a relationship. It really is the quality of the time spent, more than the quantity, that determines the strength of the connection between two people. I know plenty of couples who have nothing but time on their hands, and can't seem to find a loving, nurturing place between them.

Another myth is that a relationship will drain your energy. Let me rephrase that; a *bad* relationship will certainly be a drain, but a *good* one has the potential to actually give you energy. That's what they're talking about in all those not-so-silly love songs. Why do the days look brighter and the nights seem lighter, and all the rest of it? Because there is a power that comes from a being in a relationship with an available person. It's why you bought this book. And it's why I wrote it. But as long you believe that even a healthy relationship takes something away from your life as opposed to adding to it, you probably won't be available for love.

I've known many people who have what I call a "single dream." Maybe there's one big thing you've always wanted to accomplish before you settle down. Whether it's traveling around the world, trying a singing career, or bungee jumping off the Golden Gate Bridge—by all means, do it. (If a sex change is on the list, then definitely do it before you go looking for Mr. or Mrs. Right.) If it's really the reason you feel you can't commit, then just do it and get on with your life. But remember that a real relationship is *supposed* to be a place where you can be yourself. If bungee jumping is important to you, then it should be a part of your life *with* the person you're with.

Your life is happening and progressing whether you acknowledge it or not. It reminds me of an interview I once saw with a woman who was quite old. The interviewer asked why she had never married and she replied, "Because I didn't know that the last man who asked me would be the last man who asked me." I'm not saying (and I don't think she was saying) that the last man who asked her was Mr. Right. But if they're all Mr. Wrong because you're just too busy or too picky, then you're doing everything you need to do to stay single and unavailable.

THE FLIP SIDE

Maybe you're dating someone who is putting off a relationship until certain goals are reached. Is your relationship one of the eventual goals? There's a big difference between waiting until you can save up enough money to put a down payment on a house and waiting until you can afford to retire comfortably. As ridiculous as it sounds, I actually know someone who put off his marriage until he had a retirement fund that was sufficient to last both of them well into their second century. Now, I'm all for financial prudence, but I'd like to say a word or two at this time about "adventure." The whole purpose of a relationship is to have someone with whom to share a loving experience of life, including the adventure of it! If you're flat broke and don't have a hint of a prospect, then you might want to wait a while, until your "situation" improves, before making such a serious commitment. But the idea of having everything in place before taking the plunge strikes me as downright cowardly, not to mention not smart! Where do you think memories come from? Do you think they come from everything that goes smoothly and easily? I invite you to consider any book or movie you might have enjoyed in your life. There was conflict in that story; I guarantee it. There was struggle. A relationship is about two people facing life together, supporting each other, learning from each other and about each other. How can you do that when every moment of your lives together has been booked and paid for in advance? Leave some room for adventure. If you have a specific goal in mind, then go after that goal together. Maybe you really will be a couple once it's accomplished.

Take a good look at his list of goals and how you figure into them. Do they look like goals, or do they smell like obstacles? How much do you want to be a part of his life and vice versa? I know many couples (and I'll bet you do as well) who are really just two people, leading separate lives, living under the same roof. Is that what you want? Is that on your "wish list?" Or do you want someone who is "available" for you to truly be in his life and he in yours? To be in his dreams, his plans, his struggles? And for him to be in yours? Never make the mistake of thinking that once you become ingrained in someone's life, things will dramatically change. If this is who they are, if their plans and their goals are their own, then that's probably who they are.

Consider this; if you are with someone who is using obstacles to keep from making a real commitment, you may be the one who doesn't want a relationship. Look at your history. Have you been in this position before? How much time have you spent with people who aren't really available to you? If it's a significant chunk of your life, then please reexamine your patterns and your objectives. If you honestly believe you are ready for a life partner, then stop and consider why you are picking people who are, in one way or another, unavailable.

YOU'RE A RESCUER

You can't buy love, but you can pay heavily for it.
—HENNY YOUNGMAN

Being a Rescuer is a never-ending, time-consuming position—and the benefits package is lousy. Still, there is job security because you can always, always, always find people who are willing to let you be in charge of their lives. And isn't it a whole lot easier to fix someone else's life than your own? In fact, the whole (hidden perhaps, but true nonetheless) purpose of being a Rescuer is to keep the attention off your own problems by focusing on someone else's. It's a great distraction for not dealing with what's going on in your own life. Of course, a Rescuer rarely thinks this is what's going on. All the Rescuer sees is that someone's in need and that he or she can help. Indeed, we all have a touch of the Rescuer in us, and that's not a bad thing. One of the best qualities any of us can have is the quality of compassion and a desire to help those who are truly in need. It's part of what makes us human. There is a fine line between "helping" and "enabling" but it's a line you would be wise to examine. If you're enabling someone, then you are not only hurting yourself; you're also hurting the very person you think you're helping. Furthermore, if you want to be in a loving and equal relationship, it's important that you're able to recognize this behavior in order to address it. Those six most dangerous words in the English language, "I was only trying to help," rear their ugly head once again. Of course, it takes two to make this damaging equation work. A Rescuer must have someone who feels as if they're in need of, or entitled to being, rescued. Someone who has an inflated sense of entitlement can smell a Rescuer at a thousand yards. I don't know how they do it; something in the pheromones, I suppose. All I know is that they rarely miss their mark. And how do I know this? Well, maybe because I have battled with this syndrome in my own life. I've had plenty of experience with people who have a deeply rooted belief that the world revolves around the winds of their emotional state. And, for my part, I've been guilty of "being there" to listen, to understand, to "rescue" and "enable" people, over and over again. I called it "help," but I know now that it served my purposes as well as it served theirs. It has taken me a long time, a lot of work, and much self-examination to discover the reasons why I have been susceptible to this type of person. Many tears were shed while I tried to figure out why someone else's needs seemed to have so much more value than my own. And then, the painful realization that it was my involvement in other people's needs, the endless hours and emotional drain, that was keeping me from my own life, my own needs, my own happiness. Of course, I always thought I was just being a nice person. I never once woke up in the morning, stretched, and said out loud, "Let's see how much time I can waste today trying to fix someone else's life. And while I'm at it, why don't I be sure and pick someone who doesn't *really* want his or her life fixed in the first place. That way we can do this little dance year after year after . . ." Nope, I never once said that. But that's what I was doing. Now I know how stuck I was in a dynamic that began in my childhood (the same childhood I escaped at a very early age by getting married). Because my relationship with my mother was particularly difficult, I was most fond of rescuing my women friends. I was famous for taking in girlfriends of mine, letting them stay in the guest room of my house for months, sometimes years. And while there's nothing intrinsically self-destructive about offering a spare room to a friend, I would too often lose sight of my own boundaries, my own agenda. Crisis became the coin of the realm and some of the "conversations" went on for years; different problems, different men, etc., exact same behavior. They went on for years because they were *designed* to go on for years. Not consciously, but unconsciously. We were "remastering" a dynamic we had failed to complete in our childhood. And all the while I was so wrapped up in the drama that I was "unavailable" for a healthy relationship.

This same dynamic can be found in many male/female relationships as well. We all know someone who falls into the "Project Rescuer" category, a person who seeks out troubled or damaged people and then feels compelled to fix them. Where some see a "loser," they see "potential." With enough love and hard work they can save them. It's their calling and they're completely committed to it. In fact, this type of person would probably feel lost or out of a job if they actually restored a broken human. They'd have to find another fixer-upper to mend.

With some Rescuers it's clearly an issue of self-esteem. For whatever reason he feels he doesn't deserve any better. Frequently such a person will pick a partner worse off than he is in order to feel better about himself. Often he feels that someone worthwhile and healthy wouldn't be able to love him.

The "Master Rescuer" is a person who insists on doing everything for you, but he does it with a secret agenda in mind; he wants you to feel obligated. You can never do enough for the "Master Rescuer," and they always think they've done more than you deserve. Ultimately, these relationships are exhausting because the "Master Rescuer" has put all his time and energy into doing one more thing for you than you do for them.

The danger that is common to all these "Rescuer" types is that they are all "hierarchical," meaning that they all, in their own unique ways, have an imbalance built into their very structure, from the foundation on up. And the flip side of imbalance is resentment. It may come sooner, or it may come later, but it will arrive, this I promise.

If you choose to become involved in such a relationship, know that it will serve to keep you unavailable to someone who doesn't need repair. Again, I'm not suggesting you "cure" the part of you that wants to do good work for others, but if you're doing it to avoid being with yourself and your own problems, you need to look at where that's coming from. It's not an easy process. I know from my own experience. But it can be done.

Of course you should continue to be kind to others, but be

kind to yourself too. You'll have a lot more to give if you fill up your well. Try to remember that you deserve the same love, the same caring, the same nurturing that you're trying to give someone else. Next time you're spending your precious time lecturing someone about how to fix their life—even if it feels as if you're helping—*stop* . . . and ask yourself if you're throwing yourself into their life-drama in order to avoid your own.

THE FLIP SIDE

The other side of the Rescuer dynamic is the people they rescue. If you find that, more often than not, you're the one being fixed, saved or improved—you could be the project of the Rescuer. They need willing victims to fix. Maybe you're comfortable in that role. Maybe you like being taken care of. If so, then know you are fostering a relationship that has a built-in imbalance and will likely run into some serious resentment issues somewhere along the line. Maybe it's just a temporary situation, due to a particularly difficult set of circumstances. If so, then you're probably just weathering one of those "seasons" I keep talking about. But if you *repeatedly* find yourself being fixed then either you have needs which you must address in a therapeutic setting, or you're sending messages you're not aware of. The problem is that, no matter how good it feels to be the recipient of someone's attention, the Rescuer, ultimately, isn't available to a healthy person. When you decide to take control of your own life and your own fixing, then you'll be available for someone who likes you the way you are. And the first person who has to feel that way is you. You want to be a Rescuer? Rescue yourself. There aren't so many strings attached.

3. YOU HAVE A PHANTOM LOVER

> *Stay with me. I want to be alone.*
> —JOEY ADAMS

Having a Phantom Lover is like having an imaginary friend; they don't really exist except in your head. They're great to have when you're six years old, not so okay when you're twenty-six and older. A Phantom Lover is anyone who doesn't spend real time with you physically or emotionally. Real time is at least some weekends, definitely your birthday, Christmas absolutely, and hopefully Valentine's Day. Putting aside an emergency or a surprise call from the armed forces, if you don't get any of these days with the person you consider your true love, it's probably a mythical relationship.

Take my friend, Sarah. She has a great career in New York and is an incredibly bright woman—at least in her professional life. But Sarah's hit a triple! She picked a man who lives on the opposite coast, he's waiting for his kids to grow up, *and* (here comes the hat trick) he's still married. Sarah is so desperate *not* to be in a real, available relationship that she's organized things so her lover doesn't even have to show up. She loves having a "we" to talk about without actually being a "we."

It's the emotional equivalent of playing Ping-Pong with yourself. It's exhausting and takes up all your time.

Other men ask Sarah out but she tells them she has a boyfriend in Los Angeles. She will tell you all about how he's the best guy she's ever met—the only problem, she'll say, is that he's taken. But how could he really be the best guy she's ever known? First of all she doesn't *really* know him, not if she's only spent scattered hours with him at some airport-adjacent hotel midway between LA and New York. More importantly, if this is the *best* person she's ever met—a married man, living three thousand miles away, with three young children—if this is the very best person she's ever met, then she needs to meet more people. If you've never spent real, significant time with someone, you can't know who he or she really is. What you have is a "relationship" consisting of your fantasy of who and what you *think* they are—and, more significantly, what you hope they are.

The flip side

And what motivates the "Phantom Lover" to string someone along? To waste years of someone else's life while all the time professing great and undying love? First and foremost, they do it because they're afraid of the vulnerability that is risked within a complete, available relationship. And secondly, they do it because they can. Because people like my friend Sarah allow them to do it. It may sound romantic—stolen moments of passion—but the Phantom Lover is nothing but a totally unavailable person. Sarah's married boyfriend isn't just unavailable to her; an even bigger part of him is absolutely unavailable to his own wife and children.

You don't have to be married to be the Phantom Lover in this type of relationship. The primary requirement is that you are unavailable to do the normal things people do in a relationship—and that you find someone who is damaged enough to go along with that. If you are seeing a person and you never spend more than a few hours at a time with him or her, never go out to a movie, out for a meal, or go out in public period, you are in a Phantom Relationship. If you don't share the life of your work, your dreams and goals; if you are allowing the mystery and the fantasy of a relationship to take the place of reality, then you're in a Phantom Relationship. Know that it is wasting your life and the life of the other person involved in this life-deadening arrangement. And know too that you have found a way to stay completely and totally unavailable.

4. YOU DON'T LEAVE THE HOUSE/YOU'RE STUCK IN A ROUTINE

Her life was okay. Sometimes she wished she were sleeping with the right man instead of with her dog, but she never felt she was sleeping with the wrong dog.

—JUDITH CALLAS

In this day and age, it's becoming more and more common for people to work out of their home. With a computer you can buy your groceries, books, furniture, whatever; all without leaving the comfort of your home. It can be a positive and productive experience. It can also be lonely and isolating. For the unavailable person, it can help keep you that way. Maybe it's possible for you to go days without human contact. Or if you do go out, perhaps you go to the same places and see the same people. That's fine if your life is working the way you want it to. But if you want to bring someone into your life, you're going to have to do something different. You're going to have to change your routine.

A person who has a rigid or inflexible schedule doesn't leave much room for life, not to mention love. Many people are tired and weary at the end of a workday. Perhaps you have children to tend to. Maybe you can't muster the effort or interest to shake up or add something new to your already fixed schedule. But that's what it takes. The truth is, no one is going to show up at your door and ask you to fall in love. You have to *do* something. It doesn't have to be expensive. It just has to be different.

Why not take a class, any class, outside the home? Go for a walk. Get coffee and read the paper at a new spot. Visit bookstores, museums, and parks. Better yet, volunteer somewhere. Not only is it a good thing to do, and you'll feel good about yourself, but it will expose you to people who support similar causes.

Sometimes your routine gets shaken up for you. Take Cis. She rarely left her house. She worked at home as a script reader, shopped on-line, and then wondered why she wasn't meeting new people after her last relationship ended. Occasionally she would "meet" someone in a chat room, but she would always find a reason not to actually meet them in person. Cis's work was so solitary, it didn't even require her to talk to another person. She did all her communicating by phone and E-mail.

She was finally forced out of her house by her father's illness. She had to find a nursing home for him after he broke his hip. At first she visited him only grudgingly. She loved her father but hated the idea of venturing outside the safe cocoon of her well-regulated life. In the end, it was her love for her father that helped her to overcome her fear and dread of the outside world. She would go every day to visit him. There, she met *several* nice men and women who were visiting their parents or relatives at the same time. They became friendly and she began to actually look forward to the visits.

Even after her father was well enough to go home, she was inspired to start a support group for the friends and relatives of nursing patients. They would meet once a week for coffee. There she developed a crush on Raymond, a man whose mother was in the same convalescent home. Today they are involved in a wonderful relationship.

Earlier in this book I talk about the value of solitude. Solitude should be a meditation of sorts, a chance to reexamine your priorities and to learn from the events of your life. Solitude can be beneficial when it's not used as a hiding place. If you find yourself retreating from the joys of meeting new people and experiencing new places, if you've structured an isolated existence so you can avoid living your life, then you may be operating out of fear. And fear, if you let it, will put your life on hold.

THE FLIP SIDE

If you are seeing someone who never wants to leave home, you need to realize that this may not change. Obviously this person got out of the house long enough to meet you. (Maybe it was a fire, a flood, or a tax audit.) There are circumstances that will draw any hermit out once in a while. But there are people who don't want to get out and don't want to participate in your life or theirs. However, they might welcome occasional company, and this can cause confusion if you think that they're in any way available for a relationship.

5. YOU DATE PEOPLE YOU DON'T LIKE

I've had a perfectly lovely time. But this wasn't it.
—GROUCHO MARX

On Friday night, Barry has a date with a woman. By the end of the evening, he's enchanted. She's smart, funny, and charming.

They have so much in common. And, guess what, he'll never call her again. That was the beginning, middle, and end of the relationship for Barry. On Saturday night, Barry goes out with a woman who doesn't laugh when he's funny, disagrees with his political views, and chews with her mouth open. And, guess what, he will date her for the next two years. Why? Because when they do break up, and they will, it won't be any big whoop. Why? Because he never liked her anyway. No potential. No pain when it ends. That's how Barry stays single and unavailable even though he's almost always "in a relationship." That's how he protects himself from being vulnerable with another person. He looks for something that will keep him safe from having to go through a real relationship. He's afraid of the feeling he gets when he actually likes someone, so he picks women he distinctly dislikes. Of course, the ethical thing for Barry to do would be to *inform* the woman of his true feelings (or lack thereof) so she could decide whether or not she's interested in spending the next two or three years of her life with someone who doesn't even like her. And what do you think the chances are of *that* happening? Oh, he'll let her know, in subtle ways, that he's not all that crazy about her, but he'll never come right out and tell her how he really feels or why. On the contrary, he'll probably send a whole lot of mixed messages, driving the poor girl crazy.

For Barry, as for many unavailable people, the feeling of attraction is so uncomfortable and scary that it sets off a huge panic alarm inside; they will do anything to not have those feelings. They would rather choose someone they dislike, believing it's safer, than expose him or herself to the possibility of pain. It never works, of course. They only submit themselves, as well as others, to a different kind of pain. It's certainly not fair to the other person caught up in this "safe" scenario, is it? Constructing such a "safe" relationship is, by the way, no guarantee that you won't suffer. In truth, you end up creating what you think you're avoiding. But instead of feeling the sharp but very human pain of lost love or a failed relationship, you instead end up feeling empty, unloved, and lonely.

My situation with the married man, David, illustrates this point. It's hard for me to admit that I didn't like David as a person, but I didn't. He wasn't really a very decent man. He was selfish, self-centered and, obviously, he was cheating on his wife. Why would I want to be with such a man? I knew perfectly well that I couldn't have him—and I know now that I actually chose him (or allowed him to choose me) because I thought that I was "protecting" myself. Without being aware of it, I was keeping myself single and unavailable by choosing someone with whom, ultimately, I could never spend my life. My own therapist once asked me that most difficult question for people in this kind of an unavailable relationship. She asked what I would do with David if I ever "got him." I didn't have a good answer. As I've already written, we had little in common. Our values were not compatible. The way in which we viewed the world and treated people was completely different. It's a little like the dog that chases the pick-up truck down the street every evening, rain or shine. What on earth is the darn dog going to do if he ever "catches" the truck?

Today, of course, I'm grateful for the experience with David. I learned a lot of lessons from that relationship, the biggest one being that I don't need to waste years of my life on any more Davids. And neither do you.

Don't form relationships with people you don't like. I know it sounds like an obvious statement, but think about how many of these types of relationships there are in the world. They are completely and totally unavailable and you should make damn sure you're not in one for very long. Do as I write, not as I did. Don't take years to learn a lesson that you could learn in weeks, or days or, better yet, in the time it takes to read this chapter!

THE FLIP SIDE

If you're dating someone who doesn't like you the way you are—stop trying to change his mind. And don't try to become what you think he wants you to be, because the only thing he *really* wants is for you to remain unavailable. He doesn't *want* to like you, so give it up and move on to something in an available size. I'm not saying that you should bolt at the first sign of trouble. I'm not saying that all relationships should be a breeze. Relationships *should* be challenging. But they *shouldn't* be a constant challenge.

If you really want to be in a loving relationship, it won't be with a person who is *looking* for ways *not* to like you. By definition, the only way this can work is if you *don't* get too close. So, when you win, you lose. The only reason to continue such a pattern is if you feel you don't want or don't deserve an equal relationship.

My friend, Del, fits this description. He seems like a nice guy, good-looking, funny, successful. Del has been involved with a woman for three years and the relationship is beginning to take its toll on him. The woman, let's call her Carla, has practically made a career out of sending Del one mixed message after another. One minute she's telling him how much she likes him, the next minute she's got a shopping list of things that he does that drive her crazy. Del, God love him, is so locked into pleasing Carla that he puts himself through fiery hoops in order to make the changes that she's "requested." The kicker is this; every time he successfully addresses an item on her list, the list mutates and a new set of items suddenly appears. When Del dares to point out this "list with a life of its own" to her, she goes into a rage and adds his pettiness to her brand-new list of things Del needs to change. What Del can't seem to get is that he will *never* be able to please Carla. Why? Because that's not what Carla *wants*, no matter what she says! What she wants is to have the appearance of a relationship without any of the risk. No matter what Del does, it won't be enough. Now, either Del can come to terms with this fact, get the hell out and move on to somebody available, or he can spend a few more miserable years watching the list grow and change to fit Carla's not-so-hidden agenda. She wants somebody she doesn't like, not someone she does. Not a lot of love songs written about how good it feels to be that special "no one" in someone's life.

6. YOU PLACE TOO MUCH IMPORTANCE ON PHYSICAL REQUIREMENTS

It is only through the heart that one can see rightly, what is essential is invisible to the eye.
　　　　　　　　—ANTOINE DE SAINT-EXUPERY
　　　　　　　　from The Little Prince

Maybe you have a certain mental picture of the man or woman of your dreams. Perhaps you envision someone tall, thin, and blond; or maybe your idea of perfection requires someone with chiseled features and a muscled body—whatever your fantasy might be, this picture, if you put too much stock in it, can be an extremely effective way of keeping you single. The words "dream" and "fantasy" are used for a reason; they are used to differentiate them from reality. There's nothing wrong with having a fantasy about your "perfect" physical type. But when you're thinking seriously about a relationship, try to put things in some perspective. It will save you all kinds of grief if you do.

We are all physical beings. We respond to physical attraction. You do, I do, all God's children do. We all have hormones that enable us to react when we see an attractive person, a great smile, or a nice set of eyes. There's nothing bad, or wrong, or unnatural about any of this. The difficulty starts when we put too much stock in our reaction. When we begin to associate physical attributes with personality characteristics, we're headed for big-time trouble. "Skin deep" is a phrase that is often used and rarely understood. In plain English, it just shouldn't matter all that much in the long run what someone looks like. We all get old. No matter how handsome or how beautiful we might be at any given time of our lives, we will live, if we are lucky, to see our bodies change and wrinkle. Muscles will soften, no matter how many hours we spend in the gym. Hair will thin. Eyes will lose their acuity. Time happens. You can do battle with this fact, or you can embrace it. Either way, time happens.

We seem to have a particularly difficult time accepting this fact in the United States. In Europe, a much older and in some ways wiser culture, beauty and age are not considered mutually exclusive concepts. Many screen stars are considered beautiful well into their sixties and even seventies. Just before he passed away, Italian screen star Marcello Mastroianni gave an interview and was asked what effect his own startling good looks had had on his life, especially his love life. He smiled and said, "Looks buy you the first two weeks. After that, it's who you are that counts." It was a flip answer, but there's some wisdom in the words. If you want to have a two-week "fling" with someone who appeals to your physical sensibilities then, by all means, go for it. But a relationship is made up of stuff that runs much deeper. If you really want to be available for a satisfying relationship, then you would be wise to give up "looks" as your top priority. Ironically, the very thing that draws you initially to another person can end up being a huge barrier to love. You *think* it's real because he or she *looks* like your fantasy of "real love." Then, when a deeply gratifying relationship doesn't "happen," you're hurt and resentful. Do yourself a favor and redo your wish list.

For those of you who are heavily invested in a certain "look" as a requirement for love, consider the possibility that you don't really *want* a relationship. It doesn't take a Ph.D. in psychology to know that the way someone looks to us will go through changes as we get to know him or her. Haven't you had the experience of finding someone more attractive once you got close to him or her, and also the opposite reaction of finding someone less appealing if the relationship wasn't going well as time went on? That's because what we look like on the outside is just that—it's *outside* of who we are.

Look at your friends and family and the people you love unconditionally. You probably didn't pick your friends based on sheer physical attraction. There is a different kind of attraction that draws you to want to befriend someone. It's usually a combination of time spent together, similar interests, common values, and shared activities. You feel good around that person, you're attracted to their insides, you can be yourself. Why wouldn't you want to pick a life mate the same way? The answer, of course, is sex. And while I would never downplay the importance of a good sex life to a healthy relationship, don't let this one part determine the entire relationship.

When you can embrace the idea that the gift inside the package is more important than the wrapping, you're one step closer to making your list of what you want in a mate. If you had "looks" at the top of the list, try putting a sense of humor at the top, or values, or intelligence, followed by gourmet cook, country dancer, and good tennis player, or whatever makes sense when you think of sharing your life with someone.

THE FLIP SIDE

There's a big flip side to this one. What if you're the one who doesn't feel attractive enough, physically, to be in a loving relationship? What if your own standards, your own rules for yourself, are even more severe than the already outrageous role models offered by the media today? What if you actually believe that no one will love you unless you lose twenty pounds? No one can ever see your scar, your wrinkles. Whatever it is, you just don't feel good enough to be loved. You know every single flaw on your body and never miss an opportunity to point out each one.

There are dozens of very good books out that analyze the effect that fashion and advertising has had on our self-image. I happen to agree that we (especially women) have allowed ourselves to be pummeled into a state of self-loathing by the constant barrage of images which link "perfect" bodies with healthy and happy lives. It's a ridiculous concept and a damaging one. First of all, there's no such thing as a "perfect" body, just as there's no such thing as a "perfect" anything on this wonderful but flawed planet of ours. Secondly, a "healthy" body doesn't look anything like the ones that we are shown. It's a monstrous plot to create an impossible ideal and then sell us one product or procedure after another, each time with the promise of achieving that ideal *and* the alleged happiness that comes with it. It's a rat's maze, and it's a lie, and it has caused untold damage in diseases such as anorexia and bulimia as well as an overall obsession with perfection that has swelled the ranks of the seriously depressed and suicidal. But we have the power to reject these images, to look deeper than the commercials and the color-corrected photographs designed to make us feel "less than." We can be better than that, but only if we make the effort to step back from the message. We must step *towards* a deeper and saner idea of who we are, spiritually as well as physically.

Take Lily's story. Lily was an absolutely beautiful but terribly insecure woman. She spent most of her forty-nine years on the planet feeling bad about herself. In her quest for perfection, she had her nose and breasts done, and still she didn't feel worthy of being loved. When she turned fifty she found out she had breast cancer and had to have a double mastectomy. After her surgery she gave up all hope of ever having a relationship. After all, she reasoned, if she hadn't been able to attract a man when she was "whole," how could she ever hope to find love now that she was "damaged?" She felt as if her looks were "beyond hope" and so she just assumed that now she was destined to be alone. She actually relaxed for the first time in her life. She gave up the search for Mr. Right.

That's when she met Morgan. He was a forty-six-year-old man, handsome, charming, and caring. He pursued her relentlessly. She absolutely couldn't accept that he was *really* interested in her, so she finally told him she had only a massive scar where her breasts used to be. He said he hoped she'd trust him enough some day to show him her scar. Morgan didn't skip a beat. He continued his pursuit of this *person*, this wonderful, intelligent, funny, inspiring person who *happened* to have a scar. Morgan had the wisdom to know that we *all* have scars, we *all* have imperfections. Once we relax and accept that fact, only then can we go about the business of finding another "imperfect," wonderful, decent person with whom to share our life. Lily and Morgan got married when Lily turned fifty-two. Finally, Lily felt truly beautiful and loved.

When you think of the average person's life span versus the window of opportunity we have to look physically fabulous, there's a lot more time allotted to the "getting older" part of our lives. We'd better learn to make peace with that and see the beauty and opportunity of each stage. If you see your beauty, your true beauty, then someone else will too.

7. You Have Bad History/Bad Examples

To he who knows no better, horse manure tastes like caviar.
—Anonymous

Ask a successful person how he or she became that way and you're likely to hear one of two things; either they made it *because* of the things they learned during their childhood, or they made it *in spite* of them. In other words, *you're* the one who determines what you make of the cards you were dealt in this life. This is territory with which I have some familiarity. My childhood was sad and short. I was shuttled back and forth between my father and mother, both of whom had their own, how shall I say . . . "unique" version of reality. At seven years old I was sent to a convent boarding school run by nuns who had taken their vows with the Sisters of the Marquis de Sade. I'll spare you the details, but suffice it to say that I had a choice between hate and hope. I chose hope. There was enough love in my life, albeit from scattered sources, that I was able to cobble together my own version of a positive outlook. There were costs, of course. I have a streak of codependence over which I must keep a constant watch. And certainly it was my need to please people who are constitutionally impossible to please that helped me to choose so many "unavailable" people in my life.

My point is that we all have a story; what differentiates one person from another is how they *deal* with that story. Are you looking at your life as a set of circumstances over which you have no control? If so, then you're not making use of the tools that are available to help you become the person you want to be. It's perhaps an old cliché, but the image of a glass being half empty or half full is still a good one. It takes a lot of hard work and awareness to overcome bad imprinting, but it *can* be done. If I didn't think so, then I wouldn't be writing this book. It was my bad imprinting, the bad cards that were dealt to me, that helped make it possible for me to get stuck in an unavailable relationship with a married man. Only by looking at those cards, those life-shaping incidents, and facing them down, was I able to make some changes in the way I looked at the world and my place in it.

I'm speaking now about your relationship with *you*. After all, this is the relationship that *must* be in good shape before you go looking for a partner. How can you say "share my life" when you're stuck in a life (i.e., patterns of behavior that were set many years ago) that wasn't of your choosing. All those "messages" you received when you were young; they went into what I like to call the "wet cement" of a child's dependant nature. Now, as an adult, that cement has hardened and it takes a damn pickax, not to mention a steely resolve and a really good therapist, to break it up and replace the bad messages, the harmful messages, with good ones.

Following bad behavior doesn't take any effort, you just go with what you know, do what you've always done—and rest assured in the knowledge that you'll get what you always got. To do "it" differently, to make choices, to live your life a new way, requires you to acknowledge that the way you've done it and seen it done is not the way you want to keep doing it. You have to have the belief that there's another way—a better way—to do it. It's almost like reraising yourself and, make no mistake about it, it's a huge job. Use every tool you can get your hands on. If this book helps, then great. If you need to make changes in your environment, in your work situation, in your daily regimen, then that's what you need to do. If you need a professional, someone trained to "break up that cement," then do not hesitate to find someone with whom you feel a connection.

But how do you know what "better" is if you haven't even seen it? If you grew up with parents who treated each other badly then you can end up thinking that's just the way it is. Worse, you can end up feeling as if anything different is not to be trusted. There have been several studies that tracked children who were removed from their own abusive homes and placed in loving environments for a year. At the end of that time, they were given the choice to stay in the loving home or return to their offending parent. In almost every case the child chose the abusive, but familiar, parent. (The study concerned the *choice*. The children, of course, were not made to actually return to an abusive setting.) Why did they make such a choice? Because their core beliefs told them that the way they were treated by their parents was the right way, or at least the only way they *deserved* to be treated. What I'm saying is that it's our beliefs that need to be adjusted along with the behavior itself. Getting at those beliefs is hard work, but necessary if you're going to become available for a real relationship with someone else . . . as well as with yourself.

Take inventory of all the people with whom you come into contact. Think about everyone you know. Are you pleased with your interaction with most of these people? Evaluate all your relationships and write down the ones you feel the best about and the worst about. What makes the connection a good one or a bad one for you? Even though the primary focus of this book is finding a healthy relationship with your life partner, you can learn a lot about yourself by examining the other relationships in your life: your friends, your business associates, your acquaintances. When you look at these connections, how do you feel about the dynamic that you've created? Sometimes we are able to spot a pattern within a friendship quicker than in a romantic relationship.

By now we've looked at several key prototypes of "unavailable" people and situations. Use these as templates and see how the various people in your life measure up. How many "hierarchical" relationships do you have? How many relationships are with people whom you don't actually like or respect? How many are with people who think you're a great person, but think you'd be a whole lot better if you'd just do . . . ? In the end only you know how you feel when you're with a particular person. Only you know if you feel more secure or less, loved or diminished, only you know how many secrets you're keeping from this other person and how many you feel he's keeping from you.

The important thing is to look honestly at all of these relationships, see how they fit into your life as it is today, and how they fit into the life you want for your tomorrow. Is he available? Is she available? Are you?

Just because you haven't had good relationships in the past doesn't mean that's your destiny. We all have patterns of behavior, ways of looking at the world that were put into the "wet cement" of our tender hearts long, long ago. But we are all creative creatures who have the power to change those patterns. It's hard work, the hardest there is. And there are no guarantees. But it's our job, as worthy, loving people, to try. It's a job that is *never* completely finished, but it's also a job that will continue to satisfy. As the philosopher Socrates said many years ago, and as is still true today, "The unexamined life is not worth living."

And if none of the preceding does it for you, then just remember that people who are working on themselves are interesting and (many times) attractive, while people who aren't . . . aren't. If you've found someone who is truly available for a loving relationship, then he or she has probably done some of the work described in the chapters of this book.

Review

We've identified several behaviors that can keep your soul mate from finding you. How many apply to you? You know the saying, "Don't fix it if it's not broken"? Well, you also can't fix it if you *don't know* that it's broken.

Take a look at the following statements and note the areas you feel are true for you. The goal here is to make you more aware of how some of your beliefs might be helping to keep you single and unavailable.

Your answers can relate to love mates, family, friends, and/or work situations. Even if you don't consider yourself a Rescuer with your love partners, if you're a Rescuer at work or with your family and friends, it has a direct effect on your availability to a love relationship. Once you become aware of the consequence of your choices, you can begin to make better ones.

YOU HAVE OBSTACLES
1. I've never been in a committed relationship.
2. I'm waiting to lose ten pounds, or gain ten pounds, before I'm ready for a relationship.
3. I'll pursue a relationship as soon as I get my degree, buy a house, the kids leave home . . .
4. It's difficult for me to live in the "now."
5. I don't deserve happiness.
6. Nothing comes easily.
7. I am repeating a childhood dynamic.

YOUR MATE HAS OBSTACLES
1. I'm ready but he/she has a goal to accomplish first.
2. I've been in similar relationships before.
3. My happiness is dependent on another's goals and time frame.
4. I'm waiting for a married person to leave his marriage.
5. Children from a previous marriage are an issue.

THE RESCUER
1. I could do better than the mate I'm with.
2. My mate (or friends or family) depend on me quite a bit.

3. I volunteer or am volunteered for many projects.
4. I spend a lot of my time and energy helping others with their problems.
5. Often I'm the only one who sees the worthiness in a person.
6. I rarely spend time alone.
7. A lot of people feel obligated to me.

THE RESCUED

1. I crave approval.
2. I'm in a temporary relationship until the "right" person comes along.
3. No one would like me if they really knew me.
4. I'm insecure.
5. I'm ready to believe the worst about myself.
6. Others' opinions matter more than my own.
7. I would love for someone to take care of me.
8. I believe someone else should take care of me.

PHANTOM LOVER SYNDROME

1. We don't spend quality time or holidays together.
2. My significant other lives far away.
3. My significant other is married or involved with someone else.
4. Our relationship is a secret.
5. I can't refer to this person as my boyfriend or girlfriend.
6. I feel like I'm walking on eggs when we're together.
7. I don't ask for anything. I don't expect anything.
8. I don't feel really known or appreciated.

YOU NEED TO GET OUT OF THE HOUSE

1. I'm home every night and weekend.
2. I'm relieved when someone cancels plans so I can stay home.
3. I'm glad I can order what I need on-line.
4. I work at home.
5. I pass up any invitations that aren't near home.
6. I feel out of the loop.
7. I'm afraid of life and of taking risks.

8. My previous relationships have been about convenience.
9. I am about my routine.

DATING PEOPLE YOU DON'T LIKE
1. I'd rather date someone I'm not crazy about than be alone.
2. I believe maybe I'll learn to like him/her in time.
3. I don't believe I can do better.
4. I don't know anyone else.
5. I'll just date him/her until someone better comes along.
6. I also have "friends" I don't really like.
7. I don't believe I deserve better.
8. Dating someone inferior makes me feel better about my life.
9. There's no chance of being hurt.

YOU'RE THE ONE NOT LIKED
1. I try really hard to win people over.
2. I always feel like I'm auditioning.
3. I feel unworthy or inadequate.
4. I adopt others' interests and have few of my own.
5. I suffer from anxiousness and fear.
6. I feel judged.
7. I lack confidence.
8. I use alcohol or drugs to relax.
9. I've changed something about myself for another person.

TOO ATTRACTED TO PHYSICAL APPEARANCES
1. I think someone better might come along if I wait.
2. I'm very picky about others' flaws.
3. I don't have many repeat dates.
4. I feel a sense of emptiness.
5. I have a lot of material things.
6. I'm insecure around attractive people.
7. I want people to envy me.

TOO CONCERNED WITH YOUR OWN PHYSICAL APPEARANCE
1. I'm never seen without makeup.
2. I'm preoccupied about my looks or losing my looks.

3. I am preoccupied with aging and plastic surgery.
4. I feel I'm too fat, skinny, old, flabby, bald, etc. for love.
5. I feel I have a limited time to attract someone.
6. I feel I wouldn't be likeable if I weren't attractive.
7. I feel insecure about my intellect.
8. I believe no one would love me if I were damaged or disfigured.

BAD HISTORY/BAD EXAMPLES

1. I don't trust people.
2. I'm expecting the worst.
3. I always leave a relationship first.
4. I pick partners that remind me of a parent.
5. I've been in abusive relationships.
6. I feel trapped by my history.
7. I believe this is the best I can do.
8. I am in a relationship similar to my parents'.

Redo

You've looked over the list. Again, if an overwhelming number of these statements ring true for you, it can reveal a possible pattern that's been keeping you single and unavailable. Highlighting several sentences such as, "I don't believe I can do better," "I expect the worst," "I'm insecure about my intellect," "I've changed myself for another person," suggests an attitude of "less than." And if you feel "less than," then you will bring a person "less than" your ideal mate into your life. The goal here is to identify and remove the barriers that are blocking you from finding love.

See if you can change the way you do something on the list. If you have trouble finding even one thing you're willing do differently, can you at least recognize what it is and begin to monitor what triggers the unwanted negative behavior? Owning your choices as opposed to being a victim of them is a great place to start. You'll be surprised to see that once you know what your unavailable behaviors are, it is much more difficult to act them out unconsciously.

PART II

Becoming Available

NEW RULES—A NEW WAY

Fall down seven times, stand up eight.
—JAPANESE PROVERB

Desire is the first ingredient of change. If you don't want something to happen, chances are it ain't gonna happen. But desire by itself changes nothing. If your desire is to speak a foreign language, then you must go through the necessary steps of training your ear, learning the grammar, understanding the rules, and knowing when to follow those rules and when to break them.

The *desire* to become available is an important first step, but it's *only* a first step. It takes willingness, practice and, most of all, courage to become conscious, awake, and responsible for your choices. In this section, we will examine some of the tools you'll need to change the way in which you regard relationships. My hope is that you will discover new ways of thinking, new ways of understanding yourself and your needs, as well as new ways of making room for a healthy, "available" person in your life.

There are no guarantees when it comes to love. *That,* I guarantee. I make no promises about love, but I *will* share with you my sincere belief that it's when we examine our lives, face our fears, and find new ways of bringing different kinds of people into our lives that we stand the best chance of finding a healthy, nurturing, loving, "available" relationship.

Chapter 4

Facing Your Fears

All of us experience fear many times, throughout our lives. Fear, at the right time, can warn us of danger, even save our life. It keeps us alert and paying attention, and that's a good thing. Being paralyzed by fear is not. When you avoid the possibility of getting close to someone because you're afraid of what *might* happen, then you're letting fear keep you from living your life to the fullest.

Almost all the things you do today with ease and comfort were most likely events marked by fear once upon a time. From the first steps you took as a baby, to riding a bike, diving in the deep end of a swimming pool, your first day of school, a roller coaster ride, and your first kiss. Imagine what your life would be like if you had been allowed to let fear keep you from doing any of those things. Weren't you scared to death at the prospect of learning to drive? But weren't you even more afraid of not learning to drive? That's how it works. You feel the fear and you do it anyway.

The word "fear" has come up several times in this book and it will come up several *more* times. Why? Because all books about getting in touch with your feelings *must* deal with the element of fear. There are many types of fears, many degrees of strength, and many, many ways to deal with fear. One approach may work for one person, another for somebody else. One person does better by putting his toe in the water and wading in slowly, another needs to just jump into the deep end. The real danger is in steering clear of the water. In one way or another, all the "unavailable" behaviors listed in the previous chapters are fear-based. It's when we *don't* deal with our fears that we come up with patterns that make us unavailable. If someone is addicted to his work, it could be he's *hiding* at the office, hiding from some fear that lives at home, or in his heart. If someone is insanely jealous, she may be acting out a fear that nobody could possibly want to stay with her. Personally, I know how much I've suffered in my life, how much time I spent in unavailable relationships, because of my fears. I *feared* that I would be hurt if I allowed myself to become truly vulnerable to another person. I *feared* that I wasn't deserving of a complete, healthy relationship. I *feared* that if I didn't accept the relationships that were offered to me, on the terms that were offered, that nobody else would love me. I allowed myself to participate in what I call the "Sally Fields" syndrome. "You like me! You *really* like me!" she said tearfully at the Academy Awards back in 1985. Well, too many of us, men as well as women, say yes to unavailable relationships because somebody "likes us." What about the flip side of that question, "Who do *I* like?" It's a close relative to the question "What do *I* want? (In my life, for my life.)," which leads to the question at hand, "So, what am *I* afraid of?"

In order to survive, we all must learn to adapt. We see it everywhere in nature. Take a look at the lobster, for example. Long before it ends up in a water tank at your favorite seafood restaurant, this little guy has already faced danger many times over. During the course of its long life, a lobster will outgrow its shell several times. When this happens, it is forced to leave the safety of its hard outer covering and live unprotected amongst its predators for up to three days while it waits for a new, larger shell to form. It instinctively knows this is a dangerous proposition. So why does it do it? Because if it doesn't take the risk of leaving for those few days, it will die a certain death, suffocating in a shell that has become too small. In much the same way if you don't take the risks you're supposed to take, and face the fears you're meant to face, then you, too, can suffocate emotionally.

1. Fear of Rejection/Judgment/Abandonment

A ship in harbor is safe, but that is not what ships are built for.

—John A. Shedd

I've spoken about the "wet cement" of our childhood emotional lives. Many of us are unavailable for a healthy relationship in our adult lives because we had the stuffing (emotional and/or physical) knocked out of us when we were young. Alice Walker (in her book, *Drama of the Gifted Child*) and many others have written eloquently about the enormous damage done when a child's emotional state is disregarded during his or her youth. Our initial introductions to concepts such as trust, love, and pain are formed at this time and have a powerful influence over our adult behaviors. I've interviewed men and women during the course of writing this book who have told me absolute horror stories of how they were treated when they were children. One woman told me that, as a child, any time she told her mother she loved her, her mother would openly mock her, telling her that only sissies and brats said "I love you." Her mother told her that as soon as she was lovable, then she'd be sure to let her know. Her mother never said the words "I love you" to her own daughter. Never. It should come as no surprise that this woman grew up to be dangerously susceptible to anyone who said, "I love you." That's all she needed to hear and she was hooked. She had been in numerous relationships, as well as friendships, with selfish, mean-spirited, unavailable people whose only attribute was their ability to say the words "I love you." Forget about the actions that are supposed to match the words. They were incidental for this woman. Her *fear* of being unlovable, her *fear* of living her life without ever hearing the words, made her unable to ask that tough first question: What do I want? It was only after years of unhappiness that she finally took a good look at what she was doing and why she was doing it. Finally she was able to see the damage her mother had done and begin to know that it had everything to do with her mother's dysfunction and nothing to do with whether or not she was truly lovable. After coming to grips with her own history, she was able to take an inventory of the people in her life and make some critical changes. After a while, there was room for people who said "I love you" because they meant it, not because it hooked someone.

We're all vulnerable creatures. Heartbreak is probably the one affliction common to all of us. Every one of us has lost, or will lose, someone important in our lives. Most of us will experience someone who abuses our trust. So, the universal fear is that once you open yourself up to someone and become vulnerable, what if they end up kicking you in the emotional gut? This is the fear that keeps a lot of people from even trying. We will talk about ways to face this fear, but know that if you're unwilling to risk being hurt, the only thing you can be sure of is that you will remain safe and alone. If that were enough for you, I doubt you'd be reading this book.

As much as I believe in the benefits of the examined life, especially the reexamined childhood, do not think that I subscribe to the "I had a rough childhood, so . . ." defense. We've all got a story and we all have the job of dealing with that story as best we can and getting on with the business of living our life with integrity and with love. I'm not saying, "Get over it," but I *am* saying, "Find a way to get through it." I'm hoping that you agree with me on this point. We're all finding ways to "get through it" and get on with our lives.

Think about this; there are no perfect parents. Even if Mother Theresa had been your very own mother, you would most likely have grown up with an unhealthy dose of rejection and abandonment. The woman, after all, didn't spend a lot of time at home. I'm not trying to be disrespectful, I'm just saying that every scenario has its liabilities when it comes to getting the parenting we need. "Perfect" parents frequently don't provide a home life in which a child learns how to cope with emotional problems. Some of the "healthiest" people I interviewed for this book came from some of the most "difficult" homes. They didn't grow up *without* problems; they grew up *with* problems and then learned how to deal with those problems. So, they aren't *afraid* of problems the way someone might be if he or she had never really experienced a problematic environment. Of course there are childhoods that are incredibly abusive and can suffocate a child in anxiety. This can produce an adult with a level of dysfunction requiring a tremendous amount of work. But I spoke with plenty of people who fell into this category as well. I don't pretend to have any answers in such cases. There's certainly no fairness in the way some children receive care from healthy, loving parents while others receive abuse from damaged, fearful (and fearsome) ones. If there is any shred of a silver lining to this reality, it is perhaps that, no matter how difficult your upbringing, no matter how odd and complicated (and maybe even unlovable) you may consider your life, there is certainly someone who has had a similar path, an equally turbulent childhood, with whom you might be able to relate. If you think your story is so outrageous as to render you ineligible for love, go to an AA meeting sometime and listen to the stories that brought some of those brave souls to that meeting. The important thing is that you survived. Now you have to go about the business of rejuvenating your heart and your sense of trust. No easy task, but possible. And necessary if you are looking to be available for a real relationship.

In the end, love is about trust. If that trust has been violated, then it's only natural that you're going to have difficulties "opening" your heart to someone. *That's* why you (and me, and many others) spend years repeating the same scenario, even if it's inappropriate, harmful, demeaning and, ultimately "unavailable." The "holdover" from our childhood, the *constant,* if you will, is the lack of trust. This is why I ask that you go back to the very beginning. And this is why I think it wise to begin with the very basic questions. Who am I and what do I want? These are questions that you might not have been *allowed* (certainly not encouraged) to ask in your childhood. If not, then an important piece of your own emotional puzzle has gone missing. Once those pieces are replaced, then you can begin to work your way back to a new definition of words like trust, and vulnerability, and love.

One way to determine if fear is what's been keeping you single is to take a good look at your current and past relationships. How much of your relationship time has been fear-based? Is there always drama? Jealousy? Insecurity? Many times the people who fear they'll be left, judged, or replaced are the ones who set impossible standards for a partner to live up to. They sometimes create drama to distract from the possibility of a more sane connection, and even allow themselves to be mistreated because they lack confidence that they are entitled to ask for more. These are people who, for the most part, have not faced their fears. Your true happiness and mental health lie in finding peace and accepting yourself first.

We all have insecurities, whether physical or emotional, real or imagined. Maybe you have a secret, or a sexual habit, or a phobia that causes you to feel shame. It could be something that happened to you, such as abuse, neglect, or molestation. Whatever it is, if it isn't illegal or hurting someone else, and if it's something you are willing to face and work on, then someone will understand it, someone might share it, and someone can help you with it. Someone, somewhere is "available" for the kind of relationship that includes *you*. If you're looking at your life and you're working hard to be the best person you can be, then you are loveable. I will say it again because it's so damn important: *You are lovable.* Underneath so many of the phobias, addictions, and behaviors that separate people and keep them unavailable are beliefs (rarely admitted, but deeply felt) that they are not lovable for who they really are. That's why they find so many creative ways to keep their distance. They may have a million "reasons" for their behavior: work, travel, gotta wash my socks . . . There are more ways to avoid a real relationship than there are coffee choices at Starbucks. Maybe there are "Fifty Ways to Leave Your Lover," but there are five *million* ways to keep yourself from being in love in the first place. And why? Because anytime you risk it all, it's damn scary. I know. I hid from the risk of love for too many years of my life. And I didn't even know I was doing it! But if this chapter is about how love is worth the risk, it's also about becoming aware and knowing what to watch out for. I love to ski. I think it's worth the risk that comes with the sport. But I don't go off into the woods or ski recklessly. By the time you're ready to take the risk of sharing your heart and your vulnerabilities with another person, you want to have some idea about the quality of the person you've picked, or *they* could become the reason you don't try again. Don't let that happen. It's not about finding someone to say your life (problems and all) is okay; it's about being okay with yourself first and then finding someone with whom to share that.

Maybe you have a history of being judged for everything from your looks to your intelligence. It doesn't matter what your history has been; it doesn't have to determine your future unless you *decide* that it does. As Eleanor Roosevelt put it, "Nobody can make you feel inferior without your permission." But an issue worth addressing is, why have you been picking people who judge you? Are you repeating a childhood pattern of emotional or physical abuse? As I mentioned before, when we continue to repeat a relationship dynamic from our past, we are not *only* reenforcing a bad habit that will just get harder and harder to break, we are also creating a neurological pathway whose grooves get deeper each time we repeat the action.

Someone who's called stupid or fat all of his or her life by Mommy or Daddy is likely to be quite comfortable with a mate who recreates the pattern. Even though it's painful and hurtful— it's familiar. The first step to transformation is recognition. *Look* at your childhood patterns, get help if those memories are difficult to access. And when you look at your history, don't just look at the events, look at the real, raw, painful emotions that existed back then. This is, of course, much easier said than done, but it is a very necessary step in determining why you have chosen someone who is causing you pain yet is still attractive to you. It's very possible you're not even in a relationship with the person you're with. You could be in a relationship with some parent or parent figure from your past with whom you haven't had closure. You're "remastering," that is, attempting to recreate that childhood scene so that you can finally "master" it. But if you can face the original object of your hurt and anger (or whatever emotion applies), and you can work it out with *that* person, there are ways in which to come to terms with the *emotions* of the relationship. Even if they've moved away or passed away you can still truly move *past* that relationship and move *forward* into a new relationship between yourself and a *new* person. But the first step is *still* looking at the *original* fear and finding ways to deal with it.

Maybe you're with someone who makes you feel "less than" the person you are. Are you simply (or not so simply) reinforcing a voice that you heard during your growing up years? When you are with someone who makes you feel inferior, you're so busy defending yourself you don't have time to actually *be* in a real relationship. The next time you feel familiar negative feelings like anxiety and insecurity, stop and pay attention to what's going on. What happened? What buttons were pushed? If you can teach yourself to see when it happens, you can begin to see the origin of those feelings. Who first made you feel those feelings? Your mother? Father? Sisters and brothers? First boyfriend or girlfriend?

Marilyn is a very attractive woman, but she can't see it at all. She had a father who was so obsessed with physical beauty that she grew up convinced that she could never, ever live up to the standards he set. She internalized his voice and took on the same unrealistic ideal for herself. No matter who told her that she was pretty or attractive, she didn't believe them. So convinced was she that this harsh, critical voice was real that for years Marilyn was profoundly uncomfortable with her appearance. It took a long time and many hours of therapy before she began to see that it was her father's dysfunctional view of women—his overemphasis on the physical—that was at fault, not how she looked. Those voices inside our heads are incredibly powerful and rarely rational. Marilyn says that those voices are still with her, but now she's able to battle them to a draw. She also makes damn sure she doesn't allow anyone into her life who echoes those hurtful views. Robert Firestone, the same man who wrote *Fantasy Bond*, also wrote a wonderful book entitled *Voice Therapy* which deals with the specifics of these "inner voices" in great detail. The important thing to know for our purposes is that these voices are real, and powerful, and they absolutely *must* be identified before they can be faced down and vanquished.

It is these voices (and our decision to listen to them) that can cause so much confusion, allowing us to choose people (or be chosen by them) in our lives who are "unavailable" for a real, healthy relationship. Brenda Ueland, in her book *So You Want To Be A Writer*, talks about the importance of surrounding yourself with people who are enthusiastic about your dreams. She says that being a writer is such a risky business that you absolutely must have a supportive group of friends and associates around you in order to succeed. Well, I think that any time someone decides to make a substantive change in their life, they're entering into an arena that is equally risky, and I think what Ms. Ueland said about writers applies to all of us.

Ask yourself, who in your life *doesn't* want you to succeed? I'm not talking about what they say; I'm talking about their actions, the way they act and react to the ebb and flow of your life. Whom do you feel confident around? Whom do you feel safe with? How are they different from the others in your life? How are you different around them? Over time you can train yourself to react differently to those negative triggers and to avoid the people who bring out your fears and anxieties. As I said before, not only can we train ourselves, but we can and do train others to treat us the way they do. Once you're not playing the part of the abused person, the abuser will look for someone else to cast. Ironically, these words—"look for someone else"—may leave you feeling alone and abandoned. This is the "downside" of any change in our life. Even when we get rid of something or someone toxic, we must still find ways of living with what's left in their absence. It's usually anxiety and fear. That's why we brought these people into our lives in the first place, to relieve a certain anxiety. But once we realize that they can *bring* a lot more anxiety than they *relieve*, then we are able to find some strength in that knowledge as we push through the uncomfortable feelings to a healthier place and a more available person in our lives. All of these dynamics take two people to keep them going. A seesaw can't work with only one person *seeing*.

A fear of being rejected or judged can reveal itself in another way, when you're the one doing the rejecting and judging. If, deep down, you're afraid of being hurt, then taking on the role of always being the one to leave a relationship is a great way of feeling safe. Leaving first keeps the other person from leaving you. But that doesn't keep you safe; it keeps you unavailable for a real relationship.

When it comes to judging others, it may feel like you're more in control, but the end result is the same; you're still not in a satisfying relationship. Having a judgment is a lot different than having an opinion. We are all entitled to our opinions. They're part of what defines us and helps us and others know who we are. But judgments are something entirely different. If you look the word up in the dictionary you'll find that "judgments are assumed to come from a voice of authority." Unless you have a good answer to the question, "Who died and made you Bruce Springsteen?" you may want to cut back on your judgments and concentrate on your opinions. In my "opinion," judgments frequently come from a place of fear. When you feel inadequate, it's easy to judge others in order to feel superior to them. Opinions invite different and even opposing views, while judgments have an air of finality and "authority" to them. The feelings of "entitlement" that usually accompany such judgments are frequently the flip side of a deep-seated insecurity. If you find yourself passing judgment on others, then ask yourself if perhaps you're not simply distracting yourself momentarily from your own pain and fears. In the end you'll feel worse; you'll feel guilty and shamed. Why? Well, first of all, because who the hell are you to judge anyone else? (And I invite you to ask the same question of anyone judging you—Superior Court judges notwithstanding.) Secondly, and more important to your goal of becoming available for a healthy relationship, judging is, by its very nature, a hierarchical exercise. Two equals can have different opinions, but a judgment assumes that one person's is "higher" than the other. Next time you catch yourself judging another person, or allowing yourself to be judged, take a moment to register that you are now officially (at least for the moment) in a hierarchical (and therefore unavailable) relationship. What's your opinion about *that*?

2. Fear of letting go and losing yourself

Something we were withholding made us weak—
until we found it was ourselves.

—Robert Frost

Sometimes we're conscious that our fears are running the show and sometimes (most times) we're not. What are some of the ways of knowing that our fear is in the driver's seat? As much as I'd love to give you a definitive, scientific observation, I think the real answer is much more elusive. I think we all have our own voice (different from the "voice" discussed in the previous section; this voice is our own, true voice), and instinct, that give us information about a certain situation. Some people call it intuition, some consider it a helping hand from a guardian angel; whatever it is, it's an indicator of whether we're heading towards something healthy or potentially damaging. Now, between the "voices" of our youth, and our role models, our parents, teachers, society, etc., etc., it gets rather dicey to ferret out our own true voice, but that's the work we're talking about. Get to your own voice and you've gotten to a powerful helper in your quest to know what's really going on in your life.

If you've been hurt in the past, the idea of allowing yourself to be vulnerable with someone new might be unimaginable. "If I made a mistake once, and it caused me *this* much pain, how do I know I won't make the same mistake again?" You certainly didn't set out to get hurt. But if this is a pattern in your life, then you've got every right to hesitate before rushing back into what has begun to feel like a house of pain. And the truth of the matter is that *some* people *do* just keep repeating the same painful mistakes over and over again for the rest of their lives. Maybe those people aren't stopping to look at their lives. You're different in a very important way. You're determined to get to the root of the problem, face it, and find ways to change your behavior. You're different because you have stopped looking at the behavior of *others* as the sole source of your hurt and you're looking at your *own* patterns (and their causes) in order to change the one element in the equation (actually, the *only* element) that you *can* change.

When you're emotionally healthy, you can be open to a new relationship. If, on the other hand, you haven't identified your fears and seen how they affect your behavior, then you may just keep adding more and more water to your emotional moat. If you're operating from a place of fear—fear of letting go, fear of risking pain, fear of being hurt—then you are going to make choices that will reflect that fear. By definition you're unavailable for a healthy relationship and you're going to bring unavailable people into your life. If you've tried to determine whether or not you're operating out of fear, and you just can't get a handle on your feelings, then check the first three chapters of this book, and go over the checklists at the end of the chapters. How many of these "types" have you experienced in your life? If you've developed a pattern of choosing unavailable people then you're probably *not* looking at some fear that needs attention. We do this by choosing to protect ourselves rather than risk letting someone new in. Although people with armor sometimes do attempt a relationship, it doesn't mean they let you in or you let them in. They're still not getting what they *say* they want, but they can avoid the difficult job of looking at those fears by losing themselves in what passes for a relationship. If you're with someone who doesn't really mean that much to you, someone you don't love and can't imagine loving, you might think you're protecting yourself and your feelings. Maybe you believe you can't be hurt if you lose something that didn't matter that much to begin with. But that's not really true. You lose time you can never get back. And you lose the beauty and the excitement of your life, which is being robbed of the opportunity to love and love deeply.

Having said all that, I would now like to put in a good word for "dating"; old-fashioned, angst-free, dinner-and-a-movie type fun. Dating is the still the best way to get to know someone. If the pain you've experienced in the past hasn't cut too deep, then try to reframe dating as a fun way to experience people and reenter the real world after a breakup. Add the element of vulnerability only when and if it begins to feel safe; just don't use the pain of a breakup as an excuse to retreat into an "unavailable" relationship. It may look like a good way of steering clear of pain, but it's a bad bargain and a worse habit to get into. If you can, have some fun and let yourself build up some trust again. Make yourself available, but do so little by little.

Some people experience a sense of power when they're not in love. But it's a false sense of power. It may feel safe, but there is pain in being an emotional island. The right love doesn't mean you find a person who makes you feel completely comfortable; it means you feel comfortable enough or secure enough in that relationship to risk it anyway.

I wanted to be over the pain of my affair with David for so long that when it was finally over, I felt odd. I experienced the absence of pain and suffering, which is its own strange feeling in and of itself. It was during these months that I began to look at my own role in the choices I had made, especially with David. As soon as I realized how much I had done to help create my own dilemma, I knew that I could also exert some control over breaking the pattern. I made that "inventory list" I keep talking about. I spoke to a therapist who helped me see some of my own history that was damaging. I began to think of all the ways I had made myself unavailable, long before David. It was difficult and it was painful, but I finally started to see a light at the end of the tunnel. It took a long time but finally one day it happened. It was over. I didn't get nauseated when I heard his name. There was nothing. No reaction to thinking about him.

Like any addiction born out of a hole in one's soul, there were "slips" and "aftershocks." I had done the "headwork" necessary to look at what had happened, I understood my role in it, and I acknowledged the fears and insecurities that had driven me to do what I had done. Next came the feelings that accompany that awareness. Sitting tight through the anxiety took the kind of strength that I imagine all addicts must summon when they detox. First we get the toxic substance out of our bodies, then we must live through the waves of sick feelings that cried out for the "medication" in the first place.

I was lucky to have good friends around to see me through the worst of my pain. But not everyone has that. I once had a friend who told me that when he stopped drinking and joined AA, the thing he missed most wasn't the alcohol, it was the community of "friends" at the bar he frequented. "Friends" who could only relate to him as a drunk. In other words, not really friends at all. "Collateral damage" is what they call it in the military. In the civilian world it's the painful realization that there are people who don't want you to get healthy. Some of them will *say* that's what they want. But watch what they do, not what they say, when you "clean up your act." And remember what Ms. Ueland said about only keeping people in your life who want you to do well and live fully.

Sometimes people shut down and it looks as though nothing will ever get through again. Let me tell you Nina's story. Her new husband, the love of her life, went to work one day three months after they were married and never came home again. At thirty-two, Les had a brain aneurysm and died. Nina suffered indescribable grief. Her pain was the only constant for a long time. After three years of mourning, she came to a point where she was finally over the constant pain. Instead of suffering, she realized she had gotten to that point where she felt nothing. Far from being upset by this, she was actually glad. She began to experience an enormous sense of freedom. Now that she had made it through, she had no intention of ever putting herself in that vulnerable position of being at risk again. She was content with the feeling of nonfeeling.

Nothing was getting past the wall of stone that had appeared around her heart. A sad movie? No tears. A moving story? Forget it. Not even a shoe sale at Neimans could move her. (We're talking three years here!) Forget about going on a date, not so much as a glimmer of interest. No, Nina had set herself up as some kind of a character in a gothic novel and she seemed quite content to have done so. But we humans don't do well when we shut down our feelings. The heart has its own hungers and life (or the universe, or God, or whatever you please) works in some strange ways. One day a stray puppy ended up at her door. Nina was amazed at how lovable and trusting this animal was, in spite of the fact that the puppy had obviously been abused and neglected. Nina took her to a veterinarian to get her checked out and then gave her a good bath. Then she set out to find her a good home. Nina didn't name the puppy because it wasn't going to be her dog. That's the same reason she only bought a very small bag of dog food. "Puppy," as she referred to the little dog, thrived in Nina's care. All of her friends and family urged Nina to keep "Puppy," but Nina remained adamant that she wanted no part of that kind of commitment.

Nina complained about what a pain it was to take care of the dog, but the complaints didn't sound very genuine and everyone noticed that she managed to take very good care of the pup. A month later Nina got a call from a friend saying she had found a wonderful home for Puppy. Nina, of course, said that she was delighted and was looking forward to getting her freedom back. She packed up all of Puppy's belongings; her toys, the bed she bought her, her food, etc. When the couple came to take Puppy to her new home, Nina realized in an instant that Puppy had become her dog. She didn't know it then—but as with most life-changing events, in retrospect, this was a momentous occasion. Tears appeared in Nina's eyes for the first time since she had lost her husband. And once they started, they didn't stop for weeks. She took the dog in as her own and that was somehow the beginning of her true healing.

Everything fell into place after that. Nina made a decision to open her heart and love this dog. In making that declaration she was stating to the universe her desire to experience love once again. Maybe she was starting safely with a dog, but she was starting. She named the dog "Honey" and even bought a great big bag of dog food. She was saying, "I'm back and open for business." Loving an animal is not a substitute for loving a human being, but for Nina it was a test she had passed for herself and it led to other things. I tell her story as a way of saying that the heart will find a way of getting what it needs. If you're open and honest about your fears, as well as your needs, then you have a much better chance of getting what you need in a healthy way. This may entail doing something outside of your comfort zone (Nina didn't want the darn dog, she just didn't know how to say no), something that may be painful at first, but healing in the long run. For Nina it was taking in a stray puppy. Maybe for you it's joining a church, going back to school, volunteering, or taking a chance on another human being. You start to feel your passion coming back. Situations which you feared in the past, situations which require trust, slowly become manageable and, eventually, even welcome. One step at a time.

Try to remember that when you are safe from pain, you are safe from love. When you shut yourself off from one, you shut yourself off from the other. Nina had looked at love as something that takes away from you. She took a chance and got lucky when she found that her love for the puppy evolved into a much bigger decision to love. On one of Nina and Honey's daily walks in the park, they met Greg and his dog, Buster. Not only did Honey and Buster hit it off, but Greg and Nina really hit it off as well and are now engaged, with plans to marry. Would Nina have met Greg anyway, without Honey's help? Difficult to say. Either way, there's a lesson to learn here about love creating more love.

3. FEAR OF GETTING WHAT YOU WANT

I don't want the cheese; I just want to get out of the trap.
—SPANISH PROVERB

This is a hard one for some to understand. Why would anyone fear getting the love they want? Odd as it may seem, there are many reasons. The most obvious reason is the one we've already discussed; if you were vulnerable as a child (and all children are vulnerable—it comes with the territory) and you were hurt, then "getting what you want" (i.e., love) might sound like an invitation to more hurt and pain. And who wants that? Another common reason is that, somewhere inside, you don't believe you deserve to be happy. If that's the case, then you'll do all *kinds* of things (some conscious, some unconscious) to make sure you don't end up in a loving relationship. Or maybe you're the kind of person who fears that if you get what you want and you're still not happy, what then? The answer, of course, to "what then?" is that *then* you have to come face-to-face with what is *really* making you unhappy. These are frequently people who frantically go from one "unavailable" relationship to another. God forbid they have a free weekend, or even an hour that isn't occupied with the fantasy of being in a relationship. It's just *so* much easier to avoid getting what you *think* you want than having to face what may still be missing in your life. Fear of getting what you want can also apply when you consciously want to love and be loved more than anything in the world. It becomes a fantasy of sorts, your *idea* (often romantic, often unattainable) of what love *should* be, and your fear of *real* love falling short of the fantasy. Again, I recommend *Madame Bovary* by Gustave Flaubert as one of the all-time great novels about the perils of "losing" oneself to a romantic view of love.

What we're talking about in all these examples is a form of self-sabotage. It goes something like this (And if the tune sounds familiar, then hum along, by all means!). "I *say* I want a loving relationship in my life, but I *do* everything I can to thwart my chances to *have* that relationship, and *most* of the time I don't even know I'm doing it!" (For the record, *all* behaviors that keep us "unavailable" are, in some way, related to self-sabotage, but the ones just mentioned are particularly troublesome.) What is called for, aside from all the measures already discussed, is a dose of "contrary action." If you have made your lists, spent some time alone with your thoughts and your feelings, looked into your own history to ask the tough questions regarding *why* you might not be available . . . If you've done all that and you think you're at a place where you *really* do *want* a relationship, and yet you're *still* sabotaging your own best efforts, then it's time act "as if."

My belief is that, in most cases, it is better to work from the inside out when it comes to making changes in our lives. If a "change" is just a plastic add-on or remodel, then it will soon break down or, worse, show up in a different guise. By going deep inside and asking ourselves those difficult questions and confronting those dark fears, we can rewire the *causes* of the behavior and make a change that lasts. But sometimes it's necessary to "kick-start" a particular behavior or mind-set in order to get the ball rolling in the right direction.

Let me tell you a story about Cassie. Cassie was in her early forties and was forever complaining that there were no decent, eligible men "out there" for someone like her. (For the record, Cassie happens to be an attractive, charming, intelligent, and successful businesswoman.) One night Cassie was invited to join some friends for a night at the theater. After the play they all went out for a bite to eat and Cassie met Danny, a friend of Jim's who was one of the actors in the play. Cassie knew that Jim was gay and so she assumed that Danny was gay as well. Cassie was not only relaxed around Danny, she was downright flirtatious. Cassie and Danny found that they shared many interests, including a love of cooking, salsa dancing, and foreign films. They naturally hit it off big-time and were talking as if they were each other's new best friend. Numbers were exchanged and plans were made to get together soon. On the way home, the obligatory jokes were made about "If only he weren't gay," etc. The next day one of Cassie's theater buddies called and told her that, not only was Danny straight, he was also head over heels about Cassie. He just loved her openness and the easy way she had about her.

Cassie shut down faster than a kosher deli in the Vatican. Now that Danny was "available" Cassie suddenly lost interest. Suddenly she felt "foolish" about being so open and accessible the night before. Almost immediately she began to "recall" little things that Danny had said or done that were now labeled a turnoff. Danny called Cassie several times after that but Cassie found excuse after excuse until she finally got what she *really* wanted: Danny stopped calling. Cassie managed to avoid taking a chance on an available relationship.

Fear. Gripping fear. Cassie thought Danny was perfect for her *until* he was available. She was afraid of getting what she *said* she wanted. It was much easier to want it than to have it. Does this describe a behavior or reaction you might have experienced in your life? It doesn't have to be about relationships; it could be the new job you lobbied for, a move to a new city, losing weight, etc. If you are somehow disappointed when you get what you want, is it that the prize itself is disappointing? Or could it be that you've built an entire life around that disappointment and you're afraid of what might be on the other side? Are your "operating systems" *designed* to function best when you're unhappy? The truth is the older you are, the more difficult it may be to redesign those systems, but it's always, always possible. Do you have a pattern of not getting what you want? If so, perhaps it's time to reevaluate what you're doing and why. Take time to imagine realistically what life would be like if you were to have the thing you say you want.

If Cassie were a friend of mine, here's what I would have suggested. I would have tried to get her to stop and look at what she was doing, examine all the reasons why she might be doing it, and then I would have suggested that she try some "contrary action." Accept the call from Danny. Go on a date. Make it a daytime date. Make it a foreign film. Go on more "outings." Live through the anxiety that might come up if Danny turned out to be as wonderful as he seemed to be (when she thought he was gay). Even though the reality of an attractive man triggered more fears than the idea of one, I would ask Cassie to act "as if" she *really* did want to try out a relationship. Even if the anxiety proved to be too difficult, she still would have learned a lot about herself if she had let her fears rise to the surface. If *serious* pain results, then it might be time for some professional help. There are times in our lives when a therapist can really be of great assistance, as well as comfort. He or she can help you to identify what the hell's going on as long-hidden parts of your psyche come roaring up into your consciousness.

Another way to address the problem is to make use of visualization. When you can imagine something positive, create a picture of it in your head and hold it in your heart; then you are a giant step closer to bringing it into your life. I don't suggest this *instead* of all the work we've discussed in the previous chapters; rather, in addition. An architect must do the calculations and figure out all the angles in order to make a design successful. First comes the notion, or "visual," then he or she must make a drawing of the finished project which serves to keep the idea alive while the hard work is going on. Think of your visualization as the blueprint for the life you want.

In Cassie's case, perhaps if she could visualize being comfortable in a relationship with someone like Danny, someone with similar interests and joys, then maybe, the next time she meets someone who is available, it won't seem so "unimaginable."

4. Fear of Making a Mistake

There is no safety in numbers—or anything else.
—James Thurber

"What if I finally *do* take the relationship plunge, make the commitment, and then, the *real* "perfect" person comes along? Or . . . what if I commit to a relationship and then I get an incredible job offer that requires me to travel around the world?" The "what if" syndrome can paralyze you into never, ever making a decision. Let's face it, you could get hit by a runaway Zamboni ice tractor tomorrow—but you still have to go to work today. Am I right? Life doesn't stop just because we fear it. We can be so afraid of making a mistake that we end up living our life in limbo. And if we *are* in this frame of mind, then nobody is a real candidate for your heart. Why? Because . . . what if?!

How about this answer: What if . . . you ask for some help, take your inventory, look at your fears, find a way to act as if you *want* a real relationship, choose someone who is "available" for love, and then (fasten your seat belts) . . . *what if* you fall in love with somebody who loves you back? It's a bizarre concept, I know. But it just might work.

Believe me, I know it's not as easy as six lines of type. But making yourself available has to start with a belief that a positive answer to "what if?" is at least possible.

Any book on relationships, this one or any other one, must begin with the assumption that you are choosing life. Even if you're consumed by fear at this particular moment of your life, even if you can't see a way out from under, you must decide that the risk is worth the work if you're going to take a chance on love.

Obviously I think self-help books can be beneficial or I wouldn't be writing this one. They have certainly been a great help to me over the years. But I also know that, like any tool, books can be both used and abused. If you are going from one book to the next seminar to the next series of tapes, then perhaps you're missing the point. Ironically, you may be hiding behind the very tools that were designed to help you come *out* of hiding! Think about it. If you're interested in learning how to play the piano, then certainly you should find a qualified teacher and invest in some books on technique and such. But at some point you're going to have to put down the books *about* playing the piano, and *play* the piano. Put your fingers on the keys, face your fears, and risk making a few mistakes as you begin to play as best you can. It's our responsibility as human beings to put down the books and live our lives, mistakes and all. It's also our privilege.

Fear of making a mistake is the theme of Molly's life. She's another kind of unavailable person, the married kind. It may sound odd in a book entitled *Still Single*, but it's not that unusual to be married and still be unavailable. As a matter of fact, *so* many people have hidden (i.e., kept themselves unavailable) by getting married (I was one of them) that it's given the institution a rather bad name. A marriage *should* be a safe place to grow, not a sterile destination where two people can hide from life. But that's what it is to some people. Molly is one of them. Molly is a very attractive woman in her thirties who has never been available to her husband, or anyone else for that matter. Even when it was just the two of them, she kept herself so busy that they were lucky (lucky?) if they spent six waking hours together in any given month. When Molly lost her job she panicked. Money wasn't the problem; there was plenty of that. Time was the problem, because there was now way too much of *that*. An available person would have welcomed the opportunity to connect with a husband who had a busy schedule himself. But Molly quickly embarked on a series of affairs that meant very little to her heart, but still served the *real* purpose of keeping her away from her deepest fear; a real relationship with, of all people, her husband. Before Molly got married, she almost never went out. There was always a reason that the date was unacceptable. The truth was that Molly had such standards of perfection laid on her by her parents that she could never imagine *anyone* living up to her own ideal. After enough years went by, Molly was downright embarrassed by her single status, but rather than take a real look at what was going on in her life, she just married the next "unavailable" man who asked her. He was a devoted workaholic and so his expectations of the relationship were minimal at best. It was a perfect "hiding place" for Molly. Perfect, except for the fact that she would never feel the comfort of real love, never experience the excitement that comes when you are truly thinking and caring about someone else. Molly seemed willing to pass her years "stuffing" her life with "sensations" instead of feelings, one of those sad lives of quiet desperation. But Molly got a surprise one day. Something happened that she couldn't have guessed in her wildest dreams. Her husband woke up. His father passed away suddenly and it jarred something in his life, and he decided that he wanted more out of his own life than a fat paycheck and a pathetic façade of love. He divorced Molly, began working less, dating more, and started enjoying his life. After Molly recovered from the shock, she took some time to think. She really took stock of her life. She decided it was time to face her fears and take a chance on life. And that's what she's doing. With the help of a therapist, she's found ways to "slow down" her life and give herself some room to think, and to feel. Whether Molly finds her way back to her own heart remains to be seen, but she's taken the first important step in that direction.

5. FEAR OF PHYSICAL INSECURITIES

Have no fear of perfection, you'll never reach it.
—SALVADOR DALI

We are surrounded by images of youth and beauty everywhere. I wrote earlier about the damage done by these images; the anorexia, the bulimia, the erosion of self-esteem that is epidemic in our world, especially here in the United States. But there is another symptom of this constant barrage of images that isn't discussed as much as it should be. Fear. There is a shutting down; a protective shell that develops, especially during adolescence, that is born out of fear. "If I don't look like that, then there's something 'wrong' with me" is a common refrain from the inner dialogue of people today. Women, of course, are particularly vulnerable to these messages and the damage is more evident with them. They "fear" the consequences of not looking a certain way. And that fear influences their choices and their behaviors. Sometimes, when a girl can't "make herself" look the way she's been told she "should" look in order to be considered attractive, then she might shut down, or perhaps she will find ways to accelerate her own sexuality. She'll do whatever she feels she must do to alleviate this fear. And these feelings aren't restricted to adolescent girls, by any means. We are all susceptible.

The sad fact is that the ideals to which many people compare themselves are pure fantasy, and nobody can measure up to them. It's like a cruel joke; cruel because of the damage done, a joke because even the models in the advertisements don't look the way you think they do. During my years as an art director I spent plenty of time with models and I can tell you that even *they* don't recognize themselves when they appear on the pages of a magazine. After the airbrushing, the color correction, the "enhancement," etc., it's more of a painting than a photograph. It would be funny if it wasn't so sad. And recently the media geniuses have created yet a new way to make us civilians all feel like we're breathing inferior air; channel after channel, show after show, is devoted to the lives, loves, and liver transplants of every celebrity who ever so much as burped on TV. Capsule versions of their wonderful lives, usually predicated on the theory that if they're handsome, they're heroes. If they're beautiful, why, then they *must* be better than the rest of us. Every relationship is pictured as trouble free and perfect—for a few months or until they trade in one "beauty" for another. No wonder young people who watch this stuff have a fear of not being up to par. How are they supposed to know that it's all a fantasy? By comparison, "reality" seems flawed.

This is not to say that looks don't matter. Of course they do. But they should count as much as *you* want them to count, not as much as you're told they should. We can all try to cheat the clock as much as we can, with exercise, eating right, the proper amount of sun, etc. But none of us should be *afraid* of growing older. Personally, I try to look at it from the standpoint of this being "my turn" to be thirty, or forty, or (recently) fifty. Why obsess about something we can't change even if we want to?

And, of course, any discussion about our bodies and our selves must include plastic surgery. It has become an option for most people who desire it. My opinion is to do it if it makes you feel better, but know that it has very little (or it least it *should* have very little) to do with being "available" or finding someone who is "available" for a real relationship. There's a slightly coarse joke told about two men looking at a devastatingly beautiful woman at a bar. One of the men says to the other, "No matter how gorgeous she is, somewhere, someone is tired of her B.S." (I've heard it with the genders reversed, as well.) I repeat it because, underneath its banality, the joke speaks to the fact that a relationship, in the end, has very little to do with what we look like. I think that's what Mr. Mastroianni was saying when he talked about good looks only buying us two weeks. After that, it's about who we are.

Let it go. Those are my three simple words about your fears that you're not physically attractive enough. Again, I know it's not as easy as all that. But perhaps we should all try to *start* with that and work from there.

Danielle is a woman who works out at my gym. She's in great shape. Men ask her out all the time, yet she hasn't accepted a date in two years. Why? She actually believes that she looks better in gym clothes than she does naked, and she's afraid a man will be expecting a great body that she's convinced isn't there. She feels better when she's a little overweight because then she doesn't feel as if she's promising perfection. She believes that any physical flaw she might have could ruin her chances with any man she was interested in. It's been a battle she's fought her entire life.

Putting unrealistic physical demands on yourself can keep you very single and very unavailable. No matter how tempting it is, try not to focus on what's wrong with your body. If you find this impossible, then find some help. You can be so persuasive in this negative "voice" that it's only a matter of time before you convince yourself, as well as the person you're with, that you truly are flawed and unworthy of real love. It becomes a self-fulfilling prophecy and it's just so damn unnecessary.

And what are we really doing when we point out our imperfections? We're asking for approval, to be accepted for who we are. What you're hoping to hear is, "I love you the way you are." I guarantee that when you can say that to yourself, you will have taken a huge step in the right direction. A person who would reject you because of a physical flaw is not the kind of person you need in your life, especially if that person is *you*!

It does seem that body issues plague women more than men. We worry more about our wrinkles, our fat, our scars, and the effects of aging in general. Men (and this is just a casual observation on my part, not a scientific study, but I think you'll agree) seem to be more troubled about, well . . . *our* wrinkles, *our* fat, and *our* scars, etc. For the most part, they just don't seem to get all that worked up over their extra ten pounds or that new set of crow's feet. (Nobody said it was a fair world.) I remember a boyfriend I once had who proudly patted his big, soft, mushy belly and asked me in a self-satisfied way if I could believe he'd *never* done a sit-up in his life. The immediate answer that came to my mind was a great big, "Well, yeahhhh!" But I didn't say it. Why? Because the truth is that it wasn't that important (for me, anyway) that *he* have a "washboard stomach". It seemed *much* more important that *my* body be as perfect as I could make it. Why the double standard? Fifteen different scientific studies will give you fifteen different answers; nurture, nature, cultural, anthropological, cave man this, and Wonder Woman that. Whatever the "cause" might be, the "effect" is that women beat themselves up and endure ridiculous (i.e., harmful) amounts of anxiety and fear connected with their bodies and their self-images. And when that fear keeps them feeling as if they don't deserve a real relationship, then the situation is dangerous. We all have flaws. Bargain for a soft tummy and a strong sense of decency and you'll be ahead of the game when it comes to qualifications for a real relationship.

Every last one of us will age. I hate to be the one to break it to you, but you, too, will grow old. Unless you have a piece of legal-sized paper signed by the Devil, then you're headed in the same direction as the rest of us. All the plastic surgery in the world won't change that fact. If you want your sixty-year-old face to look like melting wax in a windstorm then, by all means, go for it and get an early start. But if you're *really* interested in the things that last, the things that can be shared deeply, then you'll concentrate on some of the things we've been talking about; lists, and inventories, and facing your fears, and learning to listen to what people are saying on dates, and all the rest of it. The things that, tough as they might be, will help to make you healthy and open and "available."

As long as you're striving for a centered life, a life of values and inner strength, then you'll have a purpose, not only each year, but each minute of your life. This isn't a book of philosophy per se, but, in a way, having a healthy philosophy of life is the first ingredient in any recipe for becoming "available" for love. There is a huge price to be paid for refusing to look at our lives and especially our fears. However, the payoff to *facing* those fears is that we have a better chance of living in some peace right here and right now. In his book *The Power of Now*, Eckart Tolle writes about the Now as the only time that really exists. He says, "The past wasn't created in the past and the future wasn't created in the future, it is all created in the Now. Your life is today at exactly the age and condition of your life right Now. When you think it's too late, you are wasting your Now."

If you are being rejected because of how you look, then you're looking in the wrong places. The feeling of trust that should accompany a real, "available" relationship should extend to your body and how you both feel about your bodies.

Don't allow yourself to feel judged, not by someone else and not by that "voice" of judgment that lives within. Try to think with your head and not with that competitive sense that arrived when you were young and needs to be dismissed for good. When you allow people to accept or reject you, you give away your power. If someone has the power to *give* you their approval, then they also have the power to *take it away*. Work to approve of yourself, to understand yourself as a flawed but wonderful work in progress, and you will be in a much better position to draw someone into your life who is able to think and feel the same way.

If you're okay with who you are and what you do, the right someone will be too. Sometimes, to be happy or feel good, nothing *has to* change—except your mind.

Review

Becoming available is a process. It requires listening, taking in information, gathering knowledge, and the courage to act on the combination of all three. In this chapter, we talked about facing our fears. It's probably one of the most difficult things we do in our life, but it's a necessary step towards our goal of becoming available. Fears close us down. Fears make us petty. Fears can convince us that we're not ready, or not deserving of a complete and loving relationship. Face your fears and you have faced the biggest obstacle standing between you and the person of your dreams. As you read through the following statements, highlight the ones you're ready to face.

1. I'm so afraid of being hurt that I avoid relationships.
2. I'm so afraid of rejection that I avoid relationships.
3. I'm so afraid of being hurt that I do the rejecting.
4. I've been hurt and I refuse to be hurt again.
5. I don't like to go anywhere new.
6. I won't go anywhere alone.
7. I think people are judging me.
8. I only feel safe when I'm in my routine.
9. I feel as if no one would like me if they got to know me.
10. I believe I'm too fat, too old, too poor, etc. to be considered lovable.
11. I seem to be stuck with a negative "Why try?" attitude.
12. I'm afraid to go after what I want.
13. I'm afraid of what might happen if I allow myself to feel.
14. I feel like I'm a fraud.
15. I don't feel worthy to have a good relationship.
16. I'm too shy for a relationship.

Redo

Once again, for each statement that feels true for you, write down the situation in which that emotion came up and how it has the ability to keep you unavailable. For instance, number six, I won't go anywhere alone. Write about a time when you went to a party by yourself and things didn't go as you would have liked. Maybe you felt you were "on trial" and no one spoke to you, and you left. Now stop and try to imagine the situation with a different outcome. This is the "contrary action" discussed earlier in the chapter. Remember it in as much detail as you can and then picture yourself walking up to another person and starting a conversation. Listen to the anxieties that may come up for you, even as you imagine this new scene. Think about where the fears might have come from and what you can do to do battle with them. Soldier on in your little scenario, further imagining that more people have joined you and that soon you're in the middle of a lively, engaging conversation with a whole new group of people. You find you have several things in common with more than one person. If it feels comfortable, imagine someone in the group has exhibited some of the "warning" behaviors of unavailable people, and then imagine yourself drifting away from that person and *towards* the members of the group who seem to be genuine and available. You exchange numbers and agree to meet for lunch, coffee, a movie, etc. You feel energized, confident, and hopeful.

The idea here is to go through each situation that has caused you fear or pain, and rewrite the scene with a better ending. Studies are ongoing but there is some considerable amount of support for a theory that posits that the mind has a difficult time knowing the difference between real and imagined events. If you can "see" yourself conquering a fear, then it just may go a long way towards convincing yourself that you are, in fact, capable of conquering that fear. Sports psychologists work extensively with athletes, helping them to create an image of themselves winning a point or catching a difficult pass. In essence they are creating a positive script for them to follow. You can do the same thing for yourself.

If we are capable of bringing to life a negative image, why not take the time to deliberately create a positive picture for yourself and set the path you want to take? Going over this list and "reshooting" the scene is a method that has had very positive effects in therapy. Someone who had been debilitated in a particular area of his life can be taken back—(through voice therapy, hypnosis, past-life regression, etc.)—to a sad or traumatic time in their past and then allowed to "recreate" the experience in a way that will help to empower them.

Make your own list of "positive outcome scenarios" and take the time to work them into your mental picture. Keep at it and let those images gain strength. They are the first steps of change.

Chapter 5

Twelve Steps to Becoming Available

Even if you're on the right track, you'll get run over if you just sit there.

— WILL ROGERS

We've discussed what it means to be unavailable for a real relationship. We've taken a look at various "types" of unavailable people to beware of, behaviors that can keep us unavailable, and ways in which we can better face our fears. In this chapter I would like to outline twelve individual steps designed to help you become available for the loving relationship you want and deserve.

1. BOOST YOUR SELF-ESTEEM

To bring the best relationship into your life, you must first *believe* that you *deserve* the best relationship. And the first relationship you need to look at is the relationship you have with yourself. How do you feel about yourself? Not the "self" you portray in public or at work, but the self you feel inside. The French have a wonderful expression they use when referring to the way in which an "authentic" person presents his or her true self. They say that he or she "il se sent bien dans sa peau." Literally, it means that they feel good in their own skin. It doesn't necessarily mean that they're "happy" all the time or that they have everything under control. In my opinion, to be "authentic" is a more desirable goal than simply to be happy. We are all emotional creatures and are entitled to the full range of emotions. If we have some idea that we're always supposed to be "happy," then we're bound to be disappointed in ourselves. It's a little like going on one of those fad diets that restrict you to two or three foods only. Of course you're going to lose weight at first, but very quickly your body will cry out for the things it's missing and you're right back where you started (usually plus ten or fifteen pounds). To be authentic is to realize that we are all flawed, but that we all have the capacity to be open and available for love. Feeling good in our own skin, feeling authentic, should be the first goal of anyone looking to meet someone else. Honor yourself and your right to deal with your fears as well as your right to live your dreams. If you can do this, then you are already one step closer to finding someone available with whom to share your life. Remember, we teach people how to treat us. If boosting our self-esteem means digging deep and doing hard work on ourselves, then we must do it. That's what we've been talking about in chapters one through four. If it means therapy to uncover and work through old childhood wounds, do it. If you're letting your fears get the better of you, then it's time to find a way to look at them. (See also: Chapter Four.) Look again at all the checklists at the ends of the chapters and take an inventory of everything that's standing in the way of your having a good relationship with *you*. There are hundreds and thousands of moments in our lives that have the power to damage our self-esteem. It's tedious and painful work to catalogue the ones we can track down and then to "defuse" them. But this is often what it takes to begin to undo the damage that was done. Do you have *behaviors* that keep you from feeling good about yourself? Or is it a *voice* that was set on PLAY years ago and needs to be put on STOP, or at least PAUSE? As the saying goes, "It's simple, it's just not easy." Find a way to feel good about yourself and you'll have a much better *chance* of finding someone else to feel good about you. First and foremost, you have to be the most important project you undertake. If this feels selfish, then look up the word in the dictionary. Selfishness is an *inappropriate* focus on one's own self. Taking care of your own relationship with yourself is, in the end, a *selfless* act if you are then able to enter into a healthy, loving, "available" relationship and perhaps even produce healthy, loving, "available" children who will make the world a much better place. There's a reason the flight attendants on airplanes tell you to "put the oxygen mask on *yourself* first, and only *then* should you put one on your child." You're no good to anyone if you're in trouble yourself! Take a look at this thing called self-esteem. If yours is in some need of repair, then do the work *before* you take your heart for a spin.

2. BE AWARE

Getting involved with someone is a choice. Remember that. It doesn't feel like it at the time. (*That's* why it's called an attraction.) But you *do* have a choice. Even the expression "falling in love" makes it sound like a condition over which you have no control. But love is not a cold you catch when your defenses are down, or at least it shouldn't be. You don't fall—you decide to fall. Whether it's conscious or unconscious, there are specific times during a relationship when you decide to deepen your feelings for another person. Theoretically, we "fall" in love when we are whole, and feeling good, and wanting to share our lives with someone else who is whole and feeling good. That's theoretically. In the real world we frequently "fall" in love for a myriad of other reasons; to distract, to soothe, to medicate, sometimes even to punish.

Before you "decide" to fall for the next "unavailable" person, do yourself a favor. Do what I used to tell my kids to do when they needed to think about a behavior that wasn't working; take a time-out. Take note as to why you're responding to this person at this particular time. Let the first wave of feelings pass and then really listen to what your heart is telling you, about yourself and about the person you're with. Have they revealed themselves to you? Is there a small (or a *not* so small) voice telling you that you're doing it again? Does this person have a different MO even though he or she is just as unavailable? If you've read the previous chapters, then you know what to look for. You know the "types" who are most likely to be unavailable. Are you with one of them now? Can you find the strength to back away and take it slow? We've all been there. When we first meet someone we're attracted to, we're trying so hard to make a good impression, so caught up in enjoying the "high" of that first rush, that we end up missing the clues that tell us who they are. Or we want it to work so badly that we're willing to ignore our gut telling us that something is off.

Take Elaine's situation. She had been seeing Elliot for a few months and he still hadn't given her his home phone number. He had a variety of shaky reasons for this, the most blatant one being that his sick mother lived with him and a ringing telephone would disturb her. Obviously, if you want to believe anything badly enough, you will. Elaine will tell you that she *felt* he probably wasn't telling the truth but she told herself that she didn't want to upset him by implying he was lying. More importantly, she "felt" as if she were falling in love and didn't want to stop seeing him, so she ignored her feelings. Elaine admits now that she was more hurt than shocked when she learned the truth, that Eliot was indeed married and lying to her. Some part of her "knew" right from the start. Telling this story now it would seem that Elaine just wasn't a very bright woman. But that would be wrong. Elaine happened to be *extremely* bright and successful. These "blind spots" frequently have absolutely nothing to do with intelligence. They are matters of the heart and, as we know, the heart has its own ways. So, why would a smart woman do that to herself? After beating herself up for a few months and feeling sorry for herself for a few *more*, Elaine took a look at her own role in what happened. After some soul searching Elaine realized that Elliot had only been the latest in a long line of "unavailable" men she had brought into her life. She had to look at the possibility that she was the one who was unavailable.

Theoretically, Elaine's next relationship should have been with (of course) an "available" man, right? Well, that's what she thought as well. But we are all creatures of habit and we have needs that dwell deep inside our souls, and the truth is we're not always aware of what the heck we're doing even while we're doing it. The thing Elaine did differently in her next relationship was this: She forced herself to take it slow. She didn't rush into a sexual relationship, she didn't spend every waking minute involved with this person, she didn't "fall." Instead she gave herself a "time-out," a space in which she could take a real look at what was going on. And you know what she found? Another unavailable person. The difference was that she *knew* it this time and she could make her decisions from a place of knowledge.

The change doesn't happen overnight. There will be missteps and slips, but if you're taking it slow, you give yourself a chance to recognize the mistakes instead of falling in love with them.

Spending the years I've spent writing for television has made me a sucker for a happy ending, and so I'm happy to report that Elaine found her "available" man and, because of all her hard work, was "available" herself. She's very happily married and they are expecting their third child.

3. MAKE A LIST OF WHAT YOU WANT IN YOUR MATE

Who is the right person for you? Are you hoping you'll know the minute you lay eyes on him or her that this is "the one?" Well, once again I hate to rain on anyone's parade, but you're back at the movies. The reason Boy meets Girl on the screen is because the writers have made it happen that way. "Meeting cute," it's called. And while I'm not saying that it *never* happens in real life, I *am* saying that it happens rarely. If it's happened to you, and things worked out just exactly as you wanted them to, then chances are you wouldn't be reading this book. But you *are* reading this book and there are things you can do that can *help* you to change your own "meeting disastrous" into a real-life "meeting cute." First of all, make a list of what you're looking for in a person. This will force you to focus as well as giving you something for comparison. "This is what I *say* I want, and *this* is what I have chosen." What's wrong with this picture, and why, and what am I going to do about it? Not to make light of things, but look what happens when you go to the market without a list. If you're anything like me you can end up buying everything except what you were going for.

What are the most important things on your list? If you emphasize qualities such as kind, funny, honest, generous, available, etc., you're going to have more candidates to choose from than if you narrow it down with superficial details like "blond blue-eyed six-foot-tall multimillionaire with six-pack abs who speaks five languages and will love my cat." Make sure you're not holding out for someone who doesn't exist. If your list looks like "Mission Impossible" then consider the possibility that you are using it to keep yourself single.

There are those who believe that we choose our mates from a corresponding level, meaning we pick people who are in our gettable range. Usually this means comparable age, looks, or status. Of course the playing field changes depending on who you are and what you want. For instance, if you're a seventy-year-old man who is interested only in gorgeous twenty-year-old girls, you might (I say *might*) not be doing everything you can to make yourself "available" for a real relationship (with apologies to Anna Nicole Smith). This is not to say that wealthy women don't fall in love and have wonderful "available" relationships with cash-poor men. Or vice versa. Stranger things have happened and will happen again, but some people simply make a habit of *purposely* choosing people with whom they have little in common. Why not give yourself the greatest possible chance of finding someone wonderful, realistic, and available?

So I'm asking you to ask yourself: "Am I being realistic?" There's nothing wrong with having a "crush" on a screen idol, or a fantasy about this or that famous person. But this isn't a book about "crushes" or "fantasies." This is a book about relationships. The "list" for a relationship is very different from the others.

Go over your list every so often to see if it still suits you. What can you add or subtract? The dream mate of your twenties should be different than for your forties. As you change and grow your list should change to reflect that.

When you're a sixteen-year-old girl, a cute guy with a cool job and a bitchin' car is a pretty dreamy wish list. As you grow and (hopefully) mature, your list will change to fit your growth—

although I know a few women in their thirties who would still be happy today to find a man with both a job and a car. Seriously though, as your interests and values evolve, so should your guidelines for a mate.

I have a friend who grew up reading *Seventeen* magazine and continues to read it now that she's well into her forties. If it were for nostalgia's sake, that would be one thing. But one day, not long ago, she remarked to me in all seriousness that the magazine had really gone downhill over the years and was now beginning to seem downright immature in its relationship advice. I have to admit I was speechless. It had taken her *this long* to get that she was *beginning* to disagree with advice written for a teen? Mind you this is, once again, a very successful executive in charge of dozens of workers and millions of dollars. And she does her job *very* well! But when it came to relationships, she was still looking to the pages of a teen magazine for tools with which to manage her love life. (Do I have to even say that her love life was like *The Titanic* without the love story?) Obviously it wasn't that the magazine had become immature, it was just time for my friend to buy some new magazines (do I dare hope for a book or two?) and make a new list.

The real test for a list is, in a way, very simple; is it working? What results is it producing? If the results are less than acceptable, then sit down, give it a *lot* of thought, and put together a new one designed to be more productive. If you're not doing that, then you *are* doing what you need to do to remain single.

Is a particular item on your list, a specific attraction, keeping you unavailable? You may be subconsciously sabotaging yourself. If it hasn't been working in the past, why do you think it will in the future? If you want a different way of life, then you have to do something differently. Your list is a good place to start.

4. Imagine the Relationship You Want

I've discussed "wish lists" and the attributes you want to include in your dream mate, things such as generosity, humor, kindness, honesty, or whatever your list includes. Now I want to talk about making that list come to life.

Once the list is compiled, then it's time to visualize that list. To hold an image in your mind and in your heart of what you really want in a relationship is one of the best ways to make that relationship happen. Marriage and Family Therapist Michael Topp notes that "people in a bad relationship often can only describe a healthy relationship in vague and cloudy terms; people in a *healthy* relationship can tell you just what makes it work, just what they need from their partner in order to feel cared about." Set aside a special time in your day or your week, and a special place in your home or in nature to practice your visualization. Spend whatever amount of time you need and can afford. There are dozens of books on meditation and one of them will be right for you, but whatever method you choose, find a way to quiet your mind and then visualize in detail the exact life you would like to have. See your mate. See and feel the way you would like to be treated by this person. Picture the things you would do together, the way you would laugh, how you would cook together, read the Sunday paper in bed. Imagine laughing, crying, and feeling safe with this person. Run it in your head over and over until it's a familiar movie to you. Visualizing it can't *make* it happen all by itself, but it's difficult to bring something into your life if you can't at least imagine having it. Everything begins with an idea. Everything.

Repeat the process until you can see and feel yourself comfortable with the *idea* of this relationship. See the relationship that was born out of all your hard work, your inventories, your lists, the therapy of facing your fears, the understanding of all the ways there are to sabotage yourself and, finally, the decision to set your course for new waters and make a new life. You can keep adding to it as you adopt new interests or attitudes. If you take up dancing, add this to your movie. It's your visualization. It's your life. If you've done the work, then you're in charge now. You're the writer, the producer, the director, and the star. Nobody's putting any limits on it but you. Remember that. You want a relationship in which you're appreciated and deserving of respect? *Visualize* someone who actually appreciates you and treats you with respect. If you don't give yourself these things in a relationship, then nobody else will. See this person engaged by your thoughts and conversation. See yourself calm and peaceful, sexy or excited. When you can accept that it's absolutely conceivable that you could be in a wonderful relationship, your subconscious will begin to understand what you want and it will become your ally, setting things in motion to allow all of these possibilities to come true. It's called "setting the intention."

Find some time each day to spend in this world. You can make this as simple or elaborate as you wish. It's much more meaningful to make adjustments and refinements to your list from these images that you've created and experienced. Think how significant it will be when you write the word "kind" on your list, once you've seen in your mind what a kind person doing a kind act means to you.

I can tell you from personal experience that this is an incredible tool you can use to help actualize your life. I know it helped me to get the love of my life *into my life*. He is kind, smart, funny, generous, honest, and loving—all the things I pictured, but then I can't claim total objectivity. What I *can* tell you is that he's available to be in a relationship, with me. He's the kind of man I wished for but never seemed to bring into my life, until I took a look at *my* part in keeping myself unavailable. Only then was I able to begin the process of looking at my own behaviors, my own choices, my own fears, and to do something about them. Only then did I become "available" for the kind of person I visualized as my partner in life. And this is not the first success I've had with having an event come to be that had been elusive until I made use of this gift called visualization. I have used this method many times throughout my life, with my career as a network executive, then as a television writer, and now with writing and selling this book.

The mind is incredibly powerful. I know some of you may feel your imagination is not your strongest point. Maybe you don't think you're creative enough to conjure up something that hasn't yet happened. But as we discussed in Chapter 4, many people who say they don't know how to visualize have no problem picturing something bad happening to them. It's called worrying. You conjure up the dreaded image and your mind fulfills it. The mind is just following orders. Maybe it's time to give it some orders that will make you genuinely happy.

Many people already practice meditation and consciously think worthy thoughts. That's a great start. But saying how great you are once a day during a meditation is bound to be overshadowed if the other twenty-three and a half hours are bombarded with persistent, negative thoughts.

It takes effort to reprogram those habitual perceptions, those rascally neural pathways that tell you it's better to be safe than satisfied (in a healthy relationship). You have to be incredibly vigilant, but it works. If you hang in there you'll begin to see how much control you have over your behavior patterns when you learn how to "visualize" a different way of doing things. You'll get a different kind of result. If your thought patterns are reinforcing the idea that you're undeserving, then guess what? That's probably what you're going to be and that's the kind of relationship you're going to bring into your life. If you can visualize anything you want, then why not visualize someone wonderful, and deserving, and available?

For those who feel intimidated about using their imagination to visualize a desired future, there are alternatives. Instead of picturing the life you want in your head, you can use a bulletin board and fill it with pictures from magazines, photos, sayings, vacation settings, etc. Or you can write about it in story form. In her book *Write it Down, Make it Happen*, author Henriette Anne Klauser suggests writing the scene you want as if it has already happened. You can use a journal to record the *wished for* event as if you're making a detailed entry in your diary from a memory of the *real* event.

It doesn't matter which method you use; the important thing is that you are actively spending quality time finding ways to visualize your goals, working to reprogram those behaviors that have kept you single and unavailable for too long.

5. BE WILLING TO DO THINGS DIFFERENTLY

Take Alex. Alex is a doctor who was going through a difficult time in his personal life. He felt stuck in a pattern that was creating way too much anxiety, shutting him down and cutting him off from people in ways that he didn't want. He didn't like the way he was relating to the world and he wasn't thrilled about the way the world was beginning to relate to him. And so he tried an experiment. He had to go to a conference halfway around the world. He would know nobody and nobody would know him. On the plane he decided that he would "be" someone else. Alex didn't change his name or his profession. He still gave the same lectures he was scheduled to give, but he tried on an entirely new persona to see what would happen. It was part game and part therapy. He knew he felt unhappy with the way his life had been going and he felt he needed a jolt to shake things up and see how he felt about it. Where he had been sullen and withdrawn, he did his best to be open and engaging, even flirtatious, during the conference. Where he would ordinarily decline offers to go out socially after a program, he accepted any and all invitations. He was a living exercise in "contrary action." When the weeklong conference was over and he was on the plane home, he had a variety of revelations to consider. It's not that he wanted to "become" this new person, but he knew that he had gained some perspective on himself and how he was living his life, and he did it by standing outside himself and *doing things differently.*

It's not always necessary to take the kinds of dramatic steps that Alex took. But if the way you've been meeting people or functioning in relationships all your life hasn't worked for you, then maybe it's time to try doing it another way. Try doing something you've never done, going someplace you've never gone. We've talked in previous chapters about ways in which to *think* differently; consider the possibility of *acting* differently as well. It's just another tool for you to use in building a new, improved, and available you.

What do you have to lose? When I was kid I wouldn't have dreamed of eating raw fish; now sushi is my absolute favorite. How did that happen? I tried it. And I loved it. It helped that I had friends who had already tried it and assured me it was wonderful. I'm not so sure I would have ever tried it on my own. So consider me your friend who's tried this exercise already, and I'm telling you it worked for me. Try making a list of all the things you do and then *do* something differently. You'll like some of the results, and some you won't. But you're sure to shake things up in the process.

I'm fully aware that this exercise is, by its very nature, working from the outside in. And I'm also aware that most of the suggestions in this book entail working from the inside out. But, as I just said, consider them different tools for different parts of the job. For instance, if you've only been interested in meeting a certain kind of person, and things haven't been going well, then put all your lists in a drawer, go someplace you've never been before, and take a chance on meeting someone completely and totally new. And if you want to "be" someone different, then try that too. It's only an outing. Think of it as a science experiment and check your findings and conclusions afterwards.

Doing it differently means just that. Whatever hasn't been working, look at it in a new way. Be willing to feel unfamiliar and uncomfortable for a few hours, or a few days. What if something incredible happens? What if this *new* thing you're doing not only doesn't feel bad, what if it feels *better* than doing it the old way? Maybe you don't have to go back to the old way. That one new thing just changed your life. Perhaps only in a small way, but change has a way of leading to more change. Ever see what happens when there's a small crack in a big dam?

6. LOOK FOR RELATIONSHIPS YOU ADMIRE

This is a big one. Think of the relationships in your own circle of family and friends. How many of them do you admire and aspire to? In my surveys, the number I heard most often was one (and sometimes zero). The numbers (or number, if you prefer) don't make it easy to find a whole lot of what we're looking for. How can we dream of having a wonderful relationship if we don't have any role models? Well, if you know one, then study them well. If they're close to you, relatives or friends, then spend as much time as you can watching how they relate to each other, how they connect, how they fight, how they live their lives. It won't be the exact same way you want to do it in your life, but we all know a "jumping off" place, an idea from which we can add or subtract, adjust and modify so that it fits our idea of what we want in our lives.

If you can't find couples you admire in your immediate circle of family and friends, then look in different places. Pay attention the next time you're at a social gathering. If you meet a couple who seem to have a good relationship, then make it a point to spend time with them. If that's not an option, then put "relationships" on your book list and study the subject that way. Being a writer, of course, I heartily endorse the value of the written word, but I also know how important it is to actually *see* and *hear* the way people resolve problems, the way they show affection. There are subtle clues that we can learn from, and those clues are easier to spot when we're in the same room with them.

The relationships don't necessarily *have* to be romantic couples. Look at the way some of your friends treat each other, or take a look at business partnerships that work. The dynamic will be somewhat different, but the principles are the same. Watch and you'll learn something about successful associations.

Hillary Clinton used the phrase "It takes a village" as the title of her book, and the sad truth is that we have "engineered" a society in which there are very few "villages" left. And when we lost the villages, we lost many of the support systems that were designed to provide us with direction, guidance and, yes, role models. It's now up to us to find ways of furnishing these things to our children and, when necessary, to ourselves.

If you don't know of a relationship that you admire, then find one. And if you don't find one, then keep looking until you do. I guarantee you that it will prove to be one of the most precious gifts you ever give yourself.

7. OPEN YOUR LIFE TO MORE AVAILABLE PEOPLE

Available doesn't have to mean single, but if every one of your friends is married or in a committed relationship, this obviously limits your exposure to single, unattached people. If you're always with the same group of paired-up people it's not going to open up any new avenues for you unless they're doing their bit to introduce you to *other* single (and, hopefully, available) people in their circle. This is not to say that you should rush right over to the nearest singles bar, but make sure you haven't been hiding by spending all your time with your married friends.

Of course, some single people are just as effective at taking up *all* your time and *all* your energy. When I was doing interviews for this book I heard countless stories of people who felt trapped in "pity parties" (their term, not mine). They could be male or female but the subject is often the same: "It's so hard to meet someone special." Sometimes the discussion is ostensibly entitled, "So, what can we do about it?" But even those evenings produced very few real suggestions and no tangible results. There are people who just love to fill your empty hours, time in which you could be *doing something* to make your life a better place. Well, you don't have to let them! Your time is too important. All of our time is important. If you're hanging out with people who *say* they want you to be in a healthy relationship, but *do* nothing to help you, or to help themselves, then you need to change the people you're hanging out with. At least spend less time with them. Do whatever you need to do to bless yourself and your dreams with the company of people who care, people who *want* you to succeed. When you bring those people into your life, then you put yourself closer to the starting gate of a new way of living.

Another way to limit your accessibility is by spending too much of your time as a third wheel to a couple. It's an easy habit to fall into because it *feels* as if you're actually *part* of a couple. (This is different than spending time with a couple you admire in order to learn. This is "hiding out" by attaching yourself to an already established relationship.) If that's you, then ask yourself what you may be avoiding. Maybe it's being alone. As a third wheel, it feels as if you get many of the benefits of a relationship or family without the risk of commitment. When you're really ready to be in relationship, you will need to venture out of the safety of this kind of attachment.

So take a look at your days, your weeks, your months, and see how much time you're spending in situations that *could* be keeping you single and unavailable. If you're not happy with the answer, then take some steps to change things. You've already heard me say it, but sign up for a class, go on a trip, pursue a new sport, do volunteer work. Do it for the experience, not just hoping to meet someone. But do it. Remember that once you've done all the hard work necessary to make yourself available, you still have to put yourself into the right environment to meet your mate.

8. DON'T LOOK FOR ONE PERSON WHO WILL BE YOUR EVERYTHING

When you're putting together your wish list for the perfect mate, the tendency sometimes is to get too specific. Chances are, you're not going to find one person who fits 100% of what you're looking for. This is why I have tried throughout this book to emphasize the importance of qualities such as *values, attitudes*, and *disposition*. These are general areas, but they're extremely important.

People can have wildly different "views" on a variety of topics and still form the basis of a healthy, respectful relationship. What helps is if they have similar definitions of words like decency and respect, concepts such as anger and what constitutes a fair fight. You might want to talk about words like "good" and "evil" and what they mean to both of you before you get heavy into the difference between the Gap and Banana Republic. Try to recognize the difference between the things that *really* matter and things that fall in and out of fashion. If one person is comfortable in the world of computers and another one is not, who cares? For all we know computers will one day be replaced by something else. Look at what happened to most of the Dot Coms. Try to stay focused on the things that you and your partner will carry with you into your old age. If you can do that, then you have traveled some distance down the road of not looking for *everything* in one person.

It's a sticky problem, this habit of putting all our dreams onto one "lucky guy" or "gal." It's not fair to us and it's *really* not fair to them. Quite simply, *nobody* is so damn fascinating that they can be endlessly entertaining, or interesting, or funny, or [whatever you've tacked onto your list] without a little help from a supporting cast.

Look at the way you choose your friends. Some are there for you in one type of situation, others are right for something else. I'm certainly not suggesting that you go out and find multiple "significant others," but I *am* suggesting that you be realistic when you're putting together a "picture" of what you want in a mate. Don't "get a life," *have* a life! At least have a "life in progress" complete with friends and family and outside interests, and your own views and beliefs (minimum requirement, one of each!) *before* you call yourself available for a relationship. Asking another person to be your "everything," no matter how nifty he or she might be, is a prescription for big trouble. The Eastern religions emphasize balance in all things. Relationships are no exception. Conduct your search for the elusive "balanced relationship," and you may find your love.

Once you become a couple, you will find things you have in common that weren't even on your list. As you get to know the person in your life, you will develop new interests that reflect your life together, whether it's gardening, cooking, skydiving, or stamp collecting. It's called "growing" and, provided you both use a similar inner compass, your journey will be a much smoother one.

9. TRY FRIENDSHIP FIRST

I know this caveat has appeared several times in this book, and has certainly been the subject of countless volumes all by itself. Nevertheless, I'm including it yet again in this list because it's a human quality that has so famously gotten all of us (me included) into such monumental trouble. There's no denying how exciting it is to feel the heart pounding, the butterflies in the stomach, the can't sleep kind of feeling when you're newly attracted to someone. But those quivery off-balance feelings are not evidence of true love; they're a sign of attraction—a crush. And maybe if I say it, or write it enough times, the message will get through. Obviously the reason this is such a tough concept is because it asks you to *not* listen to some of the very things that you *should* listen to when you're trying to determine if you're attracted to someone or not. Attraction equals flutters in your stomach. What I'm saying is *pay attention* to those flutters, just don't follow them all the way to Capistrano. Try to think about what steps you're going to take and how you're going to take them *before* you begin to "fall" for someone. I have a friend who purposely doesn't shave her legs before the first few dates; luckily she looks great in pants! She *knows* that she has a history of wanting to sexualize a relationship early, and she also knows (at this point) that it gets her heart into all kinds of trouble. So she does this one thing to help her decide *before* she gets lost in the moment. It may not sound like much, but it's saved her a whole lot of grief. It gives her some time to actually *think* about the choice she's making. And, often, in that "time-out," she's able to *listen* to what's being said by the other person. Then she can make a (relatively) clearheaded decision about whether she wants to move to a closer, more intimate relationship. I know it's a silly story, but whatever works. If that gut-churning feeling has been the indicator by which you measure your level of interest in someone, how has it been working for you so far?

When you are used to seeking out people who feed your adrenaline addiction, it can ruin your radar for anything real and genuine. It's possible to be so enamored of a person's looks, or appeal, or *whatever*, that you're able to convince yourself you feel much more than you actually do.

If you've had plenty of intense but short romances, maybe it's time to explore a new way of dating. If you've found someone who makes your stomach jump, why not set your actions on "slow motion." Find out who the person *is* before deciding that he's the one! If he's not someone you admire, if he's not someone who *could* be a friend, then think twice about that trip to Cancun for the weekend. Not that you're looking for a friend. You're looking for a mate, a partner, a relationship, but if "friend" is nowhere on the horizon, then you're missing a key ingredient.

If operating on intensity has been your pattern, then you know that even the hottest, sexiest relationship cools down eventually. When that happens, you probably move on. But to quote Michael Topp MFT once again: "How do couples have a satisfying sex life over a period of years, even as their bodies, their drives, and their life circumstances change? Companionship is the key. It creates more caring, more trust, and more fun." This is an important, if difficult, lesson for us all to learn. Some people are able to make the transition from lust to love and friendship comfortably. If that's not you, maybe you're picking unavailable people. Whether you are finding them sexy *because* they're unavailable is a difficult but important question to ask yourself.

It's been said that love is not only how you feel about the other person but also how you feel about yourself when you're with the other person. With your friends you can feel comfortable and really be yourself; isn't that how you want to feel around the person you love? Do you *like* this person, or are you just excited by him? I realize that, at the moment of pheromone activation, it doesn't feel like it's *just* excitement. It *just* feels like excitement! This is why I vote for a slower speed. If the excitement is real, then it will be there *big time* as the relationship develops.

Take your time. If the other person is not willing to go slow, let them move on. You don't need to give in to someone else's schedule. If going slow means that it's difficult to sustain the relationship, maybe there isn't enough there to begin with. "Hot" and "available" are definitely not mutually exclusive terms. Just make sure you're not mistaking one for the other.

10. END RELATIONSHIPS THAT DON'T SERVE YOU

Not to be blunt, but get rid of what's not working in your life. Whether it's a love relationship, a bad friendship, or a toxic work situation, find a way to end the things that aren't working in order to make room for the "healthy stuff" to fill the void. Again, I must use the phrase "easier said than done," but again I say, "do it." Every relationship is made up of good and bad, very few are all of one or the other. This, of course, makes it difficult to label any given relationship as "not working." But if you've done the work outlined in the previous chapters, then you have some idea of what kinds of things you are looking for in your life, what kind of requirements you now have. As your goals become clearer, the benefits and/or liabilities of the various relationships become clearer as well.

Courage is not something this or any other book can give you, but words can occasionally inspire. It is my sincere hope that at least some of the words, some of the stories in this book have helped you to draw upon your own reserves of courage so that you may do the things you need to do to become available for a healthy relationship. I'm the last person to advocate cutting people off prematurely. If there is *any* chance that a friendship or relationship can be addressed in such a way as to make it a positive force in your life, then do whatever you must to make that happen. But if the nature of that particular relationship is such that it *only* helps to keep you unhealthy and unavailable for a real, loving relationship, then know that you are tying a ball and chain around your leg as you "race" towards your new goals.

Imagine yourself as a pie circle of 100% energy. Then picture that everything that requires your time and your energy takes some part of this pie. Then you can see that you are "slicing" away at the very energy source you *need* to break down your old patterns of behavior and build new ones. And "bad" (i.e., difficult, hurtful) relationships are the most draining of *all*. An "unavailable" friend or relationship can become a *constant* distraction because they never leave your thoughts. Even when they're not physically spending time with you, you could be spending ten percent, twenty-five percent, maybe up to fifty percent of your time and energy trying to figure out ways to "fix" the relationship. Consider the possibility that *they* don't *want* to "fix" it. Consider the possibility that they're perfectly happy to have you stay the way you've always been, available for them, unavailable for a nurturing relationship. But whether or not there's a hidden agenda in play, it's your job to look at *all* the relationships in your life and determine whether everyone you *think* is on your team, really *is* on your team.

11. BE WILLING TO ASK FOR HELP

This stuff is not easy. If you've done all the work contained in the chapters, and you've spent the time making your lists and taking your inventories; if you've taken time alone to collect your thoughts and your dreams; if you've tried and tried again to take the "time-outs" and to really listen to what's being said during a date or a first meeting; if you've done all this and more, and you're still feeling stuck in some of the old patterns that keep you unavailable, then do not hesitate to ask for help. Obviously my hope is that this book will furnish you with some of the tools that it took me many years and many tears to acquire. But if this book serves only as the motivating force that gets you to a loving friend, a favorite pastor or rabbi, a therapist or psychologist, *anyone* you can trust and who will understand and help you in your quest, then this book will have served a wonderful function. I happen to believe in everything I've written, but I'm a grown-up and I know that life can be a complicated journey and no one book is enough. I've read many wonderful self-help books. None of them ever apply to all your problems, all the time. You're supposed to take what works for you, add your own thoughts and conclusions, and disregard what doesn't feel right. Use the words and stories contained in this book as a tool, but don't ever be afraid to ask for more tools. Whatever you might need. The only thing that matters is that you find a "you" who is open, and loving, and available for the relationship you deserve.

12. DON'T DESPAIR/DON'T SETTLE

And, finally, there is *always* the possibility that the reason you're still single is that you just haven't yet met the right person yet. If you've read this book and find that precious little relates to your life or your patterns, and yet you're still single when you don't want to be, then this paragraph is for you. Just a few words about "not settling." The flip side of "Mission Impossible" lists and dream mates who don't exist on planet Earth is "settling." It's tough to write much about settling because only you know what that word means to you. One person's Mr. Right is another person's Mr. Nightmare. However, the purpose of all the chapters in this book on lists and inventories and all the rest of it is to help you to choose a mate who is real, available, and will never represent "settling" for *you*. It's *your* list, *your* visualizations, and *your* dream that those chapters were trying to address. If *your* idea of Mr. Right comes from your true heart, and you do the work designed to spare you the "detours" of an unavailable partner, then the person you bring into your life will *not* be someone you settle for. I was married for seventeen years, single for even longer, and was fifty years old before I met someone with whom I feel the kind of bond I always dreamed of. Did luck have anything to do with it? Luck, my friends, has something to do with everything. But I like Thomas Jefferson's quote, "I find that the harder I work, the more luck I seem to have."

Review

1. Boost your self-esteem.
2. Be aware.
3. Make a list of what you want in a mate.
4. Imagine the relationship you want.
5. Be willing to do things differently.
6. Look for relationships you admire.
7. Open your life to more available people.
8. Don't look for one person who will be your everything.
9. Try friendship first.
10. End relationships that don't serve you.
11. Be willing to ask for help.
12. Don't despair/don't settle.

Chapter 6

The Questions to Ask—
The Answers to Listen For

The opposite of talking is not listening; the opposite of talking is waiting.

—FRAN LEIBOWITZ

It's something all of us do practically every day of our lives. We ask questions and we listen for answers. It's such a natural part of social interaction that we rarely have to think much about it. But if the information you're looking for is hidden beneath the surface, then the nature of the questions becomes extremely important, and the text and subtext of the answers need to be evaluated with a different degree of scrutiny than the usual Q and A. Q: "Can I get grilled onions on that?" A: "Sure, but it'll cost you half a buck extra" need not be given the same critical ear as: Q: "Do you believe that nicotine is addictive?" A: "To the best of my knowledge nicotine is not addictive." The first exchange involved fifty cents. The second cost three billion dollars and millions of lives.

Lawyers understand how important it is to ask the right questions to solicit the desired answers. They charge a lot of money to know these techniques. Unfortunately (well, fortunately for our pocketbooks) we don't have lawyers with us when we're meeting new people, so we must learn for ourselves how to ask the right questions and listen for the answers we need. When you're trying to decide whether or not your date should be pronounced "unavailable in the first degree!" every word counts.

When you're out on a date, Lord knows you've got to talk about something. Doesn't it make good sense to ask questions that will help reveal the person's character? You probably ask a lot of the right questions already, but you may not be really listening to the answers. In this chapter we're going to look at how you can get the most information out of an evening (without sounding like an assistant district attorney).

Listening has a lot to do with our subconscious. We "screen" things that we don't want to hear or that we *think* we don't *need* to hear. ("I don't remember him saying anything about having a wife, I *swear* it!") Have you ever been introduced to someone at a party and the minute they said their name you forgot it? It could be that you were just distracted, but you know that if this were a person for whom you felt a strong attraction, or someone who could advance your career, you'd remember his or her name. We remember what we *need* (or what we *train* ourselves to need) to remember. We're going to spend some time with the questions you need to ask, and answers that you need to listen for. I'm sure you've had the experience of saying to yourself, "It's damn important that I pay attention and remember this person's name and information," and, by gosh, you did. That's because you made a conscious decision about it. This chapter is about making that decision a conscious, as well as a productive, one.

You can find out a lot more about a person when you're genuinely interested in what they have to say. I know that sounds obvious, but the truth is there are many people who don't know the first thing about the art of listening. They're busy looking around the room, seeing who's there, who's not there, worrying about how they look, wondering how their new bathroom wallpaper will look! You have to be in the "now" to really listen. And listening "now" can save you hours, days, and even years of unnecessary pain. Work on being in the "now" and your *future* can be a much more satisfying and rewarding time than your *past* has been. Or, if I may quote the great philosopher Yogi Berra: "You got to be careful if you don't know where you're going, because you might not get there."

I know a thing or two about *not* listening because I used to be damn good at it. Not only did I not know what questions to ask; I wasn't all that swift at hearing the answers I *did* get. Sometimes I would even play a neat little trick on myself by *forgetting* a piece of information that didn't fit into my picture of who I *wanted* the person to be (notice I didn't say "who the person *was*," but who I *wanted* him to be). Many years of frustrating, unfulfilling, "unavailable" relationships later I finally started to get a clue. Some of these men were *telling* me they weren't available right from the get-go. I was just so determined not to hear that I didn't. Literally. Sometimes, after a relationship ended, I would be talking about it with a friend who would remind me about this or that gathering that we all had attended. My friend would recall some telling remark that my then partner had made, and I wouldn't know what the heck she was talking about. I had *no* memory of the remark having been made even though I was right there "listening" to him when he said it. That's why I know how important it is to acquire some skills in specialized Q and A. General George Patton once said that "A pint of sweat saves a gallon of blood," and while I'm certainly not comparing "Dating Wars" to World War II, I do think that the general's words apply to both.

So, when should you start asking questions? As soon as you think he might be a candidate for your heart. As I said before, we're not talking about an interrogation, we're talking about *paying attention*. If you've read the first five chapters of this book, then you have a pretty good idea of what types of behavior are indicative of an "unavailable" partner.

There's an old saying that warns that you only get "one chance to make a first impression," and it's a tough one to argue with. No matter how things go, the value of a first encounter must never be underestimated. Guards and defenses may not be in place and you frequently get a clearer view of who a person is. If you know what to look and listen for, then those first few minutes and hours can save you months, and sometimes years of "learning the hard way" (i.e., the way the author did it). They can also, if you hear the right words, give you the confidence to move deeper into a wonderful "available" relationship with someone who just might be the one for you. A friend of mine who teaches acting tells her students to *always* have paper and pen ready when they read a play for the very first time. There will *never* be another time that they will read the words and see the images in that fresh and fertile way. They will have ideas, and reactions, and feelings that they could never conjure up on a subsequent reading, and they should take copious notes on those first impressions. The same is true for a first meeting (and subsequent meetings as well, of course, but first meetings most of all) of a person you find attractive.

So many times when we're around someone new, we're trying so hard to make a good impression that we're thinking while they're talking and formulating our reply. We aren't listening. "Don't ask, don't tell," isn't a very courageous policy for the military, but it's disastrous in the dating world. If information is power (and it is), then you need all the information you can get.

As I said, this is not an interrogation. First of all, the words aren't the only thing to look for. (Remember, only seven percent of communication is through words. The other ninety-three percent of what we learn is from observing and interpreting nonverbal cues.) But it's "listening" none the less. Listen to his body language. Is he fast or slow, abrupt or gentle? Watch his face. Does he smile? Does it seem genuine? Do his words match his expressions? How is he dressed? I'm not talking about whether he's in a suit or not. I'm talking about what is being said by his choice of clothing; clean, messy, appropriate, coordinated, *too* coordinated. There's no judgment in any of this. It's all just information. But it's information that you should pay attention to. The conversation should fit the tone and pace that feels natural for the two of you. You'll know when it feels off and it's a technique that you will develop over time, so don't expect to "get it" right away.

On the first date, if he tells you he recently left a ten-year marriage and just wants to have *fun* for awhile and catch up on *sex*, and you're ready for a committed relationship, this is probably not someone to pursue. Of course, people rarely expose their true *intentions* quite so blatantly, but you'd be surprised at the information you can glean when you are really "hearing." The man described above is clearly not available right now. Unfortunately for the unavailable person, he will hold a certain appeal. If you receive clear information like this and you still find yourself wanting to move ahead, maybe you need a "time-out." He's stated that he's unavailable. Why wouldn't someone want to hear that? There are a million possible answers and the checklists at the end of the chapters of this book will help you to narrow it down. The short version is: "You're unavailable and you're behaving in a way to keep yourself unavailable." Do you want to spend the next eight months (or eight years?) wondering what happened to the wild sex that filled the first six weeks of this "relationship?" Do yourself a favor and walk away—or date him for the six weeks of fun and wild sex and know that's what you're doing.

Following are some examples of questions, answers, and possible interpretations. I'm not suggesting that you begin your conversation with "What are your hobbies?"and move down the list. This is a date, not a press conference, but if the conversation turns to one of these areas, take advantage of it. The idea is to hear what they say and listen for more. Most people love to talk about themselves. Make it the perfect opportunity to let them. These are just suggestions for gleaning information in an interested and informal way. What you're looking for is information about availability, compatibility, and whatever else you've determined to be important to *you*.

1. GETTING TO KNOW YOU—THE FIRST FEW DATES

WHAT DO YOU DO FOR FUN?

If you ask someone what he does for fun and he tells you he doesn't have much free time, that he works most nights and weekends, then he's telling you something about who he is. Later in the relationship when he has no time for you and you realize he is a workaholic, you shouldn't be surprised. He told you this the first night, didn't he?

Ask about his interests and his passions. Hopefully, if this is someone you were attracted to in the first place, there will be at least a few things you have in common. If he (or she!) loves to watch all sports *all the time*, this tells you something about how the relationship might look later on. Does he expect or want a mate to have the same passion he does for sports? Or just a tolerance? If you're attracted to a man who tells you he watches sports every single weekend, don't think he's going to suddenly *stop* watching once the two of you are a couple. He *told you* he's a sports nut. It's *your* responsibility to *hear* that. If you hate sports yet you decide to stay with this person, then know that you're choosing someone who is (at least during his favorite sport season) unavailable. It's *your* job to determine whether or not this is a real problem that will cause you distress over the length of a relationship or a marriage, or if it's just a part of who he is and it doesn't affect your life. If it's not a problem, then great. But if it is, then you will save yourself a lot of grief if you deal with it earlier rather than later. Obviously the same is true for any interest/passion. We're just talking about acquiring as much information as we can so we can make a halfway intelligent decision.

Usually it's a matter of degrees. There's a big difference between someone who likes outdoor activities and someone who wants to spend every spare second mountain climbing. If mountain climbing is a burning passion for this person, it could affect how you spend your weekends and vacations for the rest of your life. If you're the type who likes four-star hotels and this person likes roughing it, you could be spending your nights on the roof of the Ritz Carlton. I'm not saying it's a bad thing. I'm just saying that it's better to know these things up front. And it's amazing how many of these questions are answered (if you're listening) during the first few dates with a person.

WHAT KIND OF WORK DO YOU DO?

What kind of work does he or she do? Is it a career or a job? Does he enjoy it? Does he hate it? If so, what would he rather be doing? Has he ever had a job he liked? If he's tried a variety of jobs and has hated them all, is it possible that this person just doesn't like to work, period? How does he feel about his coworkers? Does he think the boss is smart? Dumb? The simplest stories can reveal character traits if you know what to look for.

Unless you or the person you're considering is independently wealthy, then work is going to play a role in your lives. It's important that the values he brings to that work are values that you respect. I know a woman who divorced her husband after sixteen years of marriage. One of her complaints, *after* the divorce, was that he was basically a crook. She had endless stories about how he embezzled from this one and strong-armed that one. She claimed that she knew very little of all this during the time it was going on. Well, of course she *did* know (not the details, perhaps, but certainly the nature of how he did business), she simply made a choice to not "listen" or look at what was going on right in front of her. It's a dangerous way to live your life.

Work is important. Attitudes about work are even more important. How important is his work? More important than family? Less? Does he have many sources of ego gratification or is his work the whole nine yards? Is he a workaholic? Is he community minded? If someone tells you that he volunteered for a couple of hours at a hospital two years ago, and then he *talks* about it for *three hours*, maybe he just wants to *appear* community minded. A comedy writer friend of mine says, "If somebody tells you he has a great sense of humor, chances are he doesn't." In other words, start to look beyond the words for the actions that go with them.

When Amanda started dating Eric, a very successful, attractive, single doctor, she couldn't believe her luck. He seemed like a dream come true. He was charming, funny, and bright. Over dinner, by asking about his work, Amanda learned that Eric was passionate about his profession—but it turned out that he was passionately pessimistic. He told her everything that he thought was wrong with the medical profession. Since there are so many valid things to complain about in the field, this certainly didn't make Eric a bad guy. At first it made him sound dedicated and devoted. However, as he went on (and on, and on, and on,) talking about his job, it became apparent that his resentment wasn't restricted to the injustices of the profession. Eric didn't think *any-thing* worked as well as it should. (So why on earth should Amanda think that *she* would be the exception?) Eric was not a happy guy. He had strong feelings of resentment regarding his colleagues who earned more money, had faster cars, or better toys than he had. Amanda listened carefully and, even though his stories were humorous, there was an underlying jealously and bitterness in his tone. He was sarcastic with regard to other peoples' relationships as well. He implied that only "other guys" seemed to get the best women (a self-fulfilling prophecy). By this time Amanda was more than insulted; she was healthy enough, and smart enough, to know that she was not going to be the one to make this man happy. She moved on.

Obviously not everyone is in the career they hope to be in at the moment you meet them. Perhaps you're meeting them in transition; we all have to start somewhere. You could meet a twenty-year-old waiter or waitress while they're hoping for their big acting break. You could meet a forty-five-year-old in the same position. There is certainly nothing wrong with waiting tables for a living, the problem occurs when you're a forty-five-year-old waiter who is bitter, angry, and feels stuck in his life. You're not going to be able to change this person, but if you're a Rescuer, or several other types of "unavailable," then you might spend several years trying.

WHERE DID YOU GROW UP? HOW MANY IN YOUR FAMILY?

Ask about his family and listen to the tone of his answers. Does he have brothers and sisters? How did they get along as children? How do they get along now? What was his position in the family? How was he treated? And, more importantly, how does he *feel* about how he was treated?

Someone who tells you about the warm, loving family get-togethers they had growing up is telling you a lot about who they are. And someone who tells you about the loud, drunken, angry, bitter family they experienced is also telling you a lot. Of course it will take time to understand the dynamics of anybody else's family, but listen to the first words spoken on the subject.

If you are meeting someone who had a secure, easy family life and you had a difficult childhood, then your communication might be more challenging. Sometimes key words like "trust," "security," "love," and "respect" have been defined another way. But many relationships work wonderfully with an opposing balance within the couple. One person has more strength, the other more sensitivity. One is outgoing, the other a loner. The important thing to ask about (and listen for) is whether there is a shared sense of values regarding the way you will treat each other. Is he capable of sharing? Does he understand the *concept* of sharing? (i.e., understand it in a manner similar to your understanding of it.) If he doesn't, then you're looking at a huge obstacle to the kind of closeness that belongs in a loving relationship. And *you* are not going to be the one to teach him. Talk about what goes into our wet cement; sharing is a concept that goes into the mix on day one.

Most of us suffer some sort of damage from our childhood. Everyone has family "issues," some large, some small. You want to weed out the ones who remain unavailable because of *unresolved* family issues that will affect you.

Did he come from an affectionate family? Did you? How important is it to show affection, and how? If *you* have family stories that you bring to the table during a first or second meeting with someone, then you've opened up a door for him to walk through. If he *doesn't* have any stories about his family, then that tells you something as well. Stories about family are the best because they tell you so much about the storyteller. Without having to ask a man directly how he feels about women, he will reveal his feelings if you know how to listen to what he's saying.

Growing up in a happy family doesn't necessarily guarantee a happy person, but at least there is a frame of reference for it. It's important to use all your resources and gather enough information to keep you from picking the unavailable person who never learned and is now incapable of loving you.

DO YOU HAVE CHILDREN?

If you're dating someone with children, or thinking about dating someone with children, you want to know as much as you can about that parent/child relationship. Where do children fit into his life? Obviously asking deep, probing questions concerning his children, and his thoughts about them, on date number one could send a guy running for the hills. But when you ask if he has children, you should be listening for a lot more than a yes-or-no answer.

Does he get excited when he talks about his kids? Does he brag about them? Or does he shrug and say his ex won't let him see them? Does he like being a dad or does he seem to resent the time he has to spend with them? Is there love and respect between them or does he talk of constant tension? It may be a while before you actually meet the children and that *could* be a good indication that the father is being appropriately protective of their feelings. But if a "dating" situation is developing into a real relationship, then sooner or later you should get a chance to see how things work between parent and child.

Children, as we all know, can be the most wonderful, lovable, loving creatures on God's good earth; they can also be an extremely powerful force in any family dynamic. If you are considering a relationship with someone who has a different attitude about where children fit into your lives, then you're looking at Big Trouble in Relationship City.

All of this, of course, works both ways. If *you're* the one with children, then you need to make sure that the two of you agree on the basics vis à vis where kids fit in and how much to include them in your daily lives. If you're someone who goes to every Little League game, every piano lesson, works on every homework assignment and then reads each of your kids a bedtime story, you should probably think twice before dating someone who sends his kids to boarding school and regularly forgets their birthdays. The two of you live in different worlds and, sooner or later, there's going to be friction. Worse, that friction is going to affect the very children you love so much.

As divorce rates have risen and families have become fragmented, we see more and more single-parent and divorced households. Amongst these single and divorced parents, children have become an important factor in dating, yet we don't see nearly enough material addressing the subjects of kids, dating, attitudes of ex-spouses and the like. As important as it is to ask the tough questions, it's not enough to just ask the questions and then accept his answers as gospel; observe his behavior and see if his actions match his words. Nobody wants to admit that he's not fond of, or comfortable with, children, especially his own; but you can see it easily enough in the way he relates to them. If it's a good, healthy relationship, you'll see it, and you'll feel it when you spend time together with his kids, or yours.

You can't expect to date someone with children and not deal with it eventually. Only you can determine the right timing for the right questions. Then observe the behavior and pay close attention to the interactions between everyone involved, including yourself!

If you are someone who has spent time in an unavailable relationship, make sure you're not choosing a situation that ultimately won't work.

HOW DID YOU/HOW DO YOU SPEND HOLIDAYS? FAMILY VACATIONS?

How does he feel about the holidays? Again, these questions are meant to reveal something more than pork or poultry preferences. If this person remembers family experiences as being terrible, lonely, frightening, or sad, it's bound to have a negative impact on how he feels about the holidays (and, perhaps, family) today. Or maybe he came from a very close family and he still spends all the holidays and vacations together (and expects you to do so, as well, no matter what your traditions have been). You're the only one who knows the right or wrong answer to these questions. If you've done your work and you have a more specific idea of who and what you're looking for in a relationship, then you will know whether or not his answers feel right. You're looking for areas of harmony and common ground. If you're a family-oriented person you might not be compatible with a person who's not. If he had a terrible family experience growing up, he might not want to spend any time with family—yours or his. On the other hand I know many people who married into a better family than they were given and adjusted to the happy group quite nicely, thank you very much.

Obviously stories about holidays are stories about families, but sometimes a specific moment during a particular holiday is a way to open up the subject and learn a lot more than simply the words.

DO YOU HAVE MANY CLOSE FRIENDS?

You can tell a lot about people by the company they keep. Sometimes you can learn more by meeting, or at least hearing about, the friends than you can by meeting the family. The friends are chosen, the family isn't.

Does he have friends of long standing? Is he telling you stories of hard times where they were there for each other through thick and thin? I always take this as a good sign that the person has some relationship skills. Just as friends are chosen, they can be *unchosen*. If someone elects to do the work to keep a friendship together over a long period of time, it *could* mean that he knows what it takes to make a relationship work. Of course, it could also mean that he's been involved in a long-term friendship that has helped to keep him "unavailable" for a *real* relationship. (See also: Chapter 5, End relationships that don't serve you).

When someone has only "new" friends or "working" friends from the office, this could point to a person who regards friends as more of a convenience than a necessity. Or it could indicate someone who doesn't put much value on, or has trouble making, real friends. Does he tell supportive stories about his friends when he's describing them? If you're hearing more negative tales than positive ones about his friends, you should be wondering why he's "stuck" in relationships that don't work. (So should he, by the way.)

One of the most attractive aspects about the man in my life, one of the things that made me think that he was significantly different from my previous relationships, is the people he has in his life. Once I began to meet his friends and family I could see the way he interacted with the people for whom he cared and it reassured me that what my instincts were telling me (that this was the right, "available" person for me) was correct. I went through all the steps that I've talked about in this book. I had already made my lists, taken my inventories, looked at the reasons I had made some of the choices I had made, faced some of the fears that had influenced those choices. Then, when we met, I asked the questions, listened to the answers, and took it slow (more about this happy ending in Chapter 7). Looking at the *other* relationships in his life helped me to see who he *really* was, not just who he *said* he was, or even who I *thought* he was. The fact that he had an incredible community of people who love and respect him said volumes about him.

If you're meeting someone with no close friends, this should be a big red flag. Unless he's brand-new to the area, or he's doing his *own* inventory and has just "cleaned house" to make room for healthier relationships, then he should have some history of friendship in his life. If not, then why not? It certainly doesn't make him a bad person, but it sure makes him look unavailable.

Another caution flag is someone with a lot of ex-friends. You know the type; they have a ton of stories about one injustice after another that has been done to them by one bad person after another. (It never seems to be their fault. Did you ever notice that?) This type usually has a running inventory of all the favors they've ever done for a series of "ungrateful" people. And what makes you think you'll be any different? Unless your wish list includes the words "and I want to be his next big disappointment," then you should move on to the next "available" person.

WHAT'S THE BEST THING ABOUT YOU?

This is a good question to ask because you get a feel for how someone perceives himself. Sometimes people are very insightful about themselves—sometimes not. I know a woman who thinks her best quality is that she's a wonderful listener; the problem is she never stops talking about what a great listener she is. Generally though, the answers to this question will give you some idea of what's important to this person. If he tells you that he's most proud of his work with Habitat for Humanity, this is a different person from the one who chooses his tight abs as a source of great pride.

Since there's no right answer (although in my opinion the "tight abs" response is about as close to a wrong answer as I can imagine), you have to determine for yourself if what they believe to be their best attribute is a plus or a minus. Is it a clue that he's not "available" for the kind of relationship you're looking for? Or is it one of the reasons that you can feel good about moving into a deeper commitment with this person?

Where do you see yourself in five years?

Companies use this question all the time in their human resources applications when interviewing prospects, and it's a good question for you to use as well. It can help give you a picture of what he has in mind for his future—and whether or not there's room in it for you.

You're looking for someone who can imagine being in a committed relationship, aren't you? Well, if their future plans are all about career and travel for the next five years and you want to settle down and get married now, this may not be the person for you.

Sometimes people change their minds. Meeting the right person can have a profound effect on future plans. Rick had a whole different life mapped out for himself when he first met Cindy. In fact he almost didn't ask her out because he knew he was moving away in six months. His idea was to move to Florida and open a restaurant. Meeting Cindy changed all that. Rick ended up staying and he and Cindy opened a restaurant together. In Rick's case, his plan of living in Florida wasn't set in stone and he still got to realize his dream of opening a restaurant. He considers it a happy ending.

This is why relationship stuff is difficult, for *all* of us. Rick didn't *look* available (travel plans, etc.) but, in his heart, he really *was*. He didn't change who he was as a person, he just changed where he wanted to be the "available" person that he was. So, by hanging in there for a while, long enough to see who Rick really was, Cindy ended up with an "available" man in her life. Please note that she didn't "hang in there" for years and years; she sensed that Rick was a loving, available man, she waited a few months to see if things would work out, and they did.

This question, "Where do you see yourself in five years?" is just as important to ask yourself as it is to ask anyone else. When you answer, be sure to listen.

2. KNOWING YOU BETTER—MORE QUESTIONS TO ASK

After the first few dates, if both people are feeling positive about where the relationship is going, they move to a different, hopefully deeper, level in their communication and their committment. This is frequently the point at which the "fall" into love becomes a "free fall," gaining speed and losing control. You're over the first obstacles to compatibility; now you're en route to the land of intimacy. If you could stay truly conscious during this time and perhaps pull the cord on one of your smaller "safety chutes," you might be able to ask the second level of questions that could give you the kind of insight you need. It's not easy. The narcotic effects of something *finally* beginning to go right can be overpowering. But if you make use of your "time-out" clause, take a deep breath, check your lists, and ask these next questions—questions that are more appropriate to a deeper relationship—then you might pave the way for a smoother trip into an "available" relationship, or a more painless exit from an "unavailable" one.

ARE YOU AVAILABLE AND OPEN TO A RELATIONSHIP?

It's date number four or five. The question is very simple, but not very easy: "Are you available for a relationship?" A "yes" answer does not automatically mean they are truly available—but a "no" will certainly tell you they're not. If you really want to be in a relationship, be willing to walk away when you hear the answer "no." Be sure that the two of you have the same definition of the words "relationship" and "available." Be sure that the obstacles getting in the way are real. (Remember Rick, who *thought* he was unavailable because he was leaving town. This turned out *not* to be a real obstacle after all.) But if all the ifs and buts still lead to the word "unavailable" then at least you know what you're dealing with. And now, if you've done your work, you know what steps you have to take if you want to save yourself some time and pain.

Another response you might get to that question could be, "I don't know." See if you can get him to elaborate on that. Does it mean he hasn't given a relationship any thought? Does it depend on something else? (Like, for instance, when his wife's leaving town for two weeks?) He might say he's not available right now and he might have a very real, very logical reason. When I first asked the man in my life this question, his answer was, "No, not right now." He was in the middle of a family crisis and didn't think he could deal with a new relationship while this was going on. Again, find out what "not now" means. You don't want to spend a year with someone who is still saying he's not ready. And you certainly don't want to spend twenty. When you make your lists and put together your inventories, give this question some thought. Before you get caught up in the passion of a love affair, decide how much time is enough to wait for an answer to this extremely important question. And then stick to the number you've written down. It won't be easy to honor it, but it will be the right thing to do if your goal is to be available for real love in your life.

WHAT ARE THE GOOD THINGS ABOUT BEING IN A RELATIONSHIP?

You're looking for someone who is optimistic about the idea of a relationship. You want to hear that this person can see the positive side of sharing and caring. Also you'd like to hear that this person values some of the same things in a relationship that you do. If being able to use the carpool lane on the freeway, filing a joint tax return, and two-for-one dinner specials are his idea of "advantages," you're in trouble (although the carpool lane can *really* come in handy in LA!)

WHAT ARE THE BAD THINGS ABOUT BEING IN A RELATIONSHIP?

It's not necessarily a bad sign to hear that your potential mate is able to cite a few arguments for the downside of a relationship. Anyone who has been in the trenches will have some war stories to tell and some scars that show. As a matter of fact, I would be worried about someone who had *nothing* but positive things to say about "the joys of relationships." If all his experiences were so darn positive, then how come he's single? (Widows and widowers are, of course, exempted from this generalization.) But, with those exceptions, my argument holds. Either they've never really been in a close relationship, or they weren't paying attention, or maybe they're not being honest. Relationships can be difficult, *very* difficult, *until* you find the right one. If you're dating someone who has an idealized picture of what a relationship *should* be, then you (*and* he) are going to have a heck of a time trying to live up to it.

Of course, if his outlook is too gloomy, then you're in a different kind of trouble. Let's say one of his fears is that he'll lose his independence. Is it a fear or is it a deal breaker? One is manageable (i.e., he can be reassured), the other is not. And is he *so* convinced that *any* type of compromise will represent this fear being realized? If it is, then good luck. *Every* relationship involves compromise. The best relationship, the most "available" relationship in the history of the solar system, requires some compromise. So his fear will *automatically* throw a monkey wrench into your relationship, no matter what you do. And this conversation may not come up *until* you've moved into the second phase of your time together. It's when things move from "getting to know you" to "I really like you and maybe we could get closer to each other" that these questions need to be addressed and you need to hear the answers.

It's hard enough to achieve true intimacy with another person. It's just about impossible when that other person is *looking* for the relationship to fail.

WHEN WAS YOUR LAST RELATIONSHIP?

It's only natural for someone to mourn a relationship that ended badly or, in his or her view, prematurely. I would be wary of someone whose attitude when discussing a failed relationship was a shrug and a "No problem." However, I would also think twice before trying to make room in somebody's heart if they're clearly not over it yet. We talked about the dangers of the "Can't Get Over A Past Love" type in Chapter 1. Whether it be anger, grief, self-pity, or any number of emotions that can linger after a relationship ends, if he's still *living* in that relationship, then there's no room for you. You should be looking for complete closure with the last—or any previous—relationship. You don't want to hear that there's lingering love—or hate—for an old flame. I've known people who were *so* invested in their last relationship that they kept it alive for a longer period of time than the relationship had actually gone on!

The truth is that if a person still has strong feelings about a past love, then the relationship isn't really over. How many friends have you heard say they *hate* their ex with a passion, and then they end up back with him or her? (After you've been honest and told them what a jerk the ex was!) So don't get giddy when you meet someone who still carries a grudge. Things can change.

If they're not over it, then you may be with someone who is (consciously or unconsciously) using this as an excuse to keep himself unavailable. A "rebound" relationship is not a relationship between two available people. It has plenty of emotion and very little substance. Listen to what he says and how he says it when he tells his stories about how they broke up and how he's doing now. If it doesn't sound like it's over, and sometimes he will even come right out and *tell* you that he's not over it, then please understand what this means to your chances of entering a healthy relationship with this person (i.e., slim at best). Again, I'm not saying that you should take this as a cue to bolt out of the restaurant before the entrée arrives. Just learn to listen, and to know what you're dealing with.

How long was your longest relationship?

"Serial monogamy" is a term that has recently come into vogue. The sexual freedoms of the Sixties came to a crashing halt with the advent of AIDS, and terms like "swinging" and "orgy" were heard less. Whether the "new morality" was born out of medical necessity or because of an embrace of more conservative values is a subject that will surely be debated in sociology departments all over academia for decades to come. The part of "serial monogamy" that should interest you when you're meeting someone new is how long did the "serial" last. Is this a person who has a (hefty) number of six-month relationships in his resume? Or has he had a few two- to five-year relationships? One pattern is not *necessarily* better than the other, but the information tells you something about how this person defines (or, at least, *defined*) the word "relationship."

You're looking for evidence that someone is capable of sustaining interest. Obviously if he is someone who moves on quickly, then you should ask questions soliciting his views on words like "commitment." Maybe they're out of there at the first sign of trouble. Not a good sign if you're actually looking for a real relationship.

Listen for information that will let you know how much *work* he's done since his last relationship. Is he aware of why the others failed? Has he thought about it? Is it *always* the other person's fault? There's no need to be judgmental as you probe these areas. It's his life and he's allowed to go through it as he pleases, but you need to know if this is someone who is on the same page as you are.

WHO ENDED THE RELATIONSHIP? WHY?

Someone ended it. It's almost never a mutual decision. It seems that relationships rarely fizzle out by mutual agreement. So a good question to ask is: Has this person ended every relationship? If so, then why? It *could* mean (but not necessarily) that he has a need to control the relationship. Many times, when someone is *always* the one to end the relationship, it's because they weren't *in* the relationship in the first place. *Then*, when it begins to move into deeper waters, he can jump ship first and do so quite easily. Look for a pattern. For instance, if a person tells you every relationship ended after six months and usually because the other person wanted more of a commitment, what makes you think it will be different with you?

How did the last one end? Listen for clues to his behavior. What kind of terms are they on today? Does it sound as if there's been time and effort spent on growth? Or is he just jumping right back onto his usual pattern, with only a name and model change (a.k.a. *you*) to make him feel like it's different. If the last few relationships ended because of someone's infidelity, then ask more questions until you know exactly what that means. Who was unfaithful, and why? If the other person was always the one who strayed, is there something he did (does?) that drives them away? If this person is unreasonably jealous, maybe it was just his suspicions that made them leave.

All of this information lets you begin to get acquainted with his pattern, his problems, and his priorities. Maybe the pattern is one that feels right for you. (You have a pattern as well. We all do.) What you don't want to do is *not* be aware of the things that caused past relationships to fail. Those failures will let you know how to make a success of the relationship, if success is on the menu.

HOW DO YOU HANDLE CONFLICTS IN A RELATIONSHIP?

There's an old Russian saying: "You don't know a person until you've eaten a pound of salt together." Like all old Russian sayings, its meaning isn't exactly clear, but I'm pretty sure it means that you really don't know someone until you've hit some big trouble. Anyone can "behave" when everything's going great. It's just not that difficult. It's when the going gets tough that the tough can beat the living daylights out of you, emotionally and physically.

How does he fight? (I take this opportunity to remind you that I have chosen to use only one gender throughout most of this book, for purposes of clarity. Obviously both genders can fight, and fight with equal amounts of fairness and respect on the one hand, and dirty-trick, below-the-belt tactics on the other. "He," in this and most other passages, represents both genders.)

I don't care how wonderful those first few days, weeks, months, or even years (rare, but I've seen it) are for both of you; eventually you will have an argument. And one of those arguments will lead to a fight. (The first can be a frank but emotional exchange of views, as the diplomats like to say. The second can be open warfare.) Chances are you're not going to get into a fight, or even an argument with someone in the first few meetings. Many new relationships go a very long time before they reach a point of conflict. That's why it's important to learn something about how he handles things when there's a difference of opinion, or when someone's feelings have been hurt. The short version of the question is: Does he fight fair? Obviously "fair" is a subjective word open to interpretation, which is why you need to find out if his definition is close to yours. Tell stories about disagreements you've had with friends or past partners, and then listen to his take on things. Does he sound too volatile? Or does he come off as uninterested and unable to stand up for what he believes? Does he know what a mixed message is, and how does he deal with them? There are a million ways to solicit information about conflict, family, work, friends, etc. The important thing is to ask the questions, and then *deeper* questions, until you have a sense of how this person is going to behave when it's time to eat a pound of salt together.

Rex and Dana got along fantastically. They couldn't imagine ever having a disagreement, much less a fight. They moved in together and things were fine for about six months. And that's when Rex found out how Dana fought. She was a complete and ugly rage-a-holic. She was the sweetest woman until she was provoked—and then she turned into a mean, vicious shrew. Rex can laugh about it now, but at the time he was downright frightened. Anger is a rational, albeit passionate, emotion. Rage is usually irrational, and frequently has little to do with the situation at hand. Anger can be dealt with; rage is like a force of nature that can cause irreparable damage to any relationship. Respect is thrown right out the window, and once respect goes, you're on a slippery slope to disaster.

Watch the way he interacts with his friends and family when there's a disagreement or a frustrating moment. Does he "lose it" in a way that feels frightening to you? And what happens when you want to talk about this *rage?* Does he even *know* he's raging, or does he think this is the way *everybody* fights? After all, it might be the way members of *his* family fought. This could end up to be one of those situations where "the only way to win is not to play."

Rex tried every which way he knew to calm Dana and get her to hang on to the element of respect when they fought. Dana never did understand what he was talking about, even long after he left the relationship, a wiser and more "available" man.

WHAT'S THE DEAL BREAKER?
WHAT WON'T YOU COMPROMISE ON?

Everybody has their Big Issues, their Deal Breakers. They're different for each of us, and they can make absolutely no sense to anyone except us. The important thing is to know what they are and to know if they're going to get in the way of real intimacy in your relationship. Most of these Deal Breakers come from an episode or a relationship in one's past. If Stacy has had liars in her past, and they've caused her incredible hurt and pain, then she's going to respond *very* unfavorably to someone who seems to play fast and loose with the truth. If it's a big enough Deal Breaker, it can interfere with even a "normal" relationship. If you're the person dating Stacy and you say you're going to be home at seven o'clock and you get stuck in traffic and your cell phone battery is dead, and you arrive at eight thirty, this could trigger a scene that is *way* out of proportion with what really happened. Did you *say* seven and is it now eight thirty? You bet. Did you lie? Well, if you ask Stacy, then you will get a "yes" answer. The element of trust, which is necessary to every relationship, is missing. And when that's missing, there's not much you can do but spend a huge amount of your time *proving* that your story is true. If the rest of the relationship is extraordinary and you feel like you can deal with this "issue," then go ahead, but know what you're getting into *before* you get into it. It's not what you'd call a "fun" surprise when you discover that you're suddenly untrustworthy in the eyes of someone you love. Again, ask the questions; find ways of telling stories that will elicit responses that will contain the information you *need* in order to know who this person is. Remember that each time you get a response that syncs up with your view of a relationship, it becomes that much easier (and safer) to let yourself get close and become vulnerable with an "available" person.

3. KNOWING YOU MORE—GETTING INTIMATE

You're at the point where you're ready to become intimate. (You know who you are!) Even at this stage, it's difficult to ask certain questions; by now you may not *want* to know the answers, especially if you run the risk of screwing up what *feels like* a great shot at a wonderful relationship. But the alternative is flying without instruments, and that's a damn good way to get into trouble.

Think about some of your past relationships. How different would the outcome have been if you had the answers to the following questions ahead of time?

WHAT ARE YOUR EXPECTATIONS FOR OUR RELATIONSHIP?

If you're thinking in terms of a serious commitment, you want to make sure the other person is thinking along the same lines. Don't assume just because you feel something that they're feeling the same level of feelings for you. Asking their intent directly won't necessarily guarantee you an honest and true answer, but you still need to ask. Then listen to his answer, and observe his behavior, in order to figure out whether or not the two of you are marching to the beat of the same drummer.

These kinds of questions are frequently asked *by accident*, at the most awkward moments, and sometimes by people who aren't even in the relationship. Two people have been seeing each other for a certain amount of time, they're at a dinner party, and someone asks them what their plans are for the future. It's intended as an innocent question, one person inquiring as to what the "happy couple" has in mind for their future. There's an awkward silence, followed by nervous laughter, then another uncomfortable silence which is mercifully broken when the hostess suggests they have their dessert on the patio. What just happened is that these two people were asked a question that they should have asked each other. The embarrassment comes as a result of neither of them knowing what the other is thinking and not wanting to expose their thoughts in front of a room full of people. It wasn't the question that was inappropriate, and it wasn't the answer. It was the fact that there *was* no answer. But, of course, there can be an answer if somebody (preferably someone in the relationship) asks the question. Why not make it you?

If you're ready for a relationship to go to a deeper, more committed, level, then you need to let the other person know that that's where you're at. Ask him how he feels about how things are going, how fast or slow he wants them to go and how *far* he wants them to go. As difficult as it is to ask this question, the answer can let you know that you're heading in the same direction. (And isn't *that* a nice thing to know!) It can save you months or years of wasted time and painful frustration.

The down side, of course, is not getting the answer you want. *If* you are ready for a real relationship, and he isn't, and now you've asked the question and received the answer, then you should know what you're going to do with that information. Are you prepared to walk away? Do you want to give him a few more weeks or months to warm up to the idea? There is no "perfect" response. You have to decide what's right for you. But somehow I don't think that "waiting five years for him to make up his mind whether to commit or not" is at the top of your wish list. I know it wouldn't have been on mine if I had *had* a wish list, or a list of questions, or any of the things I'm now writing about, and so I wasted those five years in an "unavailable" relationship.

The introduction of sex, especially great sex, can make a person think that they feel more than they do. "Love is blind and sex is stupid," said the great philosopher Schopenhauer, or was it Carmen Electra? Either way, it's frequently true, which is why I'm slaving over this chapter, so you can educate yourself to ask the important questions *before* (or after, but never during) sex has made things less than perfectly clear. As much as I'm of the belief that really great sex has the best chance of occurring within a really great relationship, I know that this is not always the case. Hence the confusion. We've already talked about mistaking sex for . . . well, for anything else but just sex. Give yourself a chance to ask the kinds of questions discussed in this chapter, and be able to hear the answers with a clear, calm perspective.

Set your own pace, but don't let things go too long before you ask the questions that really count. The really important questions, the ones you need to ask in order to save you years of waiting, are the most difficult to ask. Ask them anyway. Take a deep breath, prepare yourself for either answer, know that if the answer isn't the one you want to hear that you're doing yourself a favor in the end by moving on.

WHAT DOES SEX MEAN TO THIS PERSON?

Obviously, this question goes right along with the preceding question. You probably don't need me to tell you that sex can be a wonderful, healing, exciting, moving, mystical experience that can serve to celebrate everything from the most exalted to the most primal urges we possess. No wonder it's easy to misunderstand what it means to any given person under any given circumstances.

The only thing that really matters is that you've discussed this subject with your partner so there can be no (or at least as little as possible) misunderstanding between the two of you. If sex means commitment to you, you want to know it means the same thing to the other person as well. This is not the area in which to make assumptions.

IS THERE ANYTHING "ELSE" I SHOULD KNOW ABOUT YOU?

Now here's a question that begs for qualification. Of course, if someone hasn't told you something really important or they have a big secret, why would they answer this question? They might not. Still you need to ask.

How would you answer this question? We all have secrets. Some of us have skeletons. What you're looking for here is information that could be a potential deal breaker. Maybe they're in deep debt and owe thousands of dollars to the IRS. Maybe they've spent time in prison (they were framed, of course!), have children somewhere, are due to be deported, stuff like that.

It's the kind of information that is extremely difficult to talk about unless the person knows that it's safe. And, of course, this isn't easy early in the relationship, and later on it becomes difficult because it should have been mentioned earlier. What can you do to help? You can let him know that you will try not to be judgmental no matter *what* he has to tell you. If you have a similar kind of secret, then of course you can tell yours first and make it easier for him to do the same. Even if you've spent your life in a convent (bad example, probably *lots* of secrets there) or at least if you have a somewhat "normal" life, you can still let him know that you are a safe place for him to talk about who he really is, "warts and all," as they say.

If nothing else, you'll learn a lot about him simply by the way in which he deals with the question itself. If he's angry or hostile, that tells you something about how he handles areas of discomfort. If he's sensitive but straightforward, that tells you something entirely different. Either way, you've asked. If the answer turns out to be a lie, and the truth comes out later, at least he can't say you didn't ask. Ask the questions. Listen to the answers. Know the person as best you can. Consider the information as you get to know him. And then make your decision from a position of strength and knowledge.

Hanna met Terry in acting class. They dated for a few months and things began to get more serious. Terry wanted Hanna to move in. Hanna decided now was the time to ask the question, "Is there anything else I should know about you?" And Terry, feeling scared to death, but safe and loved by Hanna, shared a secret part of his past. He told her he had been in a homosexual relationship while he was in college. Terry let her know that this had been a brief and experimental period of his life many years ago. He didn't regret it because he learned a lot about himself. He also assured her he had practiced safe sex at all times and was in perfect health. Understandably, Hanna was shocked. She didn't run away but she needed some time to think about it. After a few weeks, Hanna knew she loved Terry and decided that his honesty helped her to make the decision to take a chance. She moved in. Shortly after she did, Hanna met one of Terry's old girlfriends from college who inadvertently (or not) let a reference to Terry's gay "friendship" slip. Because Hanna already knew this information, the old girlfriend's news didn't have the desired effect. Imagine the scene if Terry hadn't trusted her with the truth. It could've gone a different way. Hanna might have ended the relationship once Terry shared the secret. It was still the right thing to do. In the end, there are no guarantees, but telling the truth just might save you years and tears. It worked out well for Terry and Hanna. Today they're married and have two little girls.

I want to say again that all of the "types" and warnings offered in this book should never be taken as "reasons to back out of a possible relationship." Instead they should serve as guidelines and observations that *you* should put into *your* data base as you go about the business of looking at the choices you've made and the way to improve on your choices in the future. This book is about finding ways to collect information that will help you to do all of that. But the last judge is you. If you see something in his heart that speaks of something genuine and real, something that might not show up at first glance, or even second, then hang in there. Just don't stay year after year, as I did, *without knowing what you're doing!*

PART III

Success Stories

Conquering Unavailability

The world breaks everyone, then some become strong at the broken places.

ERNEST HEMINGWAY

When it *finally* began to dawn on me that I might be playing a significant role in all the "unavailable" choices I was making, that *I* might be the one who was unavailable, then I began to put together some of the observations and conclusions contained in this book. At first it was informal; I did my own work at home. I journaled, put together my own lists, spent time visualizing, and generally tried to make some sense of what had happened in my life and how I was going to live the *rest* of my life differently. After a while this process of discovery became a big part of my everyday life. I continued to write screenplays, I still had a social life, I went to movies, read books, and visited with friends, but I found myself talking about some of the things that were "coming up" for me, things that had long been buried, things that provided me with the beginnings of an explanation for why I had "hidden" in a series of limited, sometimes abusive, and always "unavailable," relationships. And an interesting thing started to happen. I would be at a party or a gathering and someone would ask me how things were going. And when I would talk about this idea of being single and (yet) unavailable, *many* people would respond with an incredible sense of recognition. Some might have had a friendship that had gone on throughout their lives that had been draining and abusive. As we talked, and I mentioned this or that bit of research I had done, they would begin to see how that relationship had served a particularly unhealthy purpose in their life. People in relationships that weren't working would listen attentively. I spoke about my own revelations regarding mechanisms I had put into place to keep me "safe" by keeping me "unavailable," mechanisms that I didn't even know existed. It was comforting to know I wasn't alone, but at the same time it was discouraging to be part of such a big group of single and unavailable people.

This, by the way, is how ideas for books are born. If this many people have been wrestling with the same problem, then it's worth putting my thoughts, my work, and my research into book form.

As I put my research methods into professional mode and really set out to find couples and therapists who could share their experiences and insights with me, I found quite a few people who had been through similar journeys. Some who had been through the process of losing their way and then doing the work to find it again. People who had lived much of their lives in the safe harbors of unavailability, who were now living differently. These were the people I wanted to talk to. These were the people who had "walked the walk" as I was trying to do in my own life. I want to end this book with some of their stories. Their pain, their loneliness, the events that forced them to face their own fears, and the courageous road back to a healthier place.

My goals for this book were threefold. One: To identify unavailable behavior in ourselves as well as the people we choose. Two: To discover ways to overcome and change it. Three: To find people who did just that, who made specific changes in their lives that enabled them to finally become open and available to love. What follows are some of their stories.

Chapter 7

Living the Solution

BARBARA

Barbara is thirty-two years old. Attractive, bright, and extremely successful, she's a woman who usually gets what she wants—at least in business. When it comes to relationships, however, she's always been a "trainee." Of course, Barbara would tell you that what she wanted more than anything else in the world was to be in love. And what was she doing to make that happen? Waiting for a man to come along and find her. Occasionally she would go out on a date, but most of the time she spent complaining. "Where are all the great guys?" was her constant mantra. Mind you, this is a very attractive, successful woman who lives in Los Angeles, a city of close to eight million people. Divide eight million by two for gender, discount thirty percent for citizens under eighteen years old, another thirty percent for married, ten percent or so for total nut cases and mimes, and you've *still* got a couple of million *potentially* great guys. But not for Barbara. Every date was a disaster. Every introduction was hell.

A successful law partner, Barbara was often asked to speak at different functions. The topic for one seminar was "How to get what you want in business." Barbara gave her usual dynamic and inspiring talk on how to get what you want in business. Using her career as an example, she spoke about the importance of being proactive. Do your homework. Ask yourself questions: Where do you want to live? What kind of people do you want to associate with? What kind of cases do you want to handle? Etc., etc. Her speech was about having a plan and carrying it out with conviction and determination. The overall message being, don't settle for being a passive player in your professional life; it's just too damn important.

Many stayed to talk to Barbara after the seminar. One woman said something to Barbara that changed her life. She said, "If I applied that same drive to finding a relationship, I bet I'd be married by now." Barbara laughed, but at the same time she realized there was a big truth there. Of course, it had been staring her in the face for years, but it took an innocent comment from a complete stranger for Barbara to make the connection. Why hadn't she approached her dating life with the same effort and drive that she put into other areas of her life? When it came to buying her house, choosing a gym, or leasing her car, Barbara never played the helpless victim. But when it came to relationships, it was a whole different story. She hadn't known it, but she was single and unavailable.

I wish I could tell you that Barbara got up the very next morning and put together a business plan and "took care of business" in her love life. But that's not usually the way this stuff works. If someone is unavailable, he or she is unavailable for a reason that is sometimes difficult to find. What Barbara *did* do is the exact same thing she would do in business. She researched and found a damn good consultant. In this arena, they're called psychologists (or therapists, or psychiatrists, or whatever works for you). She went "in search of" the reasons why she was playing it safe and settling for a life of frustration (at least in this very important part of her life). After some months of hard work (Barbara knew how to work hard and it sure helped on this project!) she began to make some breakthroughs. She realized that somewhere, deep inside, there was some sense of shame about admitting she wanted a man in her life. She didn't feel desperate or needy about pursuing the best job and going after it, so why should she apologize about wanting love?

The first thing she needed to do was find more ways to increase the number of appropriate, single men she was meeting. This would require shaking up her routine, which she was willing to do. She called certain friends and let them know she was available. Then she checked out and joined a dating service. She even utilized the Internet. Just as she advised others to do, she investigated every avenue.

The mechanics, of course, were the easy part. The tough part was the emotional work. But doing both things at the same time can help keep things moving when we get "stuck" at a certain point. Barbara was always a big believer in momentum and she was using it now to her great advantage. And when the anxiety hit, the feelings of insecurity that come with behaving differently than what we're used to, Barbara reached out to friends and family to reassure her that she really *was* entitled to have someone in her life and that she was allowed to make mistakes in this area. Her professional life had gone so smoothly (she had always been first in her class, biggest earner in the firm, etc.) that she needed to redo her expectations when it came to relationships. As much as this book is about "doing the work" and "knowing what to look for," I hope I have properly emphasized that you must give yourself plenty of room for experimentation and "failures."

Barbara had her share of both. There were disappointments and missteps, but Barbara finally met someone. They were married two years ago and, as I write this, are expecting their first child.

I believe that Barbara always *was* the wonderful, dynamic woman who went after and found an "available" man with whom to share her quite incredible life. She just had to stop long enough to realize what *she* was doing to keep herself unavailable and then to go through the steps to put her heart "on the market," as she would say.

How Barbara became available
1. She became aware of her pattern.
2. She stopped being passive and took a proactive approach.
3. She decided what she wanted and came up with a plan.
4. She asked for help and found a way to do things differently.
5. She opened up her life to available people.

BRIAN

Brian didn't think of himself as unavailable. If you had asked him a few years ago, he would've told you he was a pretty happy guy in a relationship that "worked for him." The problem was, the perfect relationship was as a third wheel to a married couple. Brian's best friend, Al, fell in love with and married Sophie. I guess you could say Sophie inherited Brian when she married Al. Lucky for Brian (and his secret mission to remain "unavailable"), Sophie liked him and enjoyed his company. She and Al made Brian feel welcome in their home from day one. Brian ate dinner at their house a few times a week. He was invited for holidays, joined them for the movies, went away with them on several vacations. Brian felt loved and part of a family, but he was safely out of the danger zone of "availability." At the time he just thought of it as having his freedom. The only thing missing was sex and he managed that occasionally on the few supersafe dates he went out on. Things went on happily like this for five years until Brian turned thirty-six.

That year he went through a real midlife crisis. He lost his job. Worse, Al and Sophie decided to move across the country and start a family. All of a sudden Brian was completely by himself. He realized he didn't have anything that was his own, neither friends nor family. It was only in the rarified air of his own solitude that Brian could see his life for what it really was, and it was only when he came face-to-face with his own pain that he could make the decision to do something about it. He was renting an apartment and renting a life, and now he made a conscious decision to change.

He resolved to pursue a long-ago dream of going back to school and becoming a chiropractor. Sticking to anything that was "his own" wasn't easy. Again, there were missteps for Brian, as there will be for all of us (including and especially the author). Brian had never much liked exercise, but he joined a gym. He had read about the connection between mind and body and decided he'd give the "body" part a chance to help out. It worked. Going to the gym helped him to focus and gave him a sense of accomplishment (his *own* accomplishment) every day that he completed his workout routine. He purposely went to the gym first thing in the morning, *before* his inner voices woke up. The voices that told him he was a screwup who might as well "latch on" to somebody else's life; if he could do that, if he could "beat" those voices, then he might have a better shot at getting through his workout. He got involved in volunteer work, and took up the guitar. He wasn't very good at any of these things at first. He even managed to mess up the volunteer work. He'd show up on the wrong day or the wrong shift. Well, of course he screwed it up at first; it was all new behavior. If any of this "doing things differently" was easy, we'd all be close to perfect, wouldn't we? But it's hard and it's painful and the temptation to quit and go back to our old way of doing things is enormous. But Brian hung in there and pretty soon something wonderful happened. He met Lynne. She was an attractive woman, so attractive that Brian couldn't really believe she would be interested in him. It took Brian a few months to realize what Lynne seemed to know. Brian had become his own person. He didn't do all the steps I've talked about in this book. Not everybody has to do every step. I did the ones *I* needed to do. You'll do different ones. Brian did the things he needed to do to carve out a "self" that was "available" for a relationship. He was now a complete (or at least as "complete" as any of us can claim to be) person and, wonder of wonders, an attractive woman found him attractive and wanted to be in a relationship with him.

I want to point out that even though "life" *delivered* unto Brian a mixed blessing (he "lost" his friends, but "gained" his life), it was *Brian* who made the brave decision to make the most of the situation. He could just as well have found some other set of friends to latch onto. There have always been and always will be couples who need a distraction from their own conflicts, and those people will always welcome a bright, entertaining guy like Brian. But Brian made a decision to do things differently. Maybe that's why he's in a wonderful relationship now.

How Brian became available
1. He reassessed his life.
2. He was willing to do something new and uncomfortable.
3. He exposed himself to new experiences.
4. He knew it wasn't too late to begin his life.
5. He chose an available woman.

MONICA

Monica is in her late forties. She's a smart, successful clothing designer for a line of men's wear. From the time she can remember, Monica's gotten her validation from dating really young, good-looking men, mostly the male models who modeled her clothing. The problem was that she never really believed they could like her for herself. Why? Well, because Monica didn't much care for Monica. Anytime someone showed the least bit of interest in her, she was sure it was her position, her money, or her power. So, you can see how she had set up a neat little self-fulfilling prophecy. She was "afraid" men only liked her for her "position," then she arranged things so that she *only* dated men who worked for her and owed their income to the business she generated. See how that works? And, of course, she didn't get to know or appreciate any of these men for themselves, either. Nothing against models, but one *might* not want to *start* with that profession if one were looking for qualities like depth and complexity. As much as she "worried" about being "used" for her position, she was using the men for their looks and (unknowingly) for their "unavailability." It wasn't satisfying but for Monica it *felt* better than being alone.

Time has a way of playing a role in all our lives. An arrangement that we might make with ourselves to keep us "safe" might work perfectly well for maybe five years, maybe ten. But sometimes we get lucky and the clock pats us on the shoulder and reminds us that we aren't going to be here forever and maybe, just maybe, that "arrangement" needs to be reexamined before it really *is* too late. That's what happened to Monica. The years went by and she was just "fine," until she wasn't any longer. At first she didn't know what was happening. She had never *let* herself be unhappy before. She had always kept busy. When she wasn't working at the frantic pace common to that business, she was out and about, going to parties, seeing and being seen with all the right people. What's to be unhappy about? But it was happening, with or without her written consent. Not only that, she was becoming less and less productive. She was feeling empty and hopeless, and those are two adjectives that just aren't *allowed* in the fashion industry. She tried to lose herself in the party scene, spent some time in the company of drugs, and then she crashed. She just completely crashed. How much of it was her body giving out, and how much of it was her own sense of survival, is anybody's guess. The important thing is that she came to a screeching halt in a place where she had nowhere to look but in the mirror. She didn't shift her gaze for several months. She took a leave of absence from her business, dropped out of her social scene, stopped dating all the pouting young men who looked good, but felt bad. Eventually she came up for air, and when she did she made a commitment to do things differently. At first she had no idea what that meant. Do *what* differently? And how? And then an idea came to her and it was this: The way she had been living her life was *not* the way she would have wanted for any real friend of hers. Over the years many of her friends from outside the fashion business had wanted to "get in" on the fast-lane kind of living that Monica was doing. And each and every time, Monica would discourage him or her. She would spend hours telling them how empty it was. She always claimed that the only reason she did the things she did was because it "came with the territory." She knew now that that wasn't true. She did the things she did because it provided a way for her to hide from herself.

So Monica decided to treat herself as if she were her own best friend. She talked to herself as if she were somebody who had been lost in this fast-paced world and needed help in getting out. She started out with (true story) lists and inventories. She wrote in a journal all about the things she liked and the things she disliked. At first this took a lot of thought. It had been so long since she had been in touch with her own feelings on these subjects. But little by little she began the process of getting to know herself again. She was acting as if she liked herself, and it was starting to work. She cooked her favorite meals, used her best dishes, and read her favorite books. Every time she started to feel anxious and jittery she called one of her friends and she let him or her "talk her down." In time she realized that somewhere along the line, while she was pretending, she truly did come to like and trust her own company.

Our relationship to our work is an important one. But we must never let it take over our lives and separate us from the ones we love, especially ourselves. Being in the television business, I've seen many lives damaged by the pressures and the insecurities of the business. The lucky ones have a solid sense of self when they get into it. The unlucky ones can get swept away.

Without the time-consuming parties and *totally* unavailable dating routine, Monica had more time to explore parts of herself she hadn't known existed. Gone was her desperate need to be validated by others. Once she rediscovered her self-respect, she was able to treat others, as well as herself, with more regard. And when you start treating yourself with respect, then one of the things that often happens is that you start asking for the things that nurture your soul, things like a partner with whom to share your life, things like a real relationship. During her hiatus from dating, she uncovered a passion for exotic fabrics. This opened up the world of travel to her, and she planned trips to interesting places in search of new materials for her work.

She met other people with similar interests. It was on one of these travels that Monica met James. He was unlike anyone she had ever been out with before (first of all, he was her age). He owned a travel agency and over several months James helped Monica plan many of her trips. They developed a friendship and began dating. Two years later, on her birthday, they were married in Florence, Italy.

How Monica became available
1. She ended relationships that weren't working.
2. She spent time alone.

3. She was honest with herself.
4. She worked on her self-esteem.
5. She did things differently.
6. She met available people.
7. She developed a friendship with James.

PAUL AND JANE

Paul was a handsome, charming businessman. He had been divorced for five years with no pressing desire to marry again. He was openly dating several women when he met Jane.

They really hit it off and Paul added her into his loop of favorite dates. In the beginning, because of her own history of unavailability, the dating arrangement with Paul suited Jane perfectly. Actually, she said that she preferred it that way and, looking at her own patterns, that would appear to be true.

So what we have so far is one man (Paul) who *knows* he's unavailable for a committed relationship and is willing to say so, and one woman (Jane) who has a history of dating unavailable men and assumes that it's okay in this case as well. So far, so good, so unavailable. No problem.

But after a few months of this arrangement, Jane made the startling realization that she was no longer content to share Paul with anyone else. For the first time in a very long time, she was having deep feelings for someone. Knowing that Paul had indicated no interest in changing his "single" status, Jane dropped out of the running. Paul was disappointed and decided to pursue her. Jane was, of course, flattered (Did I mention that he was handsome, well established, and a very nice man? He was just unavailable.) and made a very bold move, a move she'd never made before in her life. She told Paul that she needed to be exclusive or she could no longer see him. She gave Paul an ultimatum (or the "old to-mato," as my father used to say): Either we give this a real shot, or we don't. Paul heard her out and then told her he'd have to think about it. She didn't hear from him for a few weeks and it broke her heart, but the thought of sharing him hurt even more.

She had taken the first, most difficult, move towards becoming "available" for a real relationship. She was willing to walk away if the answer was "no," or even "maybe."

After a month Paul called. He told her that he missed her and that he was ready to date only her. Things went very well and, several months later, he asked her to move in. It was wonderful. They got along famously. Paul seemed to relax right into it. A little over a year later Paul and Jane were married in a beautiful ceremony and things *continued* to go spectacularly. For two years they were the couple to envy. Then, one dark and stormy night (it always is), Paul told her he had a confession to make. He had made a terrible mistake during a business trip six months before. There had been a lonely night, too much wine, an attractive woman, and an empty bed in his hotel room. It had been one night of infidelity but the woman was now threatening to blackmail him. Rather than find ways to keep this from her, he was telling her the whole story. He was prepared for her to leave him, but he begged her not to go. Jane had a problem, to say the least. The years with Paul had been the best time of her life. But if he was incapable of staying in a committed relationship then she had better get out now. It would only be *more* painful later on. Jane moved out but they continued to talk. They spent many hours with a professional talking about what happened. Paul came to understand what had happened and how much damage he had done to the trust he'd built up, all for one night of pleasure.

Understanding that it might take years for things to be good again, and knowing that they might *never* be the same, the two of them tentatively reentered the marriage.

That was twelve years ago and the marriage is now one of the strongest anyone has seen.

I'm perfectly aware of how this story contradicts some of the very things outlined in this book. My point in telling it is to make clear the idea that none of us is perfect, we all slip off the path, but every one of us is *capable* of change. I wanted to underscore that it's up to you to decide how much time and effort and pain you will put into a relationship, because only you know how much caring and gentleness and love is there. There are thousands of men and women who say they will work on a problem and then never do. If this story had included further infidelities that occurred after Paul's promise, then you would never have met them here in this book. But as it is, two people went to work in order to repair something they thought was worth saving. Sometimes fighting the battles to *win* our availability isn't enough. Sometimes we have to fight them again. Sometimes it's worth it.

HOW JANE BECAME AVAILABLE
1. She ended the relationship the way it was.
2. She was honest about what she wanted.
3. She set boundaries.
4. She was aware of what had happened and decided to work to get her relationship back on track.

HOW PAUL BECAME AVAILABLE
1. He was willing to change the way he lived his life.
2. He chose to work on his issues in therapy.
3. He realized the price for his actions.
4. He stuck to his promise.

AUDREY
Audrey had a crush on Frank for years. Frank is this great guy; smart, successful, and kind. But Frank always seemed to be dating some absolutely horrible woman who treated him badly. The last one, Jody, he met during a skiing vacation and she ranked as a number-one contender in the "let's humiliate Frank" contest. She was downright arrogant and rude as she ordered him around in front of his friends, including Audrey. The people who loved Frank, his family and his real friends, were always baffled by his choices when it came to women. They felt he deserved better.

Audrey felt the same way, but she had her own special version. She not only thought he deserved better, she was convinced that he deserved *her*. If only she could get him to see her as something other than just a friend. She was always doing something nice for him in an effort to show him what it could be like to be with someone who would appreciate him. If he would only give her the chance, she would make him see what a good time they could have together.

This went on for several years. Audrey had a couple of boy-friends and a few casual flings, but her heart was always on hold for Frank. But eventually even Audrey tired of carrying this torch and she just plain gave up.

That's all it took. The next time she and Frank were at a party together, Frank told her that he was seeing her clearly for the first time ever. He talked to her about how tired he was of being treated badly, how he wanted someone in his life who had some kindness to give. Audrey was thrilled, to say the least. She asked him what had brought about this turnaround and Frank said it just hit him that night. (I would like to think that if Audrey had even casually thumbed through this book, she would have taken that answer as her first warning sign that all was not well with Frank and his newfound conversion to gentility among the sexes). Needless to say, Audrey rushed into the relationship she had been waiting to have for as long as she could remember. She knew *just* what to do. She would be kind and decent and supportive. She and Frank moved in together almost immediately. And almost immediately after *that*, Frank started to look very unhappy. At first, Audrey couldn't figure it out. She couldn't possibly be more accommo-dating, and it was exactly the kind of treatment that the "new and improved" Frank said he loved. But things were going from bad to worse in a big hurry. Until one day when Audrey was tired and cranky and just plain out of energy. She got snippy with Frank and he responded like a puppy with a pork chop. The rougher she got, the more Frank liked it. If she ignored him, he came chasing after her. If she berated him, he did anything he could to make it up to her. Audrey couldn't believe it; the "old" Frank was back. It was something right out of Jekyll and Hyde.

Well, if Audrey's dream was to have Frank in her life, then she now knew just how to do it. She could wrap him right around her little finger and, for a while, that's exactly what she did. The idea of giving him up just wasn't on the menu. But eventually she grew tired of trying to be somebody that she wasn't. She tried to talk to him about his behavior, and *hers*! But Frank was perfectly happy with things the way they were. He had no interest in therapy; therapy was for people who wanted to *change* a relationship.

Audrey had to go through six kinds of Hell before realizing that there was only one way out. The door. Being in a relationship that was based on a dynamic that didn't interest her was not what she wanted to do with the rest of her life, even if she had to give up a man she had *dreamed* of making happy for so many years.

To this day, Frank doesn't know why Audrey left. Maybe, somewhere deep inside, Frank didn't believe he deserved to have a good woman or be treated well. Audrey didn't want to win Frank over just because she was able to manipulate him; she wanted a real, "available" relationship with a man who loved her the way she loved him. She realized that he was too damaged for her and she was too healthy for him. She broke off their relationship and spent some serious time taking a look at what she had done and why. (I think the chapter on "limerance" would have been extremely interesting to her.) After a long period of journaling and questioning, Audrey realized that she had a "fantasy bond" with Frank that had never been real. She had a "relationship" with who she *thought* he was, not who he *really* was. She vowed, in the future, to take a long, hard look at the reality of what a relationship promised, and to try, or not to try, based on that reality, not on a fantasy in her head. She's had several relationships since Frank, and while she hasn't found "the one," at least she's felt like the connection was real.

How Audrey became available
1. She saw the relationship for what it was.
2. She found the strength to end it.
3. She vowed to spend some time alone.
4. She promised herself she would do things differently.

CHRISTINE AND DON

Christine and Don met on a blind date and hit it off immediately. Things moved quickly after that and they became inseparable. They had so much in common; they both worked in the advertising field, they were both taking swing dancing and flying lessons. It was a match made in heaven and, after two months, Don asked Christine to move in.

All of their friends thought they were moving too fast but neither was listening; they were in love. Christine gave notice at her apartment, sold her furniture, and gave away the rest of her belongings. From the moment she arrived at Don's, he began acting strangely. He was cold in a way she had never seen him be before. She noticed he also hadn't cleared out any space for Christine's things. Finally (i.e., one week later) he broke down and admitted that he wasn't ready for this relationship. He said he was feeling rushed and pressured and he wanted to break off the relationship. Christine was devastated, but she moved out that night.

Christine ended up staying with a friend for the next few months while she tried to figure out what had happened. It was a terrible time for her. A friend recommended a relationship therapist and Christine went to see her. What had happened? What sign had she missed? Christine was more bewildered than angry. She hadn't a clue that Don was so frightened about the commitment.

The therapist got her to finally let go of worrying about why she wasn't good enough. This was about Don's fears, not hers. But the therapist also talked about why Don might have acted the way he did. She discussed why Don's fears might have been warranted. The fact of the matter was that the relationship moved extremely fast and Christine had been a willing participant in that. She loved the feeling of falling headlong in love. And perhaps Don was also caught up in the romance (or thrill; call it what you want) and maybe he let himself get carried away. The therapist wasn't *excusing* Don's behavior, she was just trying to understand it and see if there was anything to be salvaged. After all, there had been a lot of sincere, loving feelings between these two people, at least in the beginning.

Christine agreed that there was something there with Don. Her friends thought she was crazy to still like him after what he did, but Christine decided to follow her heart, albeit with both eyes open this time.

Christine didn't go rushing back into the relationship. She knew she had some work to do on herself. She didn't like that "desperate" feeling that had pushed her to move so fast before. After many hours of talking, and journaling, Christine began to feel better about herself alone. She realized that her rush to live together came from a lack of the kind of confidence she was now feeling. She continued to work and got a new apartment, but she would periodically send Don a card; for his birthday, Christmas, etc. For a long time, she didn't get an acknowledgment. He, too, was taking a look at what had happened and his part in it. Without mentioning it to Christine, Don had also begun to see a therapist.

It took almost a year before he called to thank her for the latest birthday card. He asked if they could meet for coffee. Don told her how ashamed he was for what he had done. He had been afraid and hadn't known how to handle it. He had his own insecurities and Christine was interested to hear that it had nothing to do with her not being "good enough." To the contrary, Don was so convinced that he would *lose* somebody as wonderful as Christine that he did everything he could to "lock" her into a relationship. Then, when they were face-to-face in an apartment only a couple of months after meeting, Don didn't know what to do. The relationship hadn't had a chance to actually *become* a relationship. He knew that now. He told her how much work he had done on himself and how he believed that he was ready now to try again if she was willing.

Christine was willing. This time they'd take it slow, let the feelings blossom at their own pace. They began going to the movies, the museum, flying outings. At first they kept things simple and nonsexual. This time they really got to know each other. By the time they became romantically involved, it felt comfortable and natural, and even better than before. This time it was real. After a year and two months, Christine and Don married. They just celebrated their eleventh anniversary and have eight-year-old twin boys.

HOW CHRISTINE BECAME AVAILABLE

1. She asked for help.
2. She did the work and admitted her part in what had happened.
3. She started over with Don slowly, as a friend.

HOW DON BECAME AVAILABLE

1. He ended the relationship the first time with Christine because he wasn't ready.
2. He faced his fears and worked on them.
3. He spent time alone.
4. He was willing to try a friendship with Christine and let it grow naturally into a relationship.

MY STORY

In a way I have my affair with David, the married man, to thank for helping me to become "available," at long last, for a loving, healthy relationship. The hours of self-doubt and unhappiness that I experienced during my time "with" him, the months and (I'm embarrassed to say) years of mixed messages, the choreographed mornings designed to fool us both into thinking something existed between us. The casual conversations that were labeled "deep and meaningful" because that's the kind of conversations "real" couples have. The emptiness that hurt my heart and never crossed his mind. It all coalesced into a wound that even I couldn't ignore. It was the pain that finally got my attention and forced me to look where I had never looked before; to myself. When I think of David now I can see how I protected myself, never showing my hurt, never *ever* allowing myself to be vulnerable with him. Somewhere inside I knew he wasn't to be trusted. If he happens onto these words, he will be surprised to read that I was in such pain. Oh, I tried to tell him a couple of times but it was a fool's game. He handled tears (or any *real* emotion) the way all narcissists handle genuine emotion; not well.

But thank you, David, wherever you are. Without even trying, you brought me to a place where I could see my life passing by me without a love to call my own. And thank you for making the experience empty enough so that I vowed to "do things differently" in the future.

That was the beginning.

Then came the work. Or, to borrow the title of an excellent book by Jack Kornfield, *After the Ecstasy, the Laundry*.

But the "laundry" becomes somewhat easier to do once you have some idea of how to treat the stains. After spending time alone, working on a journal, putting together my own lists of just *how* I wanted to do things differently and *what* I wanted to bring into my life, only then did I slowly begin to get a picture of my behavior patterns and how to change them. It was the beginning of my realization that *I* had made myself just as "unavailable" as all of the "unavailable" men I had dated. I chose these people for a reason. And now I was beginning to see what that reason was.

The truth about David was that I didn't even particularly *like* him; I didn't respect his values, didn't like the way he treated other people, hell, we didn't even have any common interests. So, why were we so "perfect" for each other all those years? Because we were *both* unavailable for a healthy relationship. I needed to look at that, and look especially hard at my part in it.

This was a painful time for me, as you might imagine. But, as Winston Churchill was famous for saying: "If you're going through Hell, keep going." I looked at my own past and acknowledged the early pain that had caused me to spend so many years "hiding" in the "safety" of unavailability. I had always prided myself on the variety of choices I had made in the men I brought into my life. As far as I knew I didn't have a "type." I didn't much care if they were handsome (although I didn't hold it against them if they were), money meant very little to me as I have always been lucky enough to have earned my own. I always thought that I had chosen men (or been chosen by them) based on personality, and humor, and a view of the world that I found interesting. But now I was seeing, for the first time, that they all had one glaring similarity; they were *all*, in one way or another, unavailable. How could I not have seen this? At the time it was embarrassing. To tell the truth, it's *still* embarrassing, even as I write this. It was only in talking to so many other people who had experienced the same thing that I realized that mine wasn't such a rare revelation.

This period of searching and evaluating my own actions went on for what seemed like an eternity (thank you very much, Winston Churchill).

And then I turned a corner.

After a while, the pain seemed to lose some of its strength. (It's like a bully, this pain stuff. If you stand up to it, it will eventually back down. But you don't know that when you first confront it, do you?) This is about the time I began to think about organizing my thoughts into a book. The process of assembling material was a great help in pulling me out of a dark place and moving me forward.

I was in the middle of this project when I met Christopher. A mutual friend had introduced us.

In addition to wit and intelligence, he had a calmness and an ability to listen that made me feel instantly comfortable with him.

This was the first time I'd been charmed by someone in a very long time. I had been dating during that time, making use of my "lists" and "questions to ask," and I had met some very nice, "available" men (as well as some unavailable men whom I could now recognize rather quickly), but Chris was someone with whom I felt a real connection.

It's very interesting to be writing a book on relationships while in the process of having one. It kept me very honest and true to the premise of the book; and the premise of this book is to move slowly and know what you're getting into. I'm not saying it was easy, but I'm pleased to say that I practiced what I preached. We went very slowly. We continued to develop our friendship. I met his friends, his family. I asked him the kinds of questions that would clue me in to the kind of person he was; his values, his problems, his likes, his dislikes. I liked him more and more every time we were together. This was someone with whom I could actually see myself in a relationship. I was at that point in a relationship where anyone in her right mind does *not* want to rock the boat. But that is what I'm asking you to do in this book, and that's what I did with Chris. I did what I've never done before with anyone in my life: I told him that my desire was to be in a relationship and I asked him if that's what he wanted as well. I was clear that I wasn't trying to *rush* our situation, I was just making sure that he was open and available for the same thing. I wasn't interested in anything "casual" and it was important that he know it sooner rather than later. I told him that I understood completely if he wasn't ready or didn't want the same thing, but that I would have to move on if he *knew* he didn't want the same thing I wanted. "Tough meeting to take," as they used to say at the network. But I thought that things were going so well that I had a pretty good chance of hearing words that would make us both smile.

Christopher said no.

He told me how wonderful he thought I was, how well we got along, how much fun, how smart, all the things that go with "yes." But he didn't think this was a good time for him to commit to a real relationship. He didn't go into detail, only that there were things going on in his family. He said that he was concerned about his younger brother who was ill and that he might be spending a lot of time with him. It wasn't my place to question a "family problem," but I have to admit that I was disappointed. Even decent people make "polite excuses" when they want to deliver bad news gently, and that's what I thought was happening now. Chris said that he hoped we could continue to see each other as we had been.

It was a terribly vulnerable moment for me. I didn't want to miss out on what I thought might be a wonderful person, but I didn't want to spend time with someone who had honestly answered that he wasn't available, whatever the reason. So, as difficult as it was, I took a deep breath and I did the right thing. I thanked him for his honesty and I told him I could no longer date him.

Chris was single, but he was unavailable for the kind of relationship I was looking for. And I walked away. And that was that.

About a month later, Chris called me just to say hi. He wanted me to know that he really had liked me and he hoped we could stay in touch as friends from time to time. Well, anyone over twenty has heard these words before and it usually means *either* that someone wants to stay in touch so that a sexual relationship can be pursued, *or* it's just a way for a person to feel better about himself when he's leaving.

I felt sad. I felt bad. But the truth is that I felt something else. I felt exhilarated and proud. I had done it. I had spoken up for what I wanted and it felt really good. It had been hard enough for me to walk away from a terrible situation with a married man, but to walk away from someone I liked and a situation I was enjoying because I believed that it was the "healthy" thing to do— well, let me tell you, I've raised two children and worked since I was fifteen years old; I've done some difficult things in my life. But this was the most difficult.

In my old pattern, Christopher's "rejection" would've been the incentive for me to try harder, be smarter, and feel worse. Those days were over. And that would be a fine ending to the story. It would be still be a success story. Because the win for me was that I had finally been able to recognize and break a lifelong pattern of being with unavailable men. But it's not the end of the story.

Chris *did* call me and we *were* friends, and only friends, for quite some time. His brother's condition, sadly, worsened and it was discovered that he had a very serious form of cancer. Chris was going through an extremely difficult time with doctors and hospitals, trying to get the best care for his brother. But through it all, we seemed to spend time together that was calming, and safe and (believe it or not, in the midst of tragedy) fun. He was *right* not to take on a committed relationship in the middle of all this, and so our friendship was the right thing for both of us. As we got to know each other on a deeper and deeper level, Chris began to feel relaxed enough to share the kinds of things that people share when they trust each other. It was the type of trust that we all long for, especially in times of stress. And I know that I also felt that trust, so much so that I made myself vulnerable to him in ways that were frightening at first, but wonderful as the weeks went on. I kept asking my questions and listening for the answers; and I liked what I heard, as well as what I saw. We discovered a long list of things we share; values, humor, priorities, family dynamics, the way we deal with problems, goals, as well as an even longer list of stuff we just like doing together.

The friendship grew into a relationship as naturally as anything I've ever seen. Nothing was forced. Every step felt right, and loving, and mutual. We took it slow and we kept our eyes open. No "fantasy bond" here. I'm perfectly aware that wonderful, "available" relationships can have rocky starts and bumpy roads and, in a way, ours did as well. We "broke up" just weeks after meeting because I needed to know where we were going. Even today I'm glad that I did it the way I did. When we made our way back to the relationship that we have now, we both knew how important it was, and is, to invest in the reality, not the fantasy. I know what the word "relationship" means to him, and he knows what it means to me. Not that there won't be problems, and difficulties, and pain, and frustration, and all the rest of it. And nobody knows what the future will hold, but I do know how I feel being in a relationship with an available person, and it's better, and safer, and more fulfilling than anything I've ever experienced in my life.

And it's what I want for you. More importantly, it's what I want *you* to want for you.

I want to end with a story. It's something that happened to me and it left me with a picture in my mind's eye that helped me tremendously during my struggle to step off a path that was causing me pain, and to find a way to do things differently in my life.

It was several years ago and I had been invited to join some friends on a trip to a lake. Someone had rented a couple of Jet Skis (those water scooters that ride like a motorcycle, but have no brakes!) and we were all taking our turn with them on the warm, summer water. I took my turn and was having a blast when suddenly the Jet Ski got away from me and took off on its own. It wasn't going that fast so I tried swimming to catch up with it. I was mortified that it had broken loose, afraid that it would be my fault if it did any damage or (God forbid) hit anyone. Faster and faster I would swim. A couple of times I actually caught up with it and got a hand on it, but it would always break free of my grip. I started to panic as I realized that I might not be able to control this motorized beast. But I kept trying, again and again, chasing after it. Finally, the panic caught up with me and I stopped, gasping for air. I could swim no more and I almost started to cry in frustration as I watched the Jet Ski pull away.

But then I saw something that I couldn't possibly have seen while I was swimming so close behind. I saw that the Jet Ski was traveling around and around in circles. It had been engineered to do this and was in absolutely no danger of running onto shore, or anywhere else. I started to laugh as I realized what was going on. I looked to the beach and saw that all my friends were laughing as well. Of *course* I couldn't see that it was going in circles; I was following too close, on a path I *thought* I needed to follow. It was only by stopping that I could see what was really happening.

And I guess that's what I've been trying to say in this book. If you've been swimming your heart out, following after something, or someone, that can't be caught, then try to resist the urge to swim faster. Try to stop, and listen, and look; not only at the behavior of what you're chasing, but at your own behavior. Chances are you can't do a thing about *his* or *her* patterns, but you can do everything about your own.

Keep this picture in your head. Out of breath, stopped in the warm embrace of the water. Looking, and seeing for the first time what you've been doing. And realizing you don't have to go there after all.

Then think of all the time and all the energy you'll have for a different kind of relationship; a relationship that will nurture you, excite you, make you feel safe, and fill your heart with hope.

Swim back to shore and find it. I did.

Best of luck to you. Every one of you.